Encyclopedia
of
Mdina

Encyclopedia of Mdina

Justin Corfield

GENTEXT PUBLICATIONS
2016

Gentext Publications
An imprint of Corfield and Company

This edition first published in Australia, 2016
by Gentext Publications
59 Smeaton Close, Lara, Victoria, 3212, Australia

ISBN: 978-1-876586-36-2 (hardback)

CONTENTS

INTRODUCTION

In terms of its population, Mdina is one of the smallest cities in the world. Dating back to Phoenician times, it is known locally as the Città Vecchia ('Old City') or Città Notabile ('City of Nobles'). Mdina does have a cathedral, a long-established prerequisite for a settlement to be known as a 'city'. Its current population is estimated in March 2011 to be only 306, however including Rabat, and the nearby area, the population is some 11,000.

Mdina was the capital city of the island of Malta for many centuries until the arrival of the Knights of Malta in 1530. It is a walled city and the walls remain one of the major tourist sites of the island. On a clear winter or spring day it is possible to stand on a bastion at Mdina and see Mount Etna on the northern horizon. Indeed William Domeier in Malta noted that ice that was used in lemonade had been brought over from Mount Etna.

The origins of Mdina date back to the Phoenicians who seem to have established a settlement at the site of the city in about 1000 BC. They called the village 'Malet' (place of shelter) and the Romans took control of Malta at the start of the Second Punic War. Hannibal had invaded Italy and the Romans were anxious to keep their control over the Mediterranean to prevent reinforcements arriving by ship. The Romans enlarged Mdina which they called Melita – the same name they gave to the island, and it was to Mdina that Paul of Tarsus (later St. Paul) came after being shipwrecked on his way to Rome.

The Arabs gave the city the same Mdina (pronounced in Maltese as 'Imdina'), which was Arabic for 'walled city'. The area beyond the walls of the city was known as 'rabat' (suburb) and these two names are used to this day. However when the Christians retook Malta, the city became known as Città Notabile ('The Noble City') because most of the nobles of Malta had their family seats in the city. It was suggested by the writer A. A. Caruana as early as 1898 that during medieval Malta, the original street pattern of the Arabs was continued; and later examinations have shown that this was

A re-enactment for the Medieval Mdina Festival.
Photograph © McCarthys PhotoWorks / Fotolia

probable. This saw a number of palatial residences, and smaller buildings for the poor.

In 1530 the Knights Hospitaller (later the Knights of Malta) arrived in Malta and soon decided to make Birgu their capital because it was closer to their naval base and they were keen on becoming a sea power. This led to the city being called Città Vecchia ('Old City'). By the nineteenth century it was known as the Silent City and H.V. Morton noted that 'from the heights of its ramparts, the lowlands of Malta stretch away into the distance like a length of fawn-coloured Harris tweed.' From the 1980s tens of thousands of tourists have descended on the city each year, with about 500,000 tourists a year visiting the city.

Located on a hill, and surrounded by walls, Mdina has always had a great fascination for me from a young age. On my fist trip to Malta when I was eight, we arrived at night, and my first view of the walls of the city was the following morning from the balcony of the Grand Verdala Hotel. I was eleven when I read Ernle Bradford's *The Great Siege* and one day sitting in the fields nearby whilst my father was working on one of his paintings of the city, I imagined watching the attacks of the Turks as they tried to approach the walls. On re-reading Ernle Bradford's book some years later, I discovered, that the Turks made no real attempt to take the city which they, apparently, could easily have done – so my childhood drawings of the Janissaries with their plumes blowing in the breeze as they advanced up the hillside were historically inaccurate.

Mdina in 1975.
Photograph by Robin Corfield.

The funeral of Frater Richard Hamilton Alexander Cheffins was held on Monday morning at the Church of Saint James, Spanish Place.

Mdina, 1979.
Painting by Robin Corfield.

My father had built up a significant collection of books and papers on Malta – and indeed designated a spare room in his house as the Malta Room, replete with maps and his paintings of Mdina. I am also indebted to the many authors who have written about Mdina, and Maltese history, in particular Michael J. Schiavone whose two-volume *Dictionary of Maltese Biographies* has provided a wealth of information and who generously allowed me to reproduce some images from his book; as is John Montalto's *The Nobles of Malta*, and Denis de Lucca's *Mdina: A History of Its Urban Space* and Architecture. As work started on this book, I was fortunate to come across, by chance, at Any Amount of Books in London, much of the collection from the library of the late Richard Hamilton Alexander Cheffins (1945–2011), a Knight of Justice in the Order of Malta, the librarian of the British Association of the Order of Malta and a bibliographer, as well as a book collector. I never met Mr Cheffins but I must acknowledge the use of so many of his books and magazines, of which I am now the custodian.

Justin Corfield

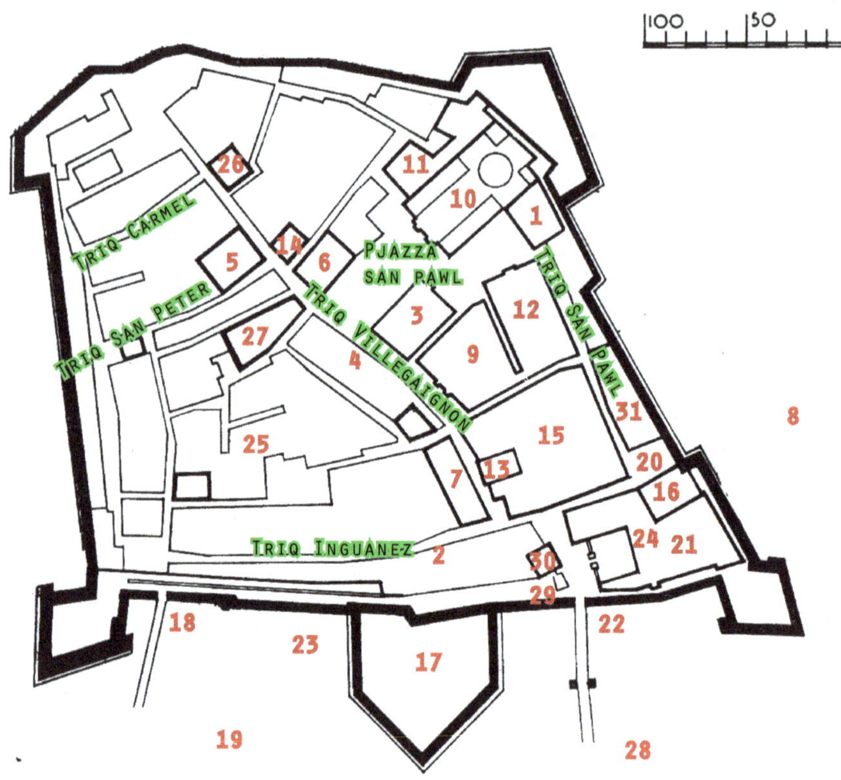

Mdina

1. Archbishop's Palace
2. Bacchus (restaurant)
3. Banca Giurate
4. Caffè Medina
5. Carmelite Church and Convent
6. Casa Gourgion
7. Casa Inguanez
8. Casa Isabella
9. Casa Testaferrata
10. Cathedral Church
11. Cathedral Museum
12. Cathedral Museum II (formerly the Mdina Seminary)
13. Chapel of St. Peter
14. Chapel of St. Roque
15. Convent of St. Benedict
16. Corte Capitanale
17. De Redin Bastion
18. Greek's Gate
19. Howard Gardens
20. Loggia
21. Magisterial Palace (Vilhena Palace)
22. Main Gate
23. Mdina Ditch
24. Mdina Dungeons
25. Mdina Experience
26. Palazzo Falzon (Norman House)
27. Palazzo Santa Sophia
28. Pointe de Vue
29. Police Station
30. Tower of the Standard
31. Xara Palace

ABBREVIATIONS AND ACRONYMS

AD	Alternattiva Demokratika.
AM	Anglo-Maltese Party.
CP	Constitutional Party.
CStJ	Commander of the Order of St John of Jerusalem.
DStJ	Dame of the Order of St John of Jerusalem.
EEC	European Economic Community.
EMU	European Monetary Union.
EU	European Union.
FMOM	Friends of the Sovereign Military Order of Malta.
GC	George Cross.
GCStJ	Bailiff (or Dame) Grand Cross of the Order of St John of Jerusalem.
KGStJ	Knight of Grace of the Order of St John of Jerusalem.
KJStJ	Knight of Justice of the Order of St John of Jerusalem.
KM	Knight of Malta.
KOWR	King's Own Malta Regiment.
KStJ	Knight of the Order of St John of Jerusalem.
Lm	Maltese Lira.
MAM	Medical Association of Malta.
MCA	Malta Communications Authority.
MEP	Member of the European Parliament.

MFA	Malta Football Association.
MP	Member of Parliament.
MJHA	Ministry for Justice and Home Affairs.
MLP	Malta Labour Party.
MMDNA	Malta Memorial District Nursing Association.
MPA	Malta Police Association.
MPF	Malta Police Force.
MSSP	Missionary Society of St Paul.
MTA	Malta Tourism Authority.
MWP	Malta Workers' Party (Partit Tal-Haddiema).
NATO	North Atlantic Treaty Organisation.
NBM	National Bank of Malta.
NTOM	National Tourist Organisation of Malta.
OCarm	Order of Our Lady of Mount Carmel (Carmelites).
PCP	Progressive Constitutional Party.
PDN	Partito Democratico Nazionalista.
RAF	Royal Air Force.
RMA	Royal Malta Artillery.
RMFR	Royal Malta Fencible Regiment.
RUM	Royal University of Malta.
SJAB	St John Ambulance Brigade.
SMOM	Sovereign Military Order of Malta (Sovrano Militare Ordine di Malta).
UM	University of Malta.

CHRONOLOGY

BC

5200 The first Neolithic settlements were established on Malta around this time.

3600 The start of the 'temple' period in Malta's history.

1000 Phoenicians from Tyre start to colonize Malta and probably establish Mdina soon afterwards.

800 The Greeks start arriving in Malta.

700 Phoenician fortifications around Mdina are constructed.

400 The start of Carthaginian rule over Malta.

218 At the start of the Second Punic War, the Roman Republic takes over Malta.

AD

60 Paul of Tarsus (later St. Paul) is shipwrecked on the island of Malta, and goes to Mdina where he meets the Roman governor Publius (later St. Publius).

440 The Vandals, from North Africa, take Malta.

533 The Byzantine general Belisarius captured Malta from the Vandals.

870 The Fatimid Arabs take the island of Malta, and the capital gets its current name Mdina.

1091 Count Roger I of Sicily arrives on Malta and tries to establish Norman rule.

1191 Tancred of Sicily appoints Margaritus of Brindisi as the first Count of Malta

1194	The Normans introduce Latin as the language of government; with the Swabians starting their rule over Malta.
1223	The entire male population of the town of Celano in central Italy is deported to Malta after they attempted to resist Emperor Frederick II.
1240	Expecting an attack on Malta, a formal Norman garrison is established on the island.
1266	The Angevins start their rule over Malta which lasts until 1283.
1283	Malta is ruled by the rulers of Aragon.
1530	The Knights Hospitaller arrive on Malta which has been ceded to them by Emperor Charles V. The Grand Master Philippe Villiers de L'Isle-Adam formally enters Mdina and promises to maintain the laws and privileges of the Maltese nobility (13 November). The Knights make Birgu their capital.
1565	The Great Siege of Malta (18 May – 11 September) sees a large Turkish force attack the fortresses of the Knights of Malta. The cavalry based at Mdina play a crucial role in attacking the Turks.
1568	The construction of Valletta sees a decline in the importance of Mdina.
1693	An earthquake damages several buildings in Mdina including the Cathedral (11 January).
1798	The French under Napoleon land at Malta (9 June), and after it refuses to supply them with water, they take the island. Napoleon leaves a garrison behind and then sails for Egypt. The British under Horatio Nelson lay a naval siege to Malta.
1800	A general uprising against the French starts at Mdina (2 September) and quickly spread to much of the rest of the island with the French retreating to Valletta and finally capitulating (5 September).
1802	Malta formally becomes a part of the British Empire.
1815	British rule over Malta is reconfirmed by the Treaty of Vienna.
1869	The opening of the Suez Canal leads to Malta becoming an important British naval base.

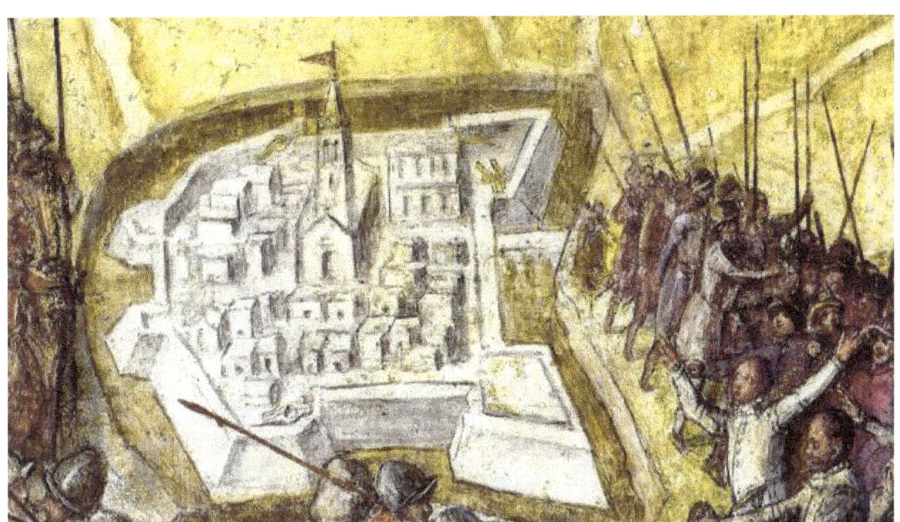

Paintings of Mdina by Salvio d'Antonio, completed between 1493 and 1525.

1898	Pointe de Vue opens as a tavern.
1909	King Edward VII visits Malta and names the Connaught Hospital after his brother (22 April).
1914–18	During World War I, many British soldiers and sailors convalesce on Malta.

1921	The British grant self-government (30 April) with an elected legislative assembly, and a senate (abolished in 1949).
1934	English and Maltese are declared the sole official languages (1 January).
1939–45	Throughout World War II, Malta continued to be an important British base suffering heavy damage from bombing raids by the Germans and Italians.
1942	The George Cross is awarded to the people of Malta (15 April).
1944	The last Axis air raid on Malta (28 August).
1945	US President Franklin Delano Roosevelt, in Malta for the Malta Conference with British Prime Minister Winston Churchill, goes on a tour of Malta including Mdina (2 February).
1949	The Xara Palace opens as a hotel.
1956	Some 75% of the people of Malta vote for integration into the United Kingdom.
1964	Malta becomes an independent country as a constitutional monarchy with Queen Elizabeth II as the head of state (21 September) and is admitted to the United Nations (1 December).
1967	Queen Elizabeth II attends a reception held in her honour at the Archbishop's Palace in Mdina (16 November).
1971	The Malta Labour Party under Dom Mintoff narrowly wins the elections and begins major social and governmental changes (17 June).
1972	The Maltese pound is adopted (16 May).
1973	The Connaught Hospital is reopened as the National Museum of Natural History (22 June).
1974	Malta becomes a Republic (13 December).
1975	The titles of the Nobility of Malta are abolished by an act of parliament (25 June).
mid–1970s	Malta undergoes a major tourism boom and remaining within the Sterling area, British tourists restricted by currency regulations, start travelling to the island in very large numbers.

1979	The last British forces leave Malta (31 March).
1990	Pope John Paul II arrives in Malta, making the first ever papal visit to Malta (25 May). Pope John Paul II holds a service at Rabat on his last day in Malta (27 May).
1999	The heavily refurbished Xara Palace reopens as a boutique hotel.
2000	Formal negotiations begin between Malta and the European Union (15 February).
2001	Pope John Paul II visits Mdina as part of his pilgrimage in the footsteps of St. Paul (8–9 May).
2003	A referendum is held in which a majority vote for Malta to join the European Union (8 March).
2004	A Medieval Mdina Festival is held (14–15 April). Malta joins the European Union (1 May).
2006	Archaeological work uncovers a Bronze Age settlement and a Roman site at the Santa Margerita Cemetery in Rabat (31 October).
2008	Malta starts using the Euro alongside the Maltese Lira (1 January); with the dual currency period ending (31 January).
2009	Medieval Mdina Festival is held (18–19 April).

2010	Medieval Mdina Festival is held (9–11 April).
2011	George Pullicino unveils plans to turn Mdina ditch into a recreational space (11 January). Medieval Mdina Festival is held (7–8 May)
2012	Medieval Mdina Festival is held (14–15 April). Protests take place at Mdina ditch against the closing of a football pitch and tennis club and turning it into a public garden (May).
2013	Medieval Mdina Festival is held (6–7 April). Mdina hosts the Grand Prix (10–13 October).
2014	Medieval Mdina Festival is held (3–4 May). A tools museum with the collection of Joseph Zammit Tabona opens in the Palazzo de Piro (17 August). The Medina Restaurant in Mdina was named, with the Bull at St George's Bay, the best restaurant in the country (13 December).
2015	Medieval Mdina Festival is held (18–19 April). Mdina Cathedral Contemporary Art Biennale opens (12 November). The second Malta International Organ Festival takes place (19 November – 7 December). Prince Charles and the Duchess of Cornwall visit Mdina Glass (28 November).
2016	Medieval Mdina Festival is held (23–24 April).

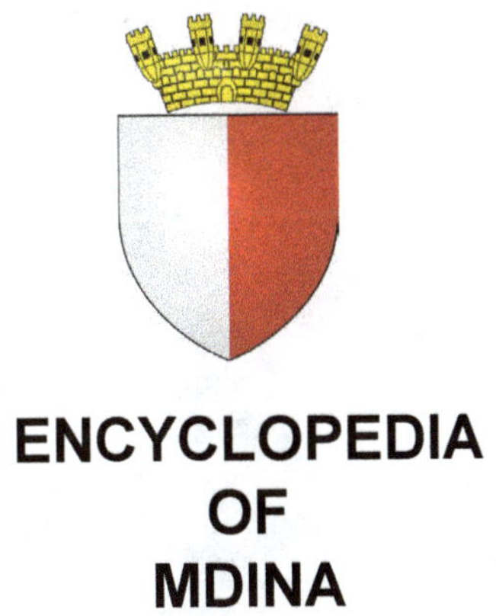

ENCYCLOPEDIA OF MDINA

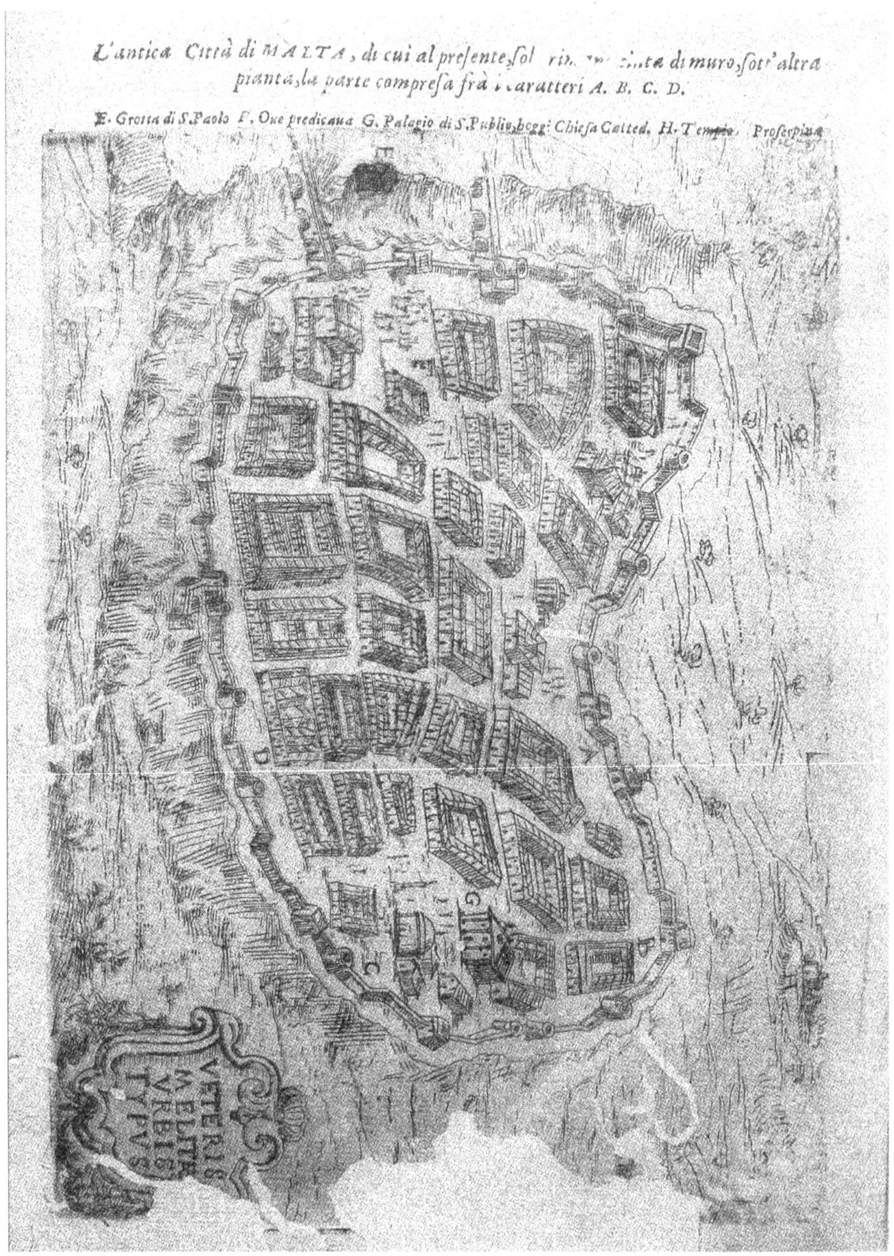

Skiers using the cable cars
Photograph © Evgenia Tubol / Fotolia.com

- A -

ABELA, LEONARDO (1541–1605). The Titular Bishop of Sidonia and Apostolic Delegate, he was born in Mdina and was from a noble family, his two brothers serving as inquisitors in Malta. After studying law he became a doctor of canon and civil law and in 1578 was nominated Vicar General of Malta. Later that same year he moved to Rome and in 1582 was named Bishop of Sidonia, in Asia Minor (modern-day Turkey). In 1582 he was a signatory to a report urging for the adoption of the Gregorian calendar. Fluent in Arabic, as well as Hebrew, Chaldean and Syrian, he moved to Aleppo , Syria, in 1582, and after some years there, he returned briefly to Malta where he started work on the construction of a palace at Tarxian. He died on 2 May 1605 in Rome, and was buried in the Basilica of St. John Lateran. He remains the only Maltese to be buried there.

References: G. Bonello, 'The Great Bishop Leonardo Abela', *The Sunday Times* (Malta) (31 March 2002); G. Bonello, 'Leonardo Abela – a forgotten intellectual of the Cinquecento', *The Sunday Times* (Malta) (8 July 2007 & 15 July 2007); Michael J. Schiavone, *Dictionary of Maltese Biographies*, Malta: pubblikazzjonijiet Indipendenza, 2009, vol 1, pp. 13–14. Portrait courtesy Michael J. Schiavone.

ACACIUS. The bishop of Malta from 451, he preached at the old Christian Cathedral (on the site of the **Cathedral Church**) in Mdina soon after the Vandals arrived in Malta.

AGIUS-FERRANTE, ANNE (1925–   ). A politician, she was born on 29 August 1925 at Mdina as Anne Pullicino, the tenth child of Sir **Phillip Pullicino** (1885–1960), a prominent judge, and his wife Maude Samut, daughter of Achilles Samut. Educated at St. Dorothy's Convent and then at Sacred Heart School, she married Lieutenant Commander Lee-Watson in 1945 and they had a daughter, Susan Mary, born later that year. Four years later she married **Thomas Agius Ferrante** and they had a son, Timothy Luke,

born in 1953. She was the Malta Commissioner for the Girl Guides Association from 1957 to 1960, she was managing director of La Cittavecchia Ltd from 1964 to 1985. An active member of the **Rabat** branch of the Nationalist Party (PN), she contested the 1976 general election. In December 1980 she was elected to fill a casual vacancy in the parliament after the death of Dr Georg Borg Olivier, the former PN leader. Becoming the first PN woman in parliament, she contested the Sliema district in 1981 and lost, losing again in 1987. In 1992 she wrote a book on Mdina, *No Strangers in the Silent City*.

References: Anne Agius Ferrante, *No Strangers in the Silent City*, Valletta: Andrew Rupert Publishing, 1992; Michael J. Schiavone, *Dictionary of Maltese Biographies*, Malta: pubblikazzjonijiet Indipendenza, 2009, vol 1, pp. 47–48. Portrait courtesy Michael J. Schiavone.

AGIUS FERRANTE, THOMAS JOSEPH (1916–1974). A medical doctor, he was born on 8 May 1916 at Birkirkara, the son of Albert Agius and Mary (née Ferrante). Educated at the Lyceum 1926–33, and the Royal University of Malta 1933–40 (PhC 1936, BSc 1936, MD 1940), he worked as a Houseman in a range of hospitals in Malta during World War II, and deputised as the Child Health Officer in the Mother and Child Health Association 1940–43. Going to England in 1943, he was resident post graduate scholar at the Hospital for Sick Children, Great Ormond St, London 1943–44, and then was Houseman at Ladywood Road Hospital for Sick Children in Birmingham 1944–45, being a child health officer and antenatal officer for the Shrewsbury area in 1945. Returning to Malta, Dr Agius Ferrante was Child Health Officer for the Medical and Health Department, and Paediatrician to the Malta Government from 1946. He was also lecturer in Paediatrics at the Royal University of Malta, and was a member of the university senate from 1956 to 1959. He married Mrs Anne Watson, daughter of **Sir Philip Pullicino** on 10 August 1949, and they had one son, Timothy. The family lived at The Old Priory, 3 St. Peter St, Mdina, and Thomas died on 21 January 1974.

References: *Malta Who's Who 1964*, pp. 4–5; *Malta Who's Who 1965*, pp. 6–7; *Malta Who's Who 1968*, pp. 8–9; *Malta Who's Who 1969/70*, p. 8; Michael J. Schiavone, *Dictionary of Maltese Biographies*, Malta: pubbli-kazzjonijiet Indipendenza, 2009, vol 1, p. 48. Portrait courtesy Michael J. Schiavone.

Hurricanes take off at Ta Kali during World War II.

AIRPORT. The only airport on the island of Malta is Malta International Airport, but known locally as Luqa Airport as it used to be the base known as Royal Air Force Luqa. With much of Malta's economy based on tourism, the airport handled some 28,022 flights in and out of the country in 2011. The airport is located between the towns of Luqa and Gudja and is 10.6 kms from Mdina. There are regular bus services between the airport and **Rabat**.

There was a Royal Air Force base at Ta'Qali, just 1½ kms to the east of Mdina. Known as RAF Ta Kali, it was constructed over the site of an ancient lake. It had been used by civilian planes in the 1930s, and operated through World War II and on to the mid–1950s. In 1941, the NW-SE runway was extended from 777 metres (850 yards) to 1098 metres (1200 yards). Some of the old prefabricated steel Nissen huts survive and most have been turned into workshops for what is now the Ta'Qali Crafts Village. Nearby is the Malta Aviation Museum which has a range of planes connected with aviation in Malta including a World War II Spitfire, and a Hawker Hurricane IIa which was salvaged from off the southwest coast of Malta in 1995. The runway was closed in the 1970s but on 9 October 2014 it was briefly reopened for the taking off of a World War II vintage Tiger Moth.

References: http://maltaairport.com; 'Airfields', *After the Battle* No 10: Malta GC, London, 1975, pp. 2–9; http://www.maltaviationmuseum.com/; John F. Hamlin, *Military Aviation in Malta GC, 1915–1993: a comprehensive history*, Peterborough, UK: GMS Enterprises, 1994; Kevin Schembri Orland, 'WWII aircraft takes off from Ta' Qali and will participate in Mdina Grand Prix over the weekend', *Malta Independent* (9 October 2014).

de ALAGONA, ANTONIO. He was the bishop of Malta from 21 June 1447 until his replacement in January 1479 by **Giovanni Paterno**.

de ALBRAYNIO, MAURO. He was the bishop of Malta from 21 August 1420, and was succeeded by **Senatore di Noto** in February 1432.

ALDUINUS (ALDUINO). The bishop of Malta from 1332 to 1333, it was during his term in office that major work on the **Cathedral Church** in Mdina started.

ANDERSEN, HANS CHRISTIAN (1805–1875). The famous Danish writer of children's stories, he was born in 1805 in Odense, Denmark, and during 1833–34 he was in Italy. On his return, he started writing fairy stories, achieving some fame and leaving Denmark from 31 October 1840 and 22 July 1841, during which time he visited Malta. Of Mdina, he wrote 'Outside Città Vecchia we could see over the whole island. It lay without shadow, with a golden and shining surface like the sunshine itself. Low walls, forming enclosures, criss-crossed the whole island, giving it the appearance of a map on which even the smallest boundaries were marked.' For Mdina, he noted, 'Città Vecchia, the seat of the Bishop and former capital of the island, is a not insignificant town. The church [Cathedral], dedicated to St. Peter and St. Paul, is in the same style as the Italian churches – large, airy and colourful – but the traveller who comes from Italy is so surfeited by churches that even one like this fails to impress.' Returning to Denmark, he was becoming famous for

Hans Christian Anderson.
The Graphic 14 August 1875, p. 164.

his stories (which were being translated into English), and as an artist. His connection with Malta was commemorated by a series of four postage stamps issued by the Maltese postal authorities on 3 March 2005.

References: Hans Christian Andersen, *The Fairy Tale of My Life: My Autobiography,* New York: First Cooper Square Press, 2000, pp. 162–63; Hans Christian Andersen, *A visit to Germany, Italy and Malta 1840–41,* London: Peter Owen, 1985; Erik Dal, *A Poet's Bazaar: Hans Christian Andersen and his visit to Malta in 1841*, Valletta: Malta International Book Fair, 1991; Paul Xuereb, 'Malta in the 19th Century: A Selection of Visitors' Accounts', in *Images: Nineteenth Century Malta*, Valletta: Valletta Publishing Publication, 1989, pp. 6–7.

ANDREA. A Dominican, he was the bishop of Malta from 4 July 1414 until his death, being succeeded in Mach 1418 by Bishop Giovanni Ximines.

ANGAS, GEORGE FRENCH (1822–1886). An English explorer and naturalist, he was born on 25 April 1822 at Newcastle upon Tyne, England, his father was George Fife Angas who helped with the establishment of South Australia. He had planned to go into business and join his father but after leaving school, went around Europe and wrote his book, *Rambles in Malta and Sicily*.

In this book, George Angas wrote of Mdina, 'It is surrounded with walls, and fenced with bastions and other modern fortifications, which render it very strong, considering the elevated situation on which it stands. Brydone, who visited Malta some sixty or seventy years since, mentions a park which formerly stood here, but I certainly saw no vestige of it, nor does it seem ever to have consisted of more than two or three trees scattered about, here and there. In early times this city bore the same name

George French Angas, 1849.
by Charles Baugniet (1814–1886)

with the rest of the island and was called Melita, according to Ptolemy the geographer. Upon the authority of Cicero and Diodorus Siculus, we learn that the capital of Malta formerly contained many stately buildings, and was very rich in the style of its architecture. This I can easily conceive to have been the case from several remains which are still to be seen scattered about the city, and by the vestiges of ancient baths and temples which have been discovered during the progress of the excavations, both within the walls, as well as without the suburbs.'

As a result of the success of this book, he decided to become involved in natural history and went to South Australia, and then later to New Zealand, and several years later to South Africa, returning to Australia to work at the Australian Museum in Sydney. He later returned to London where he died on 8 October 1886.

References: George French Angas, *A ramble in Malta and Sicily in the Autumn of 1841*, London: Smith, Elder & Co, 1842; E J R Morgan, 'Angas, George French', *Australian Dictionary of Biography* vol 1, Melbourne: Melbourne University Press, 1966, pp. 15–18; Paul Xuereb, 'Malta in the 19th Century: A Selection of Visitors' Accounts', in *Images: Nineteenth Century Malta*, Valletta: Valletta Publishing Publication, 1989, p. 6.

ANTONIO. A Franciscan, he was the bishop of Malta from 19 August 1370, taking over from Bishop **Mario Corrado**, and was succeeded in 1371 by Bishop **Corrado**.

ANTONIO. He was the bishop of Malta from 29 July 1409, and held his position at the **Cathedral Church** in Mdina until his death in early 1414.

APOLLO, TEMPLE OF. *See* **Temple of Apollo**.

ARCHBISHOP SQUARE. *See* **Pjazza tal-Arċisqof**.

ARCHBISHOP'S PALACE. The original palace dates to medieval times, and was adjoining the **Cathedral Church**. It was restored in 1682 but was damaged eleven years later in an **earthquake**. With the rebuilding of the Cathedral, the new Latin Cross design of the Cathedral meant that the Bishop's Palace had to be moved and this took place with what is now the Archbishop's Palace constructed from 1717 to 1719 during the Bishopric of Mgr. **Cannaves**. Construction started on it after **Lorenzo Gafà** finished his work on the Cathedral. Some of the windows are similar to those designed by

Francesco Borromini at the Collegio di Propaganda Fide in Rome. In 1798 the French General **Claude-Henri Vaubois**, on arriving in the city and being appointed Commander in Chief of Malta and Gozo by Napoleon, dined at the palace as a guest of Bishop **Vincenzo Labini**. On 1 January 1944 the Diocese of Malta was raised to an Archdiocese.

References: Richard England and Conrad Thake, *Mdina: Citadel of Memory*, Malta: Atlantis, 1995, pp. 11–12, 94–97; John Manduca, *Tourist Guide to City of Mdina*, Malta: Progress Press, 1975, p. 35–37.

ARCHITECTURE. There has long been a fascination with the architecture at Mdina. Although the city dates from before **Roman** times, and the site of a Roman villa has been excavated by archaeologists, the city walls and the old buildings date from medieval times with a few credited as having Norman origins although some modern historians doubt this. The **Cathedral Church** (which was dated by tradition to 1090) seems to date from the mid-fourteenth century, and the Norman House (now **Palazzo Falzon**) dates from 1495. It seems likely that many other old buildings also date from late medieval times, and added to during the Renaissance at which time many of the interiors were also remodelled. Gradually there have been modern changes and improvements to the city with sewage, water pipes, and later electricity

Mdina in 1975.
Photograph by Robin Corfield.

Mdina in 1975.
Photograph by Robin Corfield.

Photograph willmac / Big Stock Photo

Photograph © rosacant / Fotolia.com

Photograph willmac / Big Stock Photo

Mdina, 1978.
Painting by Robin Corfield.

and gas, as well as telephone and cable television wires. To help preserve Mdina, there are strict planning codes with the city being renovated as a part of a European Architectural Heritage Year programme in July 1974.

References: Mario Buhagiar, *Essays on the Knights and Art and Architecture in Malta 1500–1798*, Sta Venera, Midsea Books, 2009, reviewed by Charlene Vella, *Melita Historica* vol 15, no 2 (2009), pp. 221–23; Daniel Cilia and Michael Ellul, *Legacy in stone: the architecture of the Knights of St. John in Malta*, Sliema: Miranda Publications, 1991; Denis de Lucca, *Mdina: A History of Its Urban Space and Architecture*, Valletta: Said International, 1995; Francesco Menchetti, *Architects and Knights: Italian Influence in Malta during the Late Renaissance*, Valletta: Fondazzjoni Patrimonju Malti, 2013; George A Said-Zammit, *The Architectural Heritage of the Maltese Islands*, Malta: The Minor Seminary, 2008; Uwe Jens Rudolf and Warren G. Berg, *Historical Dictionary of Malta*, Lanham, Md: Scarecrow Press, 2010, pp. 29–32; Conrad Thake, 'Architectural scenography in 18th century Malta', *History Week* (1994), pp. 63–76; Conrad Thake, Mdina: architectural and urban transformations of a citadel in Malta, PhD in Architecture, University of California, Berkeley, 1996; John Ward-Perkins, 'Medieval and Early Renaissance Architecture in Malta', in Anthony T. Luttrell (ed.), *Medieval Malta: Studies on Malta before the Knights*, London: The British School at Rome, 1975, pp. 217–23.

ART. Although there are a number of important paintings in Mdina, especially in the **Cathedral Church** and the **Cathedral Museum**, there have also been many local and foreign artists who have been captivated by Mdina, with the city painted many times, especially from a distance, including Sir **Hugh Casson**, Frederick Morgan, and others.

References: Vincent Borg, *Contemporary Christian Art: Malta 2002*, Mdina: Cathedral Museum, 2002; Mario Buhagiar, *Essays on the Knights and Art and Architecture in Malta 1500–1798*, Sta Venera, Midsea Books, 2009; Nicholas de Piro, *The International Dictionary of Artists who Painted Malta*, Valletta: Audio Visual Centre Limited, 2003, p. 115, 176–78, 324, 335, 514, 523.

ASTIRIA, LORENZO (1604–1677). Born at Tirasonen, Spain, he was ordained priest in the Sovereign Military Hospitaller Order of St. John of Jerusalem, 22 April 1628. He was the bishop of Malta from 16 June 1670, ordained on 6 July, and remained in office until his death in January 1677.

ATTARD, GEORGE. He was the Mayor of Mdina from 1994 to 2000, and was succeeded by **Mario Galea Testaferrata**. A teacher for 35 years, he studied at the University of Malta, and graduated with an MA in history in 1984. He was also the first assistant editor of the history journal Storja. George Attard was also involved in working in Britain, Australia and Papua New Guinea, being a captain in the Australian Territorial Army in the late 1960s.

ATTARD, JANE (1924–). Born on 27 December 1924, she worked in the civil service as a clerk-typist in the conscription office, and then became heavily involved in the opening of the Victory Kitchen around Malta to serve food during World War II. She married John Attard and they had two children. Jane Attard worked for her husband's company, Greenhand Leathercraft. She was elected to Mdina local council when it was established in 1994, and been re-elected at subsequent elections for the Nationalist Party. She lives in Triq Villegaignon. On the evening of 11 November 2007, her house was attacked by vandals.

References: 'Mdina council deplores vandalism', *The Times* (15 November 2007).

ATTARD, PIETRO MARTIRE (1591–1666). A theologian and scholar, he was born in Mdina and studied with the Dominicans in **Rabat** from 1609, and ordained priest six years later. In 1617 he gained a theology degree at Messina, Sicily. He then spent the next 49 years teaching theology at the seminary in Mdina, and elsewhere in Malta and in Sicily. He died on 12 February 1666 at the Dominican Convent in Valletta.

References: Michael J. Schiavone, *Dictionary of Maltese Biographies*, Malta: pubblikazzjonijiet Indipendenza, 2009, vol 1, p. 108.

AUSTIN, SARAH (1793–1867). An English editor, she was born on 19 February 1793 in Norwich, England, as Sarah Taylor, the youngest child of John Taylor, a yarn maker and well-known Unitarian hymn writer, and his wife Sarah (née Hall). In 1819 she married John Austin (1790–1859) who became a prominent British jurist. John Austin was sent to Malta to work with the British soldiers posted there, and where Sarah Austin became fascinated with Maltese history. She enjoyed visiting Mdina and wrote of it, and also of her stay on the island in affectionate terms. The Austins later went to Germany, settling in Bonn. As a result, Sarah Austin worked as a translator of books from German into English, as did their daughter Lucie. Returning to England, she died on 8 August 1867 at Weybridge, Surrey, and is buried next to her husband in the churchyard of St. James, Weybridge.

References: 'Mrs Austin', *The Times* (12 August 1867), p. 10; Sarah Austin, 'Letter to Mr Murray, June 20, 1837', in Janet Ross, *Three generations of Englishwomen*, London: John Murray, 1888; Joseph Hamburger, 'Austin, Sarah (1793–1867)', *Oxford Dictionary of National Biography*, Oxford University Press, 2004; Lotte Hamburger and Joseph Hamburger, *Troubled lives: John and Sarah Austin*, Toronto: University of Toronto Press, 1985; Paul Xuereb, 'Malta in the 19th Century: A Selection of Visitors' Accounts', in *Images: Nineteenth Century Malta*, Valletta: Valletta Publishing Publication, 1989, p. 5.

AXAC, INDRI (d. 1565). Born in about 1500 in **Rabat**, he was ordained a priest and taught philosophy in Mdina and later Birgu. In 1545 the Inquisition was critical of his beliefs which it believed were heretical. There were also persistent claims that he had married. Sent to Rome to face an inquiry, he was then accused of teaching using books which had been prohibited by the Catholic Church. Again sent to Rome in 1560, he was interrogated and forced to renounce any support for the beliefs of Erasmus. This had him condemned and forced to wear a cross over his clothes, not to teach any more, and to remain in Rome which he died in 1565.

References: Michael J. Schiavone, *Dictionary of Maltese Biographies*, Malta: pubblikazzjonijiet Indipendenza, 2009, vol 1, p. 117.

AZOPARDI, FRANCESCO (1748–1809). A prominent composer of **music**, and one of the most well-known musicians in eighteenth century Malta, he was born on 5 May 1748 in Mdina. Recognised as a musical prodigy, he went to study at the Conservatorio Sant'Onofrio a Capuana, Naples, working under Carlo Cotumacci and Joseph Doll. Remaining in Naples where he finished his studies in 1767, seven years later he returned to Mdina and was appointed organist at Mdina **Cathedral** and after Benigno Zerafa resigned on 7 January 1787, Azopardi became the *maestro di cappella* at the cathedral. He later also took up the same position at St. John's Co-Cathedral, Valletta and held both positions until his death on 6 February 1809. His contribution to Maltese music was commemorated on a postage stamp issued on 25 April 1985.

References: John Azzopardi, *Nicolo Isouard de Malte*, Mdina: Friends of the Cathedral Museum, 1991; 'Biografia – Francesco Azopardi', *L'Arte* vol 1, no 13 (1863); Spiridion Vincent Buhagiar, Francesco Azopardi (1748–1809): A Maltese Classical Composer, Theorist, and Teacher, Mediterranean Institute, university thesis, University of Malta, Msida, 1999; Michael J. Schiavone, *Dictionary of Maltese Biographies*, Malta: pubblikazzjonijiet Indipendenza, 2009, vol 1, pp. 122–23; P Pullicino, *Notizia biografica di Francesco Azzopardi*, Malta: Z. Micallef tip, 1876; P Xuareb, 'Golden age of Mdina Cathedral's music', *The Times* (8 August 2001).

AZZOPARDI, FREDERICK. A mechanical engineer, he graduated with a B.Eng. (Hons) degree from the University of Malta in 1996 and completed his masters in Islands and Small States Studies in 2002. The chief engineer at the services division within the Ministry for Resources and Rural Affairs, he was elected to **Rabat** local council in 2000, and to Mdina local council in 2006, being re-elected in 2009. He is currently the only Labour Party member on the council. He is married to Nadette (née Falzon), and they have two daughters, Elisa Mae and Amaia Joy.

– B –

BACCHUS. This restaurant in **Triq Inguanez** opened in August 1976 and is located in the basement of the De Redin Bastion wich had been used as a powder magazine during the time of the Knights of Malta. It has retained the same owner and managing director, Mario Vella Gatt, and some of the original Roman masonry is visible in the walls. In 2001 the restaurant gained the status of being 'hospitality assured' with its chief chef Antoinne Mamo. It was badly damaged by fire on 30 June 2006 with the staff and all 35 being evacuated to safety. Two of the staff, however, trapped at the back, managed to climb out onto a nearby building without too much difficulty.

References: Bacchus Restaurant, www.bacchus.com.mt; Carolyn Bain, *Malta & Gozo*, Footscray, Vic, Australia: Lonely Planet, 2004, p. 121; Mark Macallef, 'Mdina restaurant gutted by fire', *The Times of Malta* (1 July 2006).

BALAGUER CAMARASA, MIGUEL JUAN. A member of the Sovereign Military Hospitaller Order of St. John of Jerusalem, he was the bishop of Malta from 12 February 1635, being ordained on 18 February and installed on 25 March. He remained in office until his death on 5 December 1663.

References: John Montalto, *The Nobles of Malta, 1530–1800*, Valletta: Midsea Books, 1979, p. 136, 141, 145, 160, 171.

BALBI, HENRY ALEXANDER (1867–1938). The owner of the **Palazzo Falzon** for several years, he was born on 9 October 1867 in Malta, the son of Raffaele Balbi and Rosina (née Pavia). In 1887 he was commissioned as Second Lieutenant in the Royal Malta Fencible Artillery, and was two years later transferred to the Royal Malta Artillery on its formation. On 14 February 1891 he was promoted to Lieutenant in the Royal Malta Artillery. He married

Eileen Mary Macdermott in 1895 and remained in the Royal Malta Artillery attaining the rank of Major in 1899. In 1906 he was the Founding President of the Senglea Athletics Football Club. Retiring from the Royal Malta Artillery in 1910, he moved to England and lived at 20 Montagu St, London WC1, and then returned to Malta to live at the Palazzo Falzon. He died on 11 July 1938 at Zammit Clapp Hospital, Malta. He gave his address in his will as 'Norman House'.

DE BALDES, PIETRO. A juror in 1451 and again in 1477, he was the **Capitano della Verga** of Mdina, 1460–61 and 1484–86. He married and had two children: Cafa Baldes and Isabella Baldes.

BANCA GIURATALE. It was long believed that this building was constructed on the site which had been occupied in Roman times by a temple to the God Apollo, but it appears the temple was slightly to the south of it. The house was built as the family seat of the Marquis of San Vincenzo Ferreri and his family. The title was created in 1716 by King Philip V of Spain and the current house was designed by **Charles François de Mondion** in the Baroque style, and built in 1726 by **António Manoel de Vilhena**, the Grand Master of the Knights of Malta from 1722 to 1736, with the Maltese master mason Petruzzo Debono supervising the construction from 1726 to 1728. During the Maltese rebellion against the French – whose headquarters were opposite in the **House of Notary Bezzina** – the local citizens declared the establishment of a National Assembly and it met in what was then known as the Palazzo Giuratale. In 1831 it was the location of the district court and gained the name Municipal Palace from this connection. In 1881 the Education department took over the building which was a secondary school until 1969 when it was leased to the Sisters of St. Dorothy who ran a private school for girls for a period. It now houses part of the **National Archives of Malta**. In the impressive hallway, there is a permanent display of portraits of prominent Maltese people. It is open to the public from 8 am to 2 pm on Mondays, Tuesdays, Wednesdays and Fridays, and from 10 am to 2 pm on Thursdays, as well as being open on Monday afternoons from 3 pm to 7.30 pm.

References: Richard England and Conrad Thake, *Mdina: Citadel of Memory*, Malta: Atlantis, 1995, pp. 52–53; John Manduca, *Tourist Guide to City of Mdina*, Malta: Progress Press, 1975, pp. 19–20; Edward Sammut, *The Monuments of Mdina*, Malta: Progress Press Co. Ltd, 1967, p. 18–20.

BANCHERINI, ANDREA. By tradition, he was the bishop of Malta from c1270, taking over from **John Normandus**, and was in office for about two years. Bancherini was a member of the Order of Preachers, the Dominicans.

BANKS. Formerly there were banking houses in Mdina, such as the **Banca Giuratale**, but now there are none. There are a few located in **Rabat**, the closest being the Bank of Valletta near the **Howard Gardens**. The souvenir shop called the Maltese Falcon near the **Cathedral** does exchange foreign currency.

References: John Consiglio, *A History of Banking in Malta 1506–2005*, Valletta: Progress Press, 2006; Uwe Jens Rudolf and Warren G. Berg, *Historical Dictionary of Malta*, Lanham, Md: Scarecrow Press, 2010, pp. 35–37.

BARTOLI, EMANUELE (1852–1933). A **music** composer, he was born on 13 February 1852 at Mdina and studied under Giuseppe Spiteri Fremond. He was the bandmaster of the Pinto Band at Qormi from 1862 to 1877, and the L'Isle-Adam Band Club of **Rabat** from 1876–79, and again from 1921–24. In February 1872 he made his debut with *L'Amore* at the Royal Theatre in Valletta. He was in charge of the choir at the Royal Opera House between 1879–80, and then in 1886–87. From 1883 until World War I, he was a tenor at Mdina **Cathedral** and also St. John's Co-Cathedral in Valletta. He died on 2 April 1933.

References: Michael J. Schiavone, *Dictionary of Maltese Biographies*, Malta: pubblikazzjonijiet Indipendenza, 2009, vol 1, p. 183. Portrait courtesy Michael J. Schiavone.

BASTION SQUARE. *See* **Pjazza tas-Sur**.

BASTION(S) STREET. *See* **is-Sur, Triq**.

BELLANTI, PAOLO FRANCESO (1852–1927). An author and historian, he was born on 5 March 1852 at Mdina, the son of Michele Bellanti, and educated at the Lyceum. In 1868 he joined the civil service and worked in various roles until he became the superintendent of the government printing office, and published the debates of the council. He wrote about the Maltese language, and in 1924 wrote *Studies in Maltese History*, covering the period from the visit of St. Paul though to the fifth century. He died on 13 February 1927.

References: Michael J. Schiavone, *Dictionary of Maltese Biographies*, Malta: pubblikazzjonijiet Indipendenza, 2009, vol 1, p. 192; William Zammit (ed), and Patricia Camilleri, Antonio Espinosa Rodriguez, Joseph Felice Pace, Albert Ganado, Mark Sagona, and Theresa Vella, *The Bellanti family: contributions to art and culture in Malta*, Valletta: Fondazzjoni Patrimonju Malti in association with Midsea Books, 2010.

BENEDICTINE NUNNERY. This nunnery located on **Triq Villegaignon**, was founded in 1418 in a building that had been used as a Hospital for Women and was dedicated to St. Peter. The nunnery was for an enclosed order and some of the building dates from a restoration in 1479. In 1575 Mgr. Pietroi Duzzina, an Apostolic Visitor sent by the Pope to report on Malta and Gozo, went to the nunnery and found there were 15 nuns living there and many of whom were illiterate. He laid down new regulations for the nunnery by which they could not take in novices under the age of 16, and that all novices had to spend at least a year there before becoming a nun. In 1625 the nunnery was substantially renovated and rebuilt.

The nunnery remains enclosed, and the only men allowed to visit without the permission of the Bishop are the doctor and the whitewasher – the latter to apply lime to the walls to disinfect the building and prevent the spread of infectious diseases. No nun after taking her vows is allowed to leave the nunnery and up until 1974 all nuns were buried in a crypt within the walls of the nunnery. In 1975 there were 22 nuns who spent much of their time in prayer and contemplation, or in embroidery or tending the garden of the convent. The chapel has a magnificent altarpiece by Mattia Preti which depicts the Madonna and Child with St. Peter, St. Benedict and St. Scholastica.

References: Richard England and Conrad Thake, *Mdina: Citadel of Memory*, Malta: Atlantis, 1995, pp. 40–41, 4–47; John Manduca, *Tourist Guide to City of Mdina*, Malta: Progress Press, 1975, pp. 18–19; Edward Sammut, *The Monuments of Mdina*, Malta: Progress Press Co. Ltd, 1967, pp. 16–17.

BERNARD, PAOLO (1763–1844). A prominent physician, he was born in Mdina, the son of Dr Salvatore Bernard and Domenica Micallef (née Inguanez). Educated at the seminary in Mdina, he became a cavalry officer with the Order of St. John. When the Maltese laid siege to the French in Valletta, he was a member of the Maltese forces, and in 1800 the British appointed him the commissioner of civil hospitals. In 1807 he was promoted to administrator of the hospital in Malta, and gained much respect for his work during the plague of 1813. Later he was auditor of accounts for the Malta diocese working under Bishop **Ferdinand Mattei**, and died on 11 December 1844 after a long illness.

He was buried in the family vault at Ta' Giezu church, Valletta.

References: Michael J. Schiavone, *Dictionary of Maltese Biographies*, Malta: pubblikazzjonijiet Indipendenza, 2009, vol 1, p. 199.

BEZZINA, PIETRO ANTONIO. He was a notary in Mdina at the time of the French Occupation of Malta in 1798, and the son of Aloiseo Bezzina and Maria Palma Bugea. In 1782 at Senglea he married Felicitia Viola. Establishing himself in Mdina, when the French invaded, he was a supporter of the new rulers. As a result when the French began to sell material taken from the **Carmelite Church** in Mdina on 2 September 1798, crowds attacked the French and the French commander Masson caused even more anger when he went with a lieutenant and soldier to loot St. Paul's Church in **Rabat**. He was then attacked and fled to the **House of the Notary Bezzina** opposite the **Banca Giuratale** on ***Triq Villegaignon***. The mob surrounded the house and stormed it, throwing him from the window.

References: Denis de Lucca, *Mdina: A History of Its Urban Space and Architecture*, Valletta: Said International, 1995, p. 116.

BLAQUIERE, EDWARD (1779–1832). A British naval officer, he was the author of *Letters from the Mediterranean* (1813). Born in 1779 in Ireland, the sixth of the eight children of James Blaquiere (1726–1803), a cavalry officer and later farmer, of Huguenot descent, Edward Blaquiere joined the Royal Navy in 1794 and gained a commission in 1801. His book, *Letters from the Mediterranean* reflects on his time as a naval officer in Malta during the Napoleonic Wars.

After the Napoleonic Wars, Blaquiere became a liberal and supported the constitutional movements in Spain and Portugal, as well as the struggle for independence in Latin America, and the Greek War of Independence. He drowned at sea off the Azores in early 1832 on the way to take part in the move by Dom Pedro IV to retake Portugal and establish a constitutional government and overthrow the Miguelites.

References: Edward Blaquiere, *Letters from the Mediterranean, containing a civil and political account of Sicily, Tripoly, Tunis and Malta*, London: Colburn, 1813, 2 Vols; F. Rosen, 'Blaquiere, Edward (1779–1832)', *Oxford Dictionary of National Biography*, Oxford University Press, 2004; Paul Xuereb, 'Malta in the 19th Century: A Selection of Visitors' Accounts', in *Images: Nineteenth Century Malta*, Valletta: Valletta Publishing Publication, 1989, p. 2–3.

BLESSED MARIA ADEODATA PISANI SQUARE. *See* **Pjazzetta Beata Marija Adeodata Pisani**.

da BOLOGNA, BERNARDINO. He was the bishop of Malta from 5 October 1506 to 23 January 1512 when he was nominated as Archbishop of Messina, Sicily, a position he held until 1513.

BONDINO, GIACOMO (1488–1546). A notary and author, he was born in Mdina and was a descendant of Lancia de Bandino (sic) who was ennobled in 1398. A school teacher, Fiacomo Bondino soon worked as a notary. After the death of his wife, he became a priest and was appointed to the parish of Zebbug. However Bishop Cubelles, during a visit to see him, claimed that there were irregularities in his receiving of benefices, and forbade him to be a priest. Grief-stricken, he died soon afterwards.

References: Michael J. Schiavone, *Dictionary of Maltese Biographies*, Malta: pubblikazzjonijiet Indipendenza, 2009, vol 1, p. 225.

BONETI, NICOLAUS. He was the bishop of Malta from 27 November 1342 until about 1343, and was succeeded by Bishop **Ogerius**.

BONNICI, ANTONIO. The **Capitano della Verga** of Mdina, 1710–13, he was probably the son of Alessandro Bonnici who, in 1710, married Nobile Caterina Abela, an hereditary noble of Hungary, and they had several children.

BONNICI, DOMENICO. The **Capitano della Verga** of Mdina, 1680–82, he was the son ofLuca Bonnici. In 1667 he married Maria Briffa and they had several children.

BONNICI, GIO' BATTA. The **Capitano della Verga** of Mdina, 1684–86, he was the son of Ignazio Bonnici and his wife Antonio (née Cassar) whom he had married in 1636. Gio' Batta Bonnici married Caterina Cassar in 1661 and they had several children.

BONNICI, GIUSEPPE. The **Capitano della Verga** of Mdina, 1814–15, he was probably the person of that name who married first Margerhita Muscat, and after her death, married Maria Gambin in 1810 at Valletta.

BON(N)ICI, GREGORIO (or **GIRGOR**) **(1612–1697).** The **Capitano**

della Verga of Mdina, 1654–56, and a philanthropist, he was born on 18 March 1612 in Mdina, from the noble family of Bonici, the son of Gio Maria Bonnici and his wife Marghareita Camenzuli who were married in 1608. In 1646 Gregorio Bonnici married Elena Barbaro and they had several children, one of whom was the ancestor of the Baron Bonici. Prior to his appointment as **Capitano della Verga**, he was the Procurator of Wheat and was posted to Licata. One of the four jurats of the city, the Maltese popular council nominated him their ambassador to Licata, Sicily, and in 1654 he became the governor of Mdina. A generous benefactor to the parish church at Zeitun, donating the land on which it was built, he also went to Rome to protest against the Order of St. John which had been taxing the local church to build more fortifications.

References: John Montalto, *The Nobles of Malta, 1530–1800*, Valletta: Midsea Books, 1979, p. 123, 275; Michael J. Schiavone, *Dictionary of Maltese Biographies*, Malta: pubblikazzjonijiet Indipendenza, 2009, vol 1, p. 237.

BON(N)ICI, GREGORIO. He was the **Capitano della Verga** of Mdina, 1797–99, and was the Baron of Qlejja. In office and a member of the council at the time of the French invasion, he presided over the meeting of the Mdina council at which it was decided that they should not resist the French troops providing that the occupiers guaranteed to respect the liberty, property and religion of the inhabitants of the city and accept the current public institutions. As a result Bonici provided the keys of Mdina to the French commander **Claude-Henri Belgrand de Vaubois**.

References: Denis de Lucca, *Mdina: A History of Its Urban Space and Architecture*, Valletta: Said International, 1995, p. 115; John Montalto, *The Nobles of Malta, 1530–1800*, Valletta: Midsea Books, 1979, p. 117, 349.

BONNICI, IGNAZIO. The **Capitano della Verga** of Mdina, 1640–42, he was the son of Dr Gio Batta Bonnici and his wife Angelica Xara Cassis dei Baroni di Ghariexem e Tabis. One of his descendants was appointed Baron of Qlejja by Grand Master Ramon Despuig.

References: John Montalto, *The Nobles of Malta, 1530–1800*, Valletta: Midsea Books, 1979, p. 32, 159.

DI BORDINO, LEONARDO. The **Capitano della Verga** of Mdina, 1455–56, he was probably the Leonardo de Borino who was the son of Antonio de Bordino, and who married Agata La Barba.

DI BORDINO, LEONARDO. The **Capitano della Verga** of Mdina, 1522–23, he was the third son of Orlando de Bordino, the 4th Signore ta' Bareri and Signore di Chalka di Ghajn Cuffuto. He was a member of the Università Dei Giurati and married Isabella de Nasis, and they had a son, Orlando. He then married Francesca de Vaccaro, 5th Baroness di Benuwarret and they had two sons, Giovanni and Goffredo, and two daughters Francia and Bettina.

BORG, EMANUEL V. (1945–). An art critic, he was born on 12 May 1945 in Mdina, and was educated at the Lyceum, and then St. Michael's Training College, then went to the Malta College of Arts, Science and Technology, proceeding to the University of Malta and graduated with a BA in history and classical civilisation. In 1962 he joined the department of education and then worked in primary schools, secondary schools and in the university. Contributing to a wide range of publications, he is one of the important art critics in Malta.

References: Michael J. Schiavone, *Dictionary of Maltese Biographies*, Malta: pubblikazzjonijiet Indipendenza, 2009, vol 1, p. 265. Portrait courtesy Michael J. Schiavone.

BOSIO, TOMMASO (d. 1539). A member of the Sovereign Military Hospitaller Order of St. John of Jerusalem, he was the bishop of Malta from 20 March 1538 until his death on 15 August 1539.

BOWER, ROBERT TATTON (1894–1975). A British Conservative politician who later retired to Mdina, he was born on 9 June 1894 at Bray, County Wicklow, Ireland, the son of Sir Robert Lister Bower KBE CMG and Annette (née Head). Educated at Cheam School and the Royal Naval Colleges at Osborne and Dartmouth, he married Hon. Henrietta Strickland in 1922. Having served in the Royal Navy in World War I at Jutland and elsewhere,

he retired in 1931 and in that year was elected to the British House of Commons as Conservative Member of Parliament for Cleveland, Yorkshire. In 1938, he was involved in an outburst during a debate in which some Labour MPs were arguing against the British government's recognition of the duke of Alba as a diplomatic representative of General Francisco Franco in the Spanish Civil War. This meant that the British were effectively recognising the Nationalists during the war. The Labour MP Emanuel Shinwell was speaking when Bower interrupted him and told him to 'go back to Poland'. Shinwell then walked over to Bower and punched him, turned to the Speaker and apologised, leaving the House of Commons. Bower then also apologised, and the matter was dropped. Commander Robert Bower was MP until 1945, serving as a Naval Liaison Officer in World War II. He then retired to Malta and lived at the **Palazzo Gatto-Murino** in Mdina. He died on 5 July 1975.

References: Harold Acton, *Nancy Mitford: a memoir*, London: Hamish Hamilton, 1975, p. 84; *Who was Who 1971–1980*, p. 86; *Malta Who's Who 1969/70*, p. 64.

BRAUN, VALENTIN GERHARD (1919–1998). An art dealer, he was born on 14 February 1919 in Cologne, Germany, a member of a German Jewish family. He left Nazi Germany in 1939 and went to Kenya where he ran an art gallery and became an art dealer and abstract impressionist. In 1963, worried about Kenyan independence, he moved to Cyprus but with political trouble there, he relocated to Malta in 1966 where he often used the additional name Dusemond. He lived with his six children at the Palazzo Gourgion (now **Casa Gourgion**) and he ran The Mdina Gallery, and also continued painting. In 1976 the government of Dom Mintoff expelled the Braun-Dusemond family from Malta and they decided to return to Germany where Gerhard Braun held two exhibitions. However he was unhappy and moved to Wells, Somerset, and died in 1998 in Taunton, Somerset.

References: Lisa Gwen Baldacchino, 'Reviving a gallery in Mdina', *The Times of Malta* (4 March 2010); *Malta Who's Who 1969/70*, p. 65.

BRIALDO. By tradition, he was the bishop of Malta from 1095, and was said to have taken over from Bishop **Gualtieri**. According to early modern historians of Malta, he helped oversee the building work on the **Cathedral Church** in Mdina.

BRYDONE, PATRICK (1736–1818). The author of *A tour through Sicily and Malta* which was first published in 1773, Patrick Brydone was born on 5 January 1736, probably at Coldingham, Berwickshire, Scotland, the son of Robert Brydone, a minister with the Church of Scotland and his wife Elizabeth Dysart, the daughter of Rev Robert Brydone's predecessor. He was admitted to St. Andrew's University in 1750–51, and then is presumed to have served in the British army. In the summer of 1770 he went to Naples, and from there to Sicily and then to Malta which he recorded in his book, first published in 1773. In his book, he wrote:

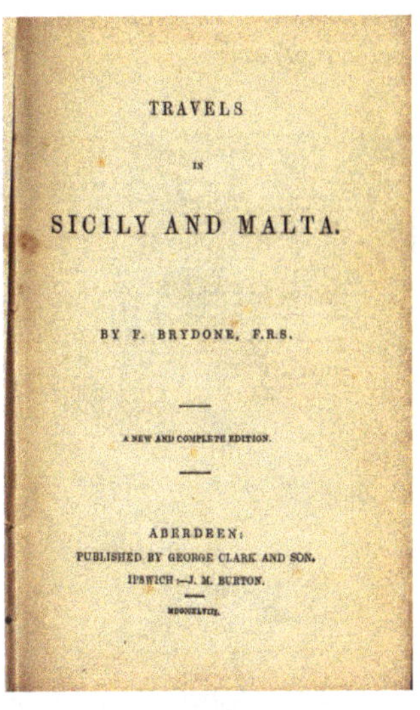
TRAVELS

IN

SICILY AND MALTA.

BY P. BRYDONE, F.R.S.

A NEW AND COMPLETE EDITION.

ABERDEEN:
PUBLISHED BY GEORGE CLARK AND SON.
IPSWICH :—J. M. BURTON.

'We went first to the ancient city of Melita, which is near the centre of the island, and commands a view of the whole; and in clear weather, they pretend, of part of Barbary and of Sicily. The city is strongly fortified, and is governed by an officer called the Hahem. He received us very politely, and showed us the old palace, which is not indeed much worth the seeing. The cathedral is a very fine church, and, although of an exceeding large size, is at present entirely hung with crimson damask richly laced with gold.'

The book introduced both Sicily and Malta to the British public, and was reprinted many times. He was later comptroller of the stamp office and lived in relative obscurity for many years. He died on 19 June 1818 at Lennel House, Berwickshire.

References: Patrick Brydone, *A tour through Sicily and Malta*, Edinburgh: William and Robert Chambers, 1840; Edward Chaney, *The Evolution of the Grand Tour*, London: Routledge, 2000; Paul Fussell, 'Patrick Brydone: The Eighteenth-Century Traveler As Representative Man', in *Literature As a Mode of Travel: Five Essays and a Postscript*, New York: New York Public Library, 1963, pp. 53–67; Katherine Turner, 'Brydone, Patrick (1736–1818)', *Oxford Dictionary of National Biography*, Oxford University Press, 2004.

BUENOS, LUCA (d. 1668). The titular bishop of Thessalonica from 15 September 1664, he was Spanish and was the bishop of Malta from 15 December 1666 until his death 7 September 1668, having taken over after the death of **Miguel Jean Balaguer Camarasa**. He was succeeded by **Lorenzo Astiria**.

References: John Montalto, *The Nobles of Malta, 1530–1800*, Valletta: Midsea Books, 1979, p. 97 n46.

BUGEJA, PIETRO PAOLO (1772–1828). A music composer, he was born on 29 April 1772 at Valletta, the son of Salvatore Bugeja and his wife Gaetana. He studied under Francesco Azopardi and when he was nineteen he went to Azopardi's former school, the Conservatorio Sant'Onofrio a Capuana, Naples. After six years there, he returned to Malta and when Azopardi died in 1809, he succeeded him as maestro di cappella at the Mdina **Cathedral**, and also at St. John's Co-Cathedral, Valletta. Composing a number of important pieces of music, his sacred oratorio, Gioas, Re di Guida was first performed at the Royal Theatre at Valletta in 1815. He also performed for the arrival of Sir Francis Hastings when he turned up in Malta to assume the position of governor of Malta in March 1824. He had married Antonia Pulis and they had three children. He died on 12 June 1828. His son Vincenzo Bugeja (1805–1860) followed in his father's footsteps and also studied at Naples.

References: Michael J. Schiavone, *Dictionary of Maltese Biographies*, Malta: pubblikazzjonijiet Indipendenza, 2009, vol 1, pp. 327–28.

BUHAGIAR, ANTONIO MARIA (1846–1891). He was the administrator bishop of Malta from 1884–88. Born on 19 November 1846 in Cephalonia in the Ionian Islands, then administered by Britain. His father Joseph Buhagiar, a merchant, was from Haz-Zebbug and his mother, Maria Concetta (née Attard) was from Floriana. He joined the Capuchin Order in Malta and then studied at the University of Malta, being ordained priest in September 1869. Pope Leo XI appointed him administrator bishop of Malta in July 1884, being consecrated on 12 August of the same year. He then served as apostolic administrator when Bishop Carmelo Scicluna was ill. Active helping people in the 1887 cholera epidemic, he was later posted to the Dominican Republic, Haiti and Venezuela, dying on 10 August 1891. He was buried at the Iglesia de San Lorenzo in Santo Domingo, in the Dominican Republic.

References: Michael J. Schiavone, *Dictionary of Maltese Biographies*, Malta: pubblikazzjonijiet Indipendenza, 2009, vol 1, pp. 336–37.

BURNS, Mrs TINA. One of the British community in Mdina, she lived in India with her husband and after his death she moved to Malta, living at No 7 Bastion Square. When she ventured out, she wore a red wig with a fringe. An oleander tree grew in front of her house and she saw it as a reincarnation of her husband.

References: Anne Agius Ferrante, *No Strangers in the Silent City*, Valletta: Andrew Rupert Publishing, 1992, p. 23.

DE BUSSAN, (PAUL) ALPHERAN (1684–1757). Born on 28 October 1684 at Aquen, he was ordained priest of the Sovereign Military Hospitaller Order of St. John of Jerusalem, on 8 December 1710. He was appointed bishop of Malta on 8 March 1728, and ordained on 14 March, being appointed titular archbishop of Tamiathis. He immediately gave the 'go-ahead' for the rebuilding of the Mdina Seminary which had been so badly damaged in the earthquake of 1693. To help the work on the Mdina Seminary (now the **Cathedral Museum**) and in 1733 he imposed an ecclesiastical tax on the population which succeeded in raising enough money for the building. He was also the institutor of the annual commemorative service held on 4 November each year at the **Cathedral Church** to remember Duke Roger of Sicily. He died on 20 April 1757.

– C –

CAFFÈ MEDINA. A popular cake shop located on **Triq Villegaignon**, it has cakes, baguettes, jacket potatoes, pasta and salad, being popular with the thousand or so tourists who visit the city each day.

References: Carolyn Bain, *Malta & Gozo*, Footscray, Vic, Australia: Lonely Planet, 2004, p. 121.

CAGLIARES, BALDASSARE (1575–1633). A member of the Sovereign Military Hospitaller Order of St. John of Jerusalem, he was born in Valletta, and had served in Portugal. He became bishop of Malta on 18 March 1615, living in a country house called Monte Cagliaresio, on a hill, near Mdina. There in 1620 he conferred Holy Orders on Domenico Magri (1604–1672), later a prominent scholar of Maltese history. He died on 4 August 1633.

References: John Montalto, *The Nobles of Malta, 1530–1800*, Valletta: Midsea Books, 1979, p. 23.

CAGLIOSTRO, ALESSANDRO (1743–1795). An occultist called Giuseppe Balsamo, he was involved in the 'Affair of the Diamond Necklace' which took place in the mid–1780s and became a scandal which was used to highlight corruption in the French Royal Court in the run-up to the French Revolution. During the 'affair', he used the name and title Count Alessandro di Cagliostro. The exact origins of Balsamo are not known with any certainty but it was long suggested that he was born in Mdina, the illegitimate son of Manuel Pinto da Fonesca, the Grand Master of the Knights of Malta from 1741 to 1773. His mother was believed to have later married Judge Maximiliano Balzan from whom he took his name. However his most recent biographer Iain McCalman traced him back to Palermo, Sicily, describing in his prologue, the run-down area where he was probably born. McCalman does note that he did flee Sicily for Malta, and lived in Mdina in 1765–66 and made mention of a claim that he was descended from a 'grand prior' of the Knights of Malta, and that he practiced as an apothecary, living next door to Grand Master's Manuel Pinto da Fonesca's 'alchemical laboratory'. Cagliostro then left for Rome, and from there went to Paris where he became involved in the Affair of the Diamond Necklace in which confidence tricksters attempted to sell a necklace which had been fashioned at great cost for King Louis XV of France in 1772 to give to his mistress Madame du Barry. The vendors then invented a scenario in which they claimed that Marie Antoinette wanted to buy the necklace but could not publically do so at a time of a budget crisis. Therefore it was to be handled by Cardinal Louis de Rohan, the uncle of **Emmanuel de Rohan-Polduc**, the Grand Master of the Knights of Malta from 1775 to 1797. De Rohan claimed that he had the authorisation of the Queen but this was not the case. Cagliostro, as he was known at the time, was arrested and held in the Bastille for nine months. He was later released and went to England and then to Rome where he was again jailed.

References: François Ribadeau Dumas, *Cagliostro*, London: Allen & Unwin, 1991; Antonia Fraser, *Marie Antoinette*, London: Phoenix, 2002, p. 277, 285, 536; Evelyne Lever, *Marie Antoinette: The Last Queen of France*, London: Judy Pitakus, 2002, p. 172; Sir Harry Luke, *Malta: an account and an appreciation*, London: G.G. Harrap, 1960, pp. 115–17; Iain McCalman, *The Seven Ordeals of Count Cagliostro: the greatest enchanter of the eighteenth century*, Sydney: HarperCollins, 2003, pp. 29–31; W. R. H. Trowbridge, *Cagliostro: The Splendour and Misery of a Master of Magic*, London: Chapman and hall Ltd, 1910.

CALAVA', LEONARDO. The **Capitano della Verga** of Mdina, 1530–31, he was the son of Francesco Calava and his wife, Preziosa dei Baroni Bernardo, the third Baroness di Majmuni and Barberi. His first wife was Paola Laureri-Saguna, and married secondly Giovanna Caxaro-Inguanez. A juror in Mdina in 1528, two years later he was the official representative of the city to welcome formally **Philippe Villiers de L'Isle-Adam** to Mdina with the Grand Master promising to uphold and maintain the political liberties of the residents of the city. Before this he had presided over the Mdina council meeting at which the members had reservations about the rule of the Knights, but Leonardo Calava convened the meeting on 17 June at which it was decided they would accept the Order of St. John.

References: John Montalto, *The Nobles of Malta, 1530–1800*, Valletta: Midsea Books, 1979, p. 62, 129 n36, 234.

CALI, MAURO. He was the bishop of Malta from 4 July 1393 to 1408 when he was nominated as Bishop of Catania, Sicily, holding that position until his death in 1411, a position contested by **Andrea de Pace**.

CALLUS, GUZEPPI 'MATTHEW' (1500/10–1561). A medical doctor, Callus was born in either 1500 or 1510 at Zurrieq, in south-west Malta, the son of Girolamo and Beatrice Callus. Initially he planned to become a priest but instead went to Sicily to study medicine. In 1530 when the Order of St. John of Jerusalem were at Syracuse, about to embark for Malta, Callus who had a good reputation in the Sicilian port was hired as a naval physician. After 1535 he was the physician in Mdina where he not only treated the sick but was also involved in debates on canon law. Records survive of evidence he gave at a court case in 1542 about whether a marriage should be annulled on medical grounds.

In 1537 Callus was given permission by Grand Master **Juan de Homedes** to start excavating in Malta to search for treasure said to have been buried by the Arabs. He made a request to embark on another search in 1558. However in that year he was involved in a legal dispute over the ownership of a schooner. He decided to use the Bishop's Court to resolve the dispute rather than the Law Court operated by the Order of St. John. Grand Master **Jean de la Valette** saw this as an attempt to circumvent the power of the Order, and in August Callus was dismissed as physician of Mdina, a position he held for 22 years. There were further political problems to follow. Most were over the promise by Grand Master **Philippe Villiers de L'Isle-Adam** in 1530 to uphold and maintain the political liberties of Mdina – and it seems likely that Callus may have been present when Philippe de L'Isle-Adam entered the city and made this solemn promise. However Grand Master La Valette, eager for more money to help fortify Malta from attack ordered Mdina to contribute money. This led to some Mdina citizens writing to King Philip II of Spain, and Callus was accused of instigating this after the petition was intercepted and handed to la Valette. Callus was arrested in September 1560 and tried for treason. Found guilty, he was hanged in 1561, probably at Saqqaija, **Rabat**.

The story of Callus was not that well-known outside Malta until Ramiro Barbaro wrote his novel in Italian, *Un martire* (1878). Guze Muscat Azzopardi translated it into Maltese and by 1921 it had been through 16 reprints. A seminar was held in December 2002 to discuss Callus, and in 2006 Evarist Bartolo, a Maltese member of parliament, wrote a play based on the life of the doctor.

References: P. Cassar, 'Dr Joseph Callus', *Heritage* no. 35 (1980), pp. 698–700; Stanley Fiorini, 'Mattew alias Joseph Callus – patriot or opportunist', *Treasures of Malta* no 36 (Summer 2006); J. Galea, 'Mattew Callus: a myth?', *Scientia* vol 2, no 2 (1945); Michael J. Schiavone, *Dictionary of Maltese Biographies*, Malta: pubblikazzjonijiet Indipendenza,

2009, vol 1, pp. 412–13.

CÁNAVES, JOAQUÍN (1640–1721). Born on 8 January 1640 in Pollensa, Spain, he was ordained priest of the Order of Santiago, he was appointed bishop of Malta on 30 August 1713, being ordained on 10 September, and installed on 4 October, remaining as bishop until his death on 3 June 1721. He was the only member of the Order of Santiago to become bishop of Malta.

CAPITANI DELLA VERGA ('Captains of the Rod'). This title was the most important position in Mdina from the 1370s until it was abolished in 1818. The person occupying this position was the governor of the city, colonel of the city's militia and a judge in the local high courts. Traditionally loyal to the kings of Sicily, after Malta was placed under the control of the Knights of St. John, the Capitano della Verga was handed the rod of office from the Grand Masters. The term of the position was from 28 August of a year, through to 18 August of the following year.

da CARAVAGGIO, MICHELANGELO MERISI (1571–1610). An Italian artist, he was born in Milan and trained as an artist under Titian. He worked in Rome from 1592 to 1606, achieving much fame and becoming celebrated as the 'most famous painter in Rome'. Managing some prestigious commissions, he was also notorious for brawling and in a fight on 29 May 1606 killed a man, probably by accident, and then fled to Naples. He then took refuge in Malta where he hoped for the patronage of **Alof de Wignacourt**. He did get some work in Malta, and in 1610 returned to Italy to receive a pardon, and died *en route* to Rome. A possible self-portrait is held at the **Archbishop's Palace** in Mdina, with three paintings – of St. Jerome, St. John with a lamb, and a Guardian Angel – in the **Cathedral Church**, with another, Cupid and the Skeleton, in the **Cathedral Museum**. The connection of the artist with Malta is commemorated on two stamps and a miniature sheet issued by the Maltese postal authorities on 20 July 2007.

References: Warren G. Berg, *Historical Dictionary of Malta*, Lanham, Md.: The Scarecrow

---

Press, 1995, pp. 27–28; Andrew Graham-Dixon, *Caravaggio: A Life Sacred and Profane*, London, Allen Lane, 2009; Peter Robb, *M: the biography of Caravaggio*, Potts Point, Australia: Duffy & Snellgrove, 1998.

CARDONA, GIO' MARIA. The **Capitano della Verga** of Mdina, 1662–64, he was from the Cardona family of Mdina which descended from Giovanni di Cardona from Aragon, Spain, a soldier in the service of King Alfonso V of Aragon (r. 1416–58), and who had been created Signore di la Guardia in 1437. His son moved to Sicily, and the family later settled in Malta.

CARMELITE CHURCH AND CONVENT. This convent, in **Triq Villegaignon**, has its origins in the arrival of the mendicant order, The Carmelites of the Old Observance who came to Malta from Sicily in 1370. Endowed by the Spanish noblewoman Donna Marghaerita D'Aragona, initially their convent was located in **Rabat** but with the worry of raids, they moved to within the city walls of Mdina in 1658 and were given a church called Santa Maia della Rocca ('Our Lady of the Castle'). It was also hoped by Grand Master Martin de Redin that religious orders would be primarily located in cities and towns rather than in the countryside.

The original church into which the Carmelites moved was soon demolished and the present church, designed by Francesco Sammut and the French architect Mederico Blondel, dates from 1659, and completed in 1675. **Lorenzo Gafà** was also involved in supervising the construction of the church as well as the adjoining convent. It has four chapels and seven altars with the altarpiece above the High Altar a painting of the Annunciation by **Stefano Erardi** (1630–1716). Elsewhere in the church there are paintings by the Maltese artist Giuseppe Cali (1846–1930) and a statue of the Virgin Mary.

Many people are buried in the crypt to the church, with the entrance through a Baroque door replete with skulls and symbols of death, along with the flames of purgatory. At the top of the portal to the gate, above the sill, a cross is there to remind people of the resurrection.

In 1798 the French arrived in Mdina and with revolutionary zeal started to destroy the power of the church. Some looting had started in July. However this was extended with the selling the possessions of many churches and on Sunday 2 September 1798 they started a sale of the treasures of this church. There was an outcry from many people, not least because of it taking place on a Sunday, and a large mob attacked the French chasing them into the **House of the Notary Bezzina** from where they defenestrated the Citizen Colonel

Masson. The French then fled to Valletta where they held out for two years.

The belfry of the church did not survive the earthquake of 1856 but was subsequently rebuilt. And during World War II, some of the staff of the accounts department of the Admiralty worked from part of the convent. On 16 July each year, the feast day of **Our Lady of Mount Carmel**, the friars organise a race for men and boys from the **Benedictine Nunnery** in Triq Villagaignon to **Pjazza tas-Sur** (Bastion Square). The Old Priory Café, located in the grounds of the church remains popular.

References: Richard England and Conrad Thake, *Mdina: Citadel of Memory*, Malta: Atlantis, 1995, pp. 54–55, 64–67; Anne Agius Ferrante, *No Strangers in the Silent City*, Valletta: Andrew Rupert Publishing, 1992, pp. 34–37; Denis de Lucca, *Mdina: A History of Its Urban Space and Architecture*, Valletta: Said International, 1995, pp. 115–16; John Manduca, *Tourist Guide to City of Mdina*, Malta: Progress Press, 1975, pp. 28–29; Laurence Mizzi, *The People's War: Malta 1940/43*, Valletta: Progress Press, 2002, p. 220; Edward Sammut, *The Monuments of Mdina*, Malta: Progress Press Co. Ltd, 1967, pp. 36–39; Conrad Thake, *Baroque Churches in Malta*, Malta: Arcadia Publishers, 1995, pp. 52–55.

CARUANA, FRANCESCO SAVERIO (FRANCIS XAVIER) (1759–1847). The bishop of Malta from 28 February 1831 until his death on 17 November 1847, he was born on 7 July 1759 at Haz-Zebbug, being ordained a priest in 1783. Teaching at the seminary, he was named canon of the cathedral chapter in Mdina in 1796. When the French invaded Malta, he reluctantly joined with the French and as a member of the government commission, persuaded them not to destroy the noble arms adorning St. John's Co-Cathedral in Valletta. However he was unable to limit the revolutionary excesses elsewhere and in the rebellion against the French, led some insurgents, and encouraged the British to come to Malta. He was the rector of the University of Malta for 22 years, and in 1822 became archdeacon. Nine years later he was made bishop of Malta. In 1835 he was nominated to be a member of the government but the Holy See instructed him to turn down the position. After 16 years as bishop, he died and was buried in the **Cathedral Church** in Mdina.

References: Michael J. Schiavone, *Dictionary of Maltese Biographies*, Malta: pubblikazzjonijiet Indipendenza, 2009, vol 1, pp. 478–79.

CARUANA, MAURUS (1867–1943). The bishop of Malta from 1915 until his death in 1943, Aloysius Caruana was born on 16 November 1867 in Floriana, and was educated at St. Ignatius College, St. Julian's College, and then to Scotland to attend Fort Augustus Abbey, becoming the school captain. He also studied at the seminary on Gozo. In 1884 taking the name Maurus, he joined the English Benedictine Congregation – the first Maltese to become a Benedictine monk – and was ordained priest in 1891 by Bishop Hugh Macdonald, Bishop of Aberdeen. Studying canon law at the Benedictine College of San Anselmo in Rome, he then taught philosophy, theology and Latin literature at Fort Augustus. His preaching was highly regarded and in 1912 was appointed Choirmaster. After the death of Bishop Pietro Pace, in early 1915 Maurus Caruana was appointed bishop of Malta, being consecrated in Rome on 10

Archbishop Caruana leading a procession in c.1920.

February, and then appointed Knight Grand Cross of the Sovereign Military Order of St. John. He returned to Malta three days later, and on 19 April he entered Mdina and was invested in the Mdina Cathedral. Becoming the first Benedictine to become bishop of Malta since 1511, he was also the titular archbishop of Rhodes, retaining the personal title after the restoration of a residential archdiocese of Rhodes in 1928.

Archbishop Caruana, as he was styled, supported the British war effort in World War I and in 1918 became the first Maltese to be created knight commander of the Order of the British Empire. He used his term as bishop of Malta to consolidate the power of the Roman Catholic Church, and this saw the start of the Catholic newspaper Lehen is-Sewwa in 1928. In 1921 he had approved the establishing of the Congregation of St. Paul, and thirteen years later the Missionary Sisters of Jesus of Nazareth. In June 1935 he hosted the first diocesan regional council to be held in Malta. He was stalwart in his support of the British during World War II, and was received by King George VI who visited Malta on 20 June 1943. Archbishop Caruana died on 17 December 1943.

References: A. E. Abela, *The Order of St. Michael and St. George in Malta and Maltese Knights of the British Realm*, Valletta: Progress Press, 1988; Arthur Bonnici, 'Death of Archbishop Dom Maurus Caruana', *Malta Review Supplement* (21 December 1943); Sir Harry Luke, *Malta: an account and an appreciation*, London: G.G. Harrap, 1960, p. 234; Michael J. Schiavone, *Dictionary of Maltese Biographies*, Malta: pubblikazzjonijiet Indipendenza, 2009, vol 1, pp. 491–92; W. L. Zammit, 'Mgr Maurus Caruana', *Heritage* No 22.

CASA GOURGION. This building, one of the most stylish in Mdina, is located on the northern side of **Pjazza San Pawl** (St. Paul Square), backing onto the southern side of Triq Santu Rokku, being almost opposite the **Chapel of St Roque**. It was built in the early 1700s by Giovanni Gourgion.

References: Anne Agius Ferrante, *No Strangers in the Silent City*, Valletta: Andrew Rupert Publishing, 1992, p. 12; Nicholas de Piro and Danial Cilia, *The sovereign palaces of Malta*, Sliema: Miranda, 2001, p. 50.

CASA INGUANEZ. This house dating from 1370, occupies an entire block,

The balcony on the Casa Inguanez.
Photograph Anibal Trejo / Big Stock Photo

3 **Triq Villegaignon**, was completed in the late fourteenth century. It has been the family seat of the Inguanez family (originally the Desguameck family from Catalonia, Spain), and in recent years the Sceberras-D'Amico-Inguanez. Citto Gatto was created Baron of Bucana in 1350 after he had managed to put down a rebellion in Gozo, and of Djar il-Bniet in 1695. The head of the family was the hereditary Governor of Notabile and also Captain of the Rod. King Alfonso V of Aragon stayed in this house when in Mdina in 1432. It was King Alonso who gave official permission for the arms of the Inguanez family to be displayed on the outside of the building.

In 1864 Baron Alexander Sceberras D'Amico, from the family second in order of precedence in the Maltese nobility, took, as his second wife, Frances Ann Whittuck who had been born in Jamaica, the daughter of Captain W. J. Whittuck, 82nd Regiment, and his wife Matilda. They had three daughters, one of whom married into the Inguanez family, and inherited Casa Inguanez.

King Alfonso XIII of Spain stayed in the same room in the house when he was in Mdina on 9 November 1927. The last of the main line of the family to live there was Mary Frances Carmen Sceberras Trigona D'Amico-Inguanez, Baroness of Buqana, Djar il-Bniet and Castle Cicciano. She married Colonel Alexander McKean of the Inniskilling Dragoons; they had no children. Anne

Ferrante wrote of her, 'she wore a black hat with little flowers and a black spotted veil that came over her face and tied under her chin – rather like a bee-keeper – we often wondered how she took her tea and ate her sandwiches but were never present to witness the event.' She and her husband were both buried in the Cathedral Church. Their nephew Ian Chesney inherited the title becoming the 21st Baron Sceberras d'Amico Inguanez. He had a great interest in history cultivated during his schooling at Downside, England, and did much to renovate and embellish the house. He served with distinction in World War I and then joined the Institute of Linguists. He saw active service again in World War II. In 1953 he represented the Nobility of Malta at the Coronation of Queen Elizabeth II in London. He was unmarried when he died on 10 April 1960, and the title then passed to his sister Frances Mary Carmen Chesney Inguanez who became the 22nd Baroness, who was also unmarried. The title was abolished in 1969, but the house was inherited by another relative, a successful orthopaedic surgeon, who was married with two daughters and two sons. The coach house attached to the house remains the location of an interesting collection of sedan chairs. Some of these featured on a series of four postage stamps issued in Malta on 11 April 1997.

References: Anne Agius Ferrante, *No Strangers in the Silent City*, Valletta: Andrew Rupert Publishing, 1992, pp. 87–91; Sir Harry Luke, *Malta: an account and an appreciation*, London: G.G. Harrap, 1960, p. 92; John Manduca, *Tourist Guide to City of Mdina*, Malta: Progress Press, 1975, p. 17–18; Edward Sammut, *The Monuments of Mdina*, Malta: Progress Press Co. Ltd, 1967, p. 17.

CASA ISABELLA. This house is located at the corner of Magazines Street

and St. Peter Street. Dating back to medieval times when it was a priory, it has its own internal courtyard and because of its location is popular as tourist accommodation, having four bedrooms, three bathrooms and able to cater for six adults and two children at any one time. Costs in 2013 were £150 per night, or £2350 per month. The owner has illustrated four books on Malta, moving to London where her husband worked at the Stock Exchange for 40 years.

References: Edward Sammut, *The Monuments of Mdina*, Malta: Progress Press Co. Ltd, 1967, p. 35.

CASA MAGAZZINI. This was the location of the gunpowder store and also the depository for weapons held by the Knights of Malta. It was a residence called Casa Magazin, with Mr and Mrs J. W. Hill living there in 1965. They had at least two children: a daughter D. M. A. 'Thea' Hill, and a son Ivan. It has recently been turned into a small museum called Knights of Malta which celebrates the history of the Order. It contains some 120 life-size figures representing various important knights of various periods of the Order's history.

Casa Testaferrata.
Photograph © robert lerich / Fotolia.com.

CASA TESTAFERRATA. Located on **Triq Villegaignon**, close to the junction where it meets Triq Mesquita, this is the home of the Testaferrata Family. It was long thought to have been built over the **Roman** Temple dedicated to the God Apollo but now it is thought the temple was in a different location in the same street. There is also a tradition that the French officer Masson was thrown off the balcony of this house at the time of the Maltese uprising in 1798, but this was actually at the **House of the Notary Bezzina**.

References: Edward Sammut, *The Monuments of Mdina*, Malta: Progress Press Co. Ltd, 1967, p. 18.

CASA VIANI. This house was built during the seventeenth century and is located on **Triq Villegaignon** and is next to the **House of the Notary Bezzina.** There is an account that in 1798, Citizen Colonel Masson, the French commander hid in this house and was defenestrated from here rather than the House of the Notary Bezzina.

References: Edward Sammut, *The Monuments of Mdina*, Malta: Progress Press Co. Ltd, 1967, p. 18.

CASINO NOTABILE. In 1886, some of the Mdina nobles were keen on a 'club' venue for socialising and they decided to build the Casino Notabile on Saqqajja Hill. This hill had long been a place where people from Mdina would go to 'take the waters', and indeed Grand Master Wignacourt built a fountain there, and also an aqueduct to take some of this water to Valletta. Archaeologists have also found the remains of a Roman wall which points to the hill's value being known since ancient times.

The prominent architect Paulson Webster (1837–1887) was hired by Casino dei Nobili, a body formed on 27 November 1885 to establish the club, From Grantham, Lincolnshire, he had moved to Malta in 1861 and had been involved in the construction of the Royal Opera House in Valletta, and many other important buildings. In October 1886, Webster presented his plans and once the lease on the land was secured, building work started on a site which had been occupied for about a hundred years by a small washroom. The building was ready for use by August 1888. However Webster died from cholera on 16 August 1887. Webster was not initially paid for the work and his wife, Fanny, claimed £400 10 s 6d for 'rights owed to her husband for the drawing of the plan and the execution of the building under his direction, until he died.' After a meeting of members of the new club, it was decided that all

28 of them should pay £15 each.

The building eventually fell into disuse and there were also problems with the foundations which rested on a fault in the rock underneath the Casino. This saw wooden poles used to prop up parts of the façade, and later scaffolding. In 2014 work started on the restoration of the building, a project spearheaded by Mdina Council with the support of European Union funds.

References: Malcolm Borg, *British Colonial Architecture: Malta 1800–1900*, San Gwann, Malta: Publishers Enterprises Group, 2001, pp. 71–72; James Debono, 'Mdina council issues tender for Casino Notabile', *Malta Today* (30 October 2014; Matthew Gauci, 'New Light on Webster Paulson and his architectural idiosyncrasies', *Proceedings of History Week* 2009, pp. 137–149; 'Restoration funds for neglected Mdina landmark', *Times of Malta* (2 November 2014).

CASOLANI, ANNETTO (1815–1866). He was the auxiliary bishop of Malta from 1848 to 1866. Born on 10 August 1815 at Valletta, the fifth son of Sir Vincent Casolani, he completed a theology degree at the University of Malta and then proceeded to Rome where he graduated with a doctorate in theology. Consecrated as titular bishop of Mauricastro in 1846, he was involved in an expedition by Jesuits to the Sudan, reaching Khartoum in 1848. Returning to Malta later that year he became the auxiliary bishop of Malta and was also actively involved in Maltese politics and was one of the elected members of the government from August 1849. He tried to get Roman Catholicism to be described as the dominant religion of Malta in the criminal code but the British government refused to allow this. However he gained much support from the populace and in 1854 was re-elected with a larger majority. He died on 1 August 1866 and was buried in the **Cathedral Church** in Mdina.

References: Charles Catania, Andrea DeBono: *Maltese Explorer on the White Nile (1848–65)*, Paula: C. Catania, 2000; Michael J. Schiavone, *Dictionary of Maltese Biographies*, Malta: pubblikazzjonijiet Indipendenza, 2009, vol 1, p. 512.

CASSAR, COSMANO. He was the **Capitano della Verga** of Mdina, 1709–10.

CASSAR, LORENZO. The **Capitano della Verga** of Mdina, 1642–44, he was the son of Michele Cassar and Imperia (née Xerri). In 1625 he married Cusmano Cumbo Navarra.

References: John Montalto, *The Nobles of Malta, 1530–1800*, Valletta: Midsea Books, 1979, p. 259.

CASSAR, MICHELE. The **Capitano della Verga** of Mdina, 1609–11, he was the son of Judge Lorenzo Cassae and his wife Imperia Xerri. His grandfather was Pietro Cassar, the ambassador for Malta to the Court of Emperor Charles V. Michele Cassar married Imperia Abela, and their eldest son was Lorenzo Cassar, later **Capitano della Verga**.

CASSAR, PIETRO. The **Capitano della Verga** of Mdina, 1652–53, he was the son of Antonio and Agata Cassar. The third cousin of **Lorenzo Cassar**, they shared the same great-grandfather Matteo Cassar.

CASSIA, GIOVANNI MARIA. The **Capitano della Verga** of Mdina, 1590–92, and 1613–15, he owned the lands at Gariexem which had been sold to his family by the Inguanez family. The son of Antonio Cassia and Catherina (née Cumbo), he was ennobled with the title Baron of Ghariexem e Tabia, and married Laurica Rosso in 1586. After her death he married secondly Caterina Cumbo.

References: John Montalto, *The Nobles of Malta, 1530–1800*, Valletta: Midsea Books, 1979, p. 34, 54 n241, 160.

CASSIA, PIETRO (d 1686). The **Capitano della Verga** of Mdina, 1659–60, he was the Baron of Gariezem sive Tabia. In 1638 he married Eugenia d'Anastasio and they had seven children.

References: John Montalto, *The Nobles of Malta, 1530–1800*, Valletta: Midsea Books, 1979, p. 127.

DE LA CASSIÈRE, JEAN LEVESQUE (1502–1581). He was the Grand Master of the Knights Hospitaller (Knights of Malta) from 1572 until his death in 1581. He had been involved in the attack on Zoara in North Africa in

1552. The town, west of Tripoli, was captured by the Knights but the Turks then counterattacked and routed the Knights with Jean de la Cassière able to save the colours of the Order. A Frenchman from the Langue d'Auvergne, he was elected on 20 January 1572 and succeeded Pierre del Monte as Grand Master. Soon he was involved in a number of disputes between the Knights and the bishop of Malta. These were eventually submitted to Pope Gregory XIII who then decided to appoint a Grand Inquisitor much to the annoyance of the Order.

He was next involved in a dispute with Venice after the Knights seized a Venetian ship and confiscated goods on board which were owned by a Jewish businessman. Venice threatened to size all the property of the Order of Malta in Venetian territory and the Pope had to intervene with the Order having to pay compensation although the Knights felt that as the goods had been owned by a non-Christian, they could be seized. Then there was a problem amongst the Spanish knights after King Philip II of Spain appointed Archduke Wenzel (Wenceslaus) of Austria, a relative but only seventeen years old, as the Grand Prior of Castile and Leon. The Spanish Knights from the Order of Malta complained and the Pope ordered them to publically apologise.

These problems contributed to an uprising in Malta itself where the Order deposed De La Cassière and confined him in Fort St. Angela appointing Mathurin Romegas, the former Grand Prior of Toulouse as acting Grand Master. The Pope summoned both Romegas and De La Cassière to Rome where he showed deference to the latter when he arrived in Rome on 26 October 1581. The Pope ordered that he be reappointed as Grand Master. Romegas died on 4 November 1581, and De La Cassière himself died on 21 December 1581, also in Rome. His body was taken back to Malta and buried in St. John's Co-Cathedral in Valletta.

References: Michael Galea, *Grand Master Jean Levesque de la Cassiere 1572–1581*,

Malta: Enterprise Group San Gwann, 1994; Victor Mallia-Milanes, *Venice and Hospitaller Malta 1530–1798: aspects of a relationship*, Marsa: Publishers Enterprises Group, 1992; H. J. A. Sire, *The Knights of Malta*, New Haven: Yale University Press, 1994.

CASSON, Sir HUGH (1910–1999). An architect, a professor of environmental design from 1953 to 1975, and the President of the Royal Academy in London from 1976 to 1984, he completed a number of watercolours of Malta including at least one of Mdina. Nicholas de Piro noted that Sir Hugh's 'economy with paint was a strength which he knew how to handle.'

References: *The Malta Year Book 1968*, p. 141; Nicholas de Piro, *The International Dictionary of Artists who Painted Malta*, Valletta: Audio Visual Centre Limited, 2003, p. 115; *Who's Who 1996*, p. 333.

CASTELLETTI, FERDINANDO. The **Capitano della Verga** of Mdina, 1733–40, the son of Gio Vincenzo Castelletti and Margherita (née Torrensi), he was the baron of Marsa, ennobled by Grand Master **António Manoel de Vilhena** by an act dated 12 June 1725. The title was because his ancestors, from the Nava family, had held land around Marsa. Erdinando Castelletti had no children and the title ended with him. However in 1878 Alessandro Sceberras D'Amico Inguanez claimed the title, but this was rejected.

References: John Montalto, *The Nobles of Malta, 1530–1800*, Valletta: Midsea Books, 1979, p. 32, 34, 38, 117, 275.

CASTELLETTI, GIOVANNI VINCENZO. The **Capitano della Verga** of Mdina, 1625–27, he was the son of Gio Francesco Castelletti and his second wife Geronima (née Surdo). In 1603 he married Aurelia de Noto, and they had several children, the oldest son being Simon who married Flavia Xara Cagliares. Their son Gio Vincenzo Castelletti was the father of **Ferdinando Castelletti**, the **Capitano della Verga** from 1733 to 1740.

References: John Montalto, *The Nobles of Malta, 1530–1800*, Valletta: Midsea Books, 1979, p. 247.

Cathedral Square in the nineteenth century.

Cathedral Church in Mdina. Photograph © JackF / Fotolia.com

DE CASTRO, JUAN. He was the Apostolic Administrator of the See of Malta from 20 March to 29 September 1506.

CATENIANO, BERNARDINO. He was the bishop of Malta from 9 April 1516 until his retirement on 22 May of the same year.

CATENIANO, BONIFACIO (d. 1522). He was the Bishop elect of Malta from 28 March 1520 but died in 1522, probably before his official installation.

CATHEDRAL CHURCH. This church is dedicated to **St. Paul** and by tradition, it is located on the site of the Palace of **Publius** who was the first bishop of Malta, with the building having been transformed by St Paul in AD 60. Demolished by the Saracens, by tradition work began in 1090 with the new building following a Norman design, and this is the basis of the current building. Again by popular tradition it was constructed on orders of Roger, Count of Sicily and each year on 4 November there is a service at the cathedral for the soul of Count Roger. The biggest service is, however, that

The bell of the Cathedral Church.
Photograph © robert lerich / Fotolia.com

Cathedral Church
Photograph © mary416 / Fotolia.com

Photograph © McCarthys_PhotoWorks / Fotolia

on 29 June each year for the feast of St. Peter and St. Paul. Recent historians have challenged this account and they date the building of the church to the fourteenth century, and the service to commemorate Count Roger was instituted by Bishop **Alpheran de Bussan** in the eighteenth century.

In 1582 Bishop Molina started work on improving the cathedral, with the aim of replacing the Norman building with a new Baroque structure. Plans were already underway and some work had started when the Cathedral was badly damaged in the earthquake of 1693. It was rebuilt in a Baroque style, in a cross pattern, designed by **Lorenzo Gafà** between 1697 and 1702; he had already been involved in designing the apsed choir, and had made a wooden model for his new design before the earthquake, and this was accepted. Gafà used pairs of Corinthian pilasters to divide the façade. The local sculptor Gerolamo Fabri and his sons worked on much of the stone carvings of the cathedral.

The Cathedral was formally inaugurated on 8 October 1702 by Bishop Cocco Palmieri whose coat of arms are above the main portal, along with those of Grand Master Ramon Perollos y Roccaful (r. 1697–1720). There was

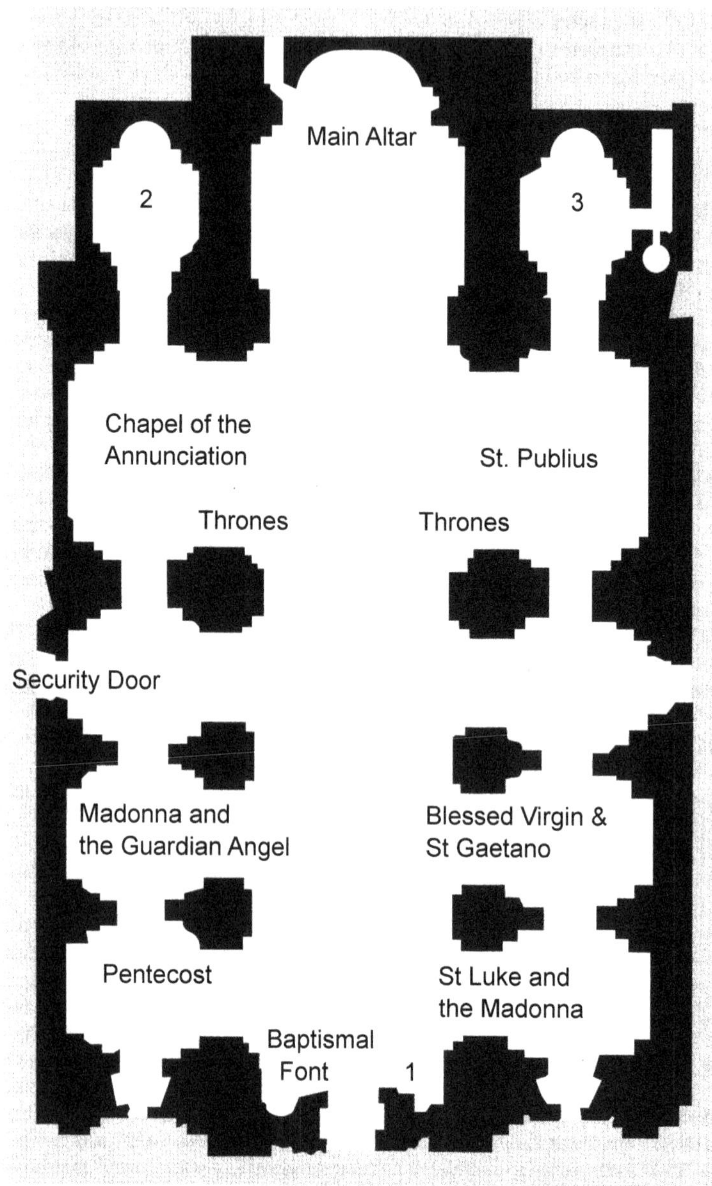

1. Statue of St. Publius
2. Chapel of the Blessed Sacrament
3. Chapel of the Crucifixion

Cathedral Church

Photograph © McCarthys_PhotoWorks / Fotolia

a dispute over which coat of arms should take pride of place with Perollos demanding that his was more important, seen as signifying the importance of the Knights of Malta. There are two bell towers and are decorated with motifs of the fire and serpent representing the first miracle of St. Paul on the island. The impressive carved door to the cathedral was pictured on a Maltese postage stamp issued on 13 July 1974.

Some Maltese nobles and others are buried within the church. These include Sir **Gerald Strickland**, the prime minister of Malta from 1927 to 1932. At the back of the cathedral, there is a massive wall-painting of St. Paul surviving the ship-wreck. There is also a clock which has two faces – one for the time, and the other for the day, although there is a popular belief that one of the faces was to show the correct time and the other was to confuse the devil.

The two massive oak doors to the cathedral were fashioned from Irish bog oak and are reputed to have been brought to Malta by Roger of Sicily. There is also a picture of the Virgin Mary attributed to St. Luke – it is now encased in silver. And the processional cross is said to have been the one Godfrey de Bouillon carried with him into Jerusalem on 15 July 1099 towards the end of the First Crusade. There are also works by the Italian artist Mattia Preti

Photograph © McCarthys_PhotoWorks / Fotolia

(1613–1699) and the Maltese painter Francesco Zahra (1710–1763). Also of importance to the cathedral is the organ which featured on a Maltese postage stamp issued on 13 October 2004.

Outside, to the right of the cathedral there was a small one-storey building dating at least from the late nineteenth century, allowing for the cathedral to dominate Cathedral Square even more than it does today.

References: Aldo Azzopardi, *Malta and its islands*, Luqa: Plurigraf, nd, pp. 118–20; Can John Azzopardi, *Mdina, Rabat, Mosta*, Terni, Italy: Plurigraf, 1988, p. 24–29; Carolyn Bain, *Malta & Gozo*, Footscray, Vic, Australia: Lonely Planet, 2004, pp. 117–18; Vincent Borg, *The Maltese Diocese during the Sixteenth Century*, Malta: Vincent Borg, 2009; Gerald Bugeja, 'A brief note on the black figure in the Mdina St. Paul polyptych', *History Week* (1994), pp. 25–31; Aloysius Deguara, *The Metropolitan Cathedral, Mdina*, Sta Venera: Midsea Books, 2008; Richard England and Conrad Thake, *Mdina: Citadel of Memory*, Malta: Atlantis, 1995, pp. 12, 80–91; Stanley Fiorini, 'Artists artisans and craftsmen at the Mdina cathedral in the early sixteenth century', *Melita Historica* vol 10, no 4 (1991), pp. 351–52; Stanley Fiorini, 'The earliest surviving accounts books of the cathedral procurators: 1461–1499', *Proceedings of History Week 1992*, Malta: Malta Historical Society, 1994, pp. 101–15; Stanley Fiorini, *The Mandati documents at the Archives of the Mdina Cathedral*, Malta, 1473–1539, Minnesota/Malta: Hill Monastic Manuscript Library & Cathedral Museum, 1993; *Images: Nineteenth Century Malta*, Valletta: Valletta Publishing Publication, 1989; Denis de Lucca, *Mdina: A History of Its Urban Space and Architecture*, Valletta: Said International, 1995, pp. 73–75; John Manduca, *Tourist Guide to City of Mdina*, Malta: Progress Press, 1975, pp. 21–27; Joseph Cassar Pullicino, 'Norman Legends in Malta', in Anthony T. Luttrell (ed.), *Medieval Malta: Studies on Malta Before the Knights*, London: The British School at Rome, 1975, pp. 96– 03; Antonio Espinosa Rodriguez, *The Paintings at the Cathedral Museum*, Mdina, Mdina: Progress Press, 2005; Edward Sammut, *The Monuments of Mdina*, Malta: Progress Press Co. Ltd, 1967, pp. 20–30; Conrad Thake, *Baroque Churches in Malta*, Malta: Arcadia Publishers, 1995, pp. 48–51; Neil Wilson, *Malta*, Melbourne: Lonely Planet Publications, 2000, p. 130.

CATHEDRAL MUSEUM. On the south side of St. Paul's Square, the building was formerly a seminary built from 1722–42 in a Baroque style closer to that of Sicily and Catalonia than the French Baroque. It has long since been turned into a museum, although the original eighteenth century octagonal chapel and refectory have been preserved. The museum houses a small but important collection of paintings and other artefacts including woodcuts by the German artist Albert Durer, and also a polyptych altarpiece depicting the life of **St. Paul**. The olive-wood carvings by the Maltese artist Anton Agius are also interesting. And the museum also has the paintings *The Annunciation, Notre Dame de la Rançon, St. Peter, St. Paul, Saint Charles Borromée, Saint François de salles*, and *Saints de l'Ordre,* as well as two of Turkish women and Greek women, all completed by the French painter Antoine de Favray (1706–1798) who came to Malta and was responsible for many of the portraits of the Grand Masters. For many years the Very Rev Mgr Emmanuel Brincat helped as the Chapter's deputy for the Cathedral Museum.

As well as the exhibits displayed to the public, there is also an important collection of artwork, objects and papers held there. The archive of the Inquisition in Malta is held at the museum, and provides one of the most detailed single sources on the life of many people in medieval Mdina. It has been indexed by academics and staff from the Malta Study Center at St. John's University, Collegeville, Minnesota, USA, and these have been consulted by a number of leading historians. The museum is open from 10 am until 5.15 pm during the week, and from 10 am until 3.15 pm on Saturdays,

References: *Antoine de Favray (1706–1798): an exhibition of paintings and drawings: the Cathedral Museum, Mdina, 5–20 June 1982*, Malta: ABC Press, 1982; Aldo Azzopardi, *Malta and its islands*, Luqa: Plurigraf, nd, pp. 115–17; Can John Azzopardi, *Mdina, Rabat, Mosta*, Terni, Italy: Plurigraf, 1988, p. 13–23; John Azzopardi, *Archives of the Cathedral of Malta*, Collegeville: St. John's University, Malta Study Center, 1977, reviewed by Giovanni Mangion, *Melita Historica* vol 7, no 2 (1977), pp. 178–79; Carolyn Bain, *Malta & Gozo*, Footscray, Vic, Australia: Lonely Planet, 2004, pp. 118–19; E.V. Borg, *The St. Paul polyptych at the Cathedral Museum, Mdina, Malta*, Mdina: Friends of the Cathedral Museum, 1987; Carmel Cassar, '1564–1696: the inquisition index of knights Hospitallers of the order of St. John', *Melita Historica* vol 11, no 2 (1993), pp. 157–96; Charles Cini, *The art of the medal: a collection of medals presented to the Cathedral Museum, Mdina, Malta*, Mdina: Cathedral Museum, 1993; Richard England and Conrad Thake, *Mdina: Citadel of Memory*, Malta: Atlantis, 1995, pp. 92–93; Stanley Fiorini, *The Mandati Documents at the Archives of the Mdina Cathedral, Malta, 1473–1539*, Mdina: Cathedral Museum, 1992; Malta Cathedral Museum, *Handlist of the Ecclesiastical Archives at the Malta Cathedral Museum, Mdina*, Collegeville, Minn,: Malta Study Center of the Monastic Manuscript Microfilm Library, 1975; Edward Sammut, *The Monuments of Mdina*, Malta: Progress Press Co. Ltd, 1967, pp. 30–34; John T. Spike, *European paintings in the Cauchi Collection at the Cathedral Museum, Mdina, Malta*, Mdina: The Museum, 1994; John Manduca, *Tourist Guide to City of Mdina*, Malta: Progress Press, 1975, pp. 32–35; John Azzopardi Vella, 'Gilbray's masterpiece at the Cathedral Museum', *The Sunday Times* of Malta (6 August 1978), p. 21; *Malta Who's Who 1969/70*, p. 68 (Brincat); William Zammit, 'New Light on the Archive of the Inquisition in Malta during French Rule 1798–1800', in Joseph F Grima, *60th anniversary of the Malta Historical Society: a commemoration*, Malta: The Malta Historical Society, 2010, pp. 275–94.

CAXARO, MANFREDO. The **Capitano della Verga** of Mdina, 1514–15, he was the third son of Luini Caxaro and his wife Zuna (née d'Amadeo). He married Miss de Aquino, and they had a son Nicholas. After the death of his wife, Manfredo married Canchia/Guarglarda La Lancia, and they had a daughter and three sons.

References: John Montalto, *The Nobles of Malta, 1530–1800*, Valletta: Midsea Books, 1979, p. 50 n113.

CAXARO, PIETRO (c.1400–1485). A notary public who had been born in Mdina, he wrote a poem called 'Cantilena' which is the earliest surviving item written in the Maltese language. He was the son of Leo and Zuna Caxaro, and on 1 April 1438 he was appointed as a notary public, becoming a judge in Gozo two years later, and in Malta a year after that. He drew up his Will on 12 August 1485 and died soon afterwards. He was commemorated on a Maltese postage stamp issued in 1985, the 500th anniversary of his death.

References: Giuseppe Brincat, 'Critica testuale della Cantilena di Pietro Caxaro', *Journal of Maltese Studies* vol 16 (1986), pp. 1–21; Michael J. Schiavone, *Dictionary of Maltese Biographies*, Malta: pubblikazzjonijiet Indipendenza, 2009, vol 1, pp. 563–64.

CEMETERIES. Although the Greeks often buried people within the city walls, the Romans tended not to do so. However archaeologists have unearthed graves from the Roman period located outside the current city walls of Mdina, but within the bounds of the Roman city. Traditionally, also, many Maltese were buried in ossaries, with important people interred within the Cathedral, or in the crypt under the **Carmelite Church**. Gradually there was a move away from this, partly on the grounds of health and sanitation, although nuns from the **Benedictine Convent** in Mdina continued to be buried in the convent until 1974.

References: Mario Buhagiar, *Late Roman and Byzantine catacombs and related burial places in the Maltese islands*, Oxford: BAR, 1986, reviewed by Anthony Bonanno, *Melita Historica* vol 9, no 3 (1986), pp. 309–10; and by Shelby Brown, *American Journal of Archaeology*, vol 94,no 3 (July 1990), pp. 518–20.

CHAPEL OF ST ROQUE. This chapel was located near the Main Gate of Mdina, at which time it was called Santa Maria della Porta. After the earthquake of 1693, because of the damage to the Cathedral Church, services were held in this chapel. It was then demolished under Grand Master **António Manoel de Vilhena** (r. 1722–36) as he tried to change the design of the city. In 1728 it was rebuilt in its current location and dedicated to St. Roque, the saint invoked during pestilences, especially the plague, although some locals call it Madonna tad-Dawi ('Our Lady of the Light'). The altarpiece was painted by Emanuel Perren from Portugal.

References: Richard England and Conrad Thake, *Mdina: Citadel of Memory*, Malta: Atlantis, 1995, pp. 58–59; John Manduca, *Tourist Guide to City of Mdina*, Malta: Progress Press, 1975, p. 27; Conrad Thake, *Baroque Churches in Malta*, Malta: Arcadia Publishers, 1995, pp. 56–57.

CHESS. Chess has been played in Malta since at least the fifteenth century and was popular with some members of the Knights of Malta. The first game of which the moves were recorded took place in 1880. With the flight of some White Russians to Malta in World War I, many significant chess matches were played. The 24th Chess Olympiad was played at Valletta, in November–December 1980, an event commemorated by a series of three Maltese postage stamps. It was famous as the event where Karpov fell ill, and the seventeen-year-old Gary Kasparov made his debut in the Olympiads. Some boys from St. Paul's Missionary College in **Rabat** have emerged as strong players such as Colin Pace, a Candidate Master, who was in the Maltese chess team at seven Olympiads. The **Mdina glassworks** continues to make chess pieces for collectors from around the world; and during the annual **Medieval Mdina Festival**, people in medieval costume play in a human chess game.

References: Malta Chess Federation, www.chessmalta.com.

CITY WALLS. The Phoenicians built walls around their settlement at Mdina, and the Romans reinforced them. The **Roman** city covered much of what is now **Rabat**, as well as the walled city of Mdina. The Byzantines would have reinforced the walls, and there is evidence that they were strengthened during the Middle Ages. When in early modern times, after attacks on the city by the Turks, the walls of Mdina were enlarged and strengthened withstanding a **siege** in 1551. In 1565 the Turks decided not to attack the city, the walls being sufficient to prevent attacks by marauders, but would not have been able to withstand a major assault because the walls were built without any strong

The City Walls Photograph © Enrico De Vita / Fotolia.com

redoubts and would not be able to withstand a sustained artillery barrage. They were also not strong enough to have gun emplacements on them. Furthermore, the western, northern and eastern walls of the city were impossible to protect as there were no bastions which meant attackers could easily approach the walls and once having done so, it was impossible for the defenders to fire at them. To protect the southern approach to the city – the most likely position for any attack, there were three bastions which, from west to east, were the San Pietro Bastion, the De Redin Bastion and the Palazzo Bastion. The city remained walled, with only two gates, the **Main Gate** and the **Greek's Gate** until the mid–1880s when it was necessary to make a third gate in the west to allow people from Mdina to easily reach the **railway** station at Mtarfa. The walls remain one of the major features of the city.

References: Richard England and Conrad Thake, *Mdina: Citadel of Memory*, Malta: Atlantis, 1995, pp. 20–31; Denis de Lucca, *Mdina: A History of Its Urban Space and Architecture*, Valletta: Said International, 1995, Chapter 2; Edward Sammut, *The Monuments of Mdina*, Malta: Progress Press Co. Ltd, 1967, pp. 11–12; Stephen Spiteri, 'The Medieval Walls of Mdina', *Treasures of Malta* vol 8, no 3 (no 24) (Summer 2002), pp. 7–13.

DE CLEMENTIS, BATOLOMMEO. He was the **Capitano della Verga** of Mdina, 1461–62.

COAT OF ARMS. The coat of arms of Mdina is similar to the Maltese flag, with a fortress as the mantle, and the motto 'Città Notabile'.

COCCO PALMERI, DAVIDE (1632–1711). Born in Peschi, on 24 February 1657, he was ordained priest in the Sovereign Military Hospitaller Order of St. John of Jerusalem. Appointed the bishop of Malta on 15 May 1684, he was ordained on 4 June, remaining in office until his death on 19 September 1711.

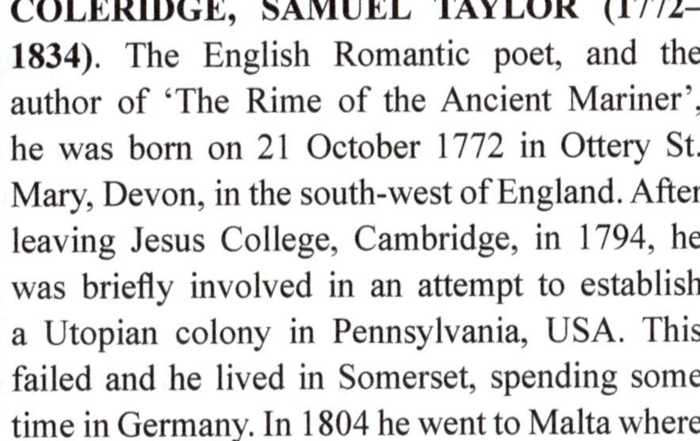

COLERIDGE, SAMUEL TAYLOR (1772–1834). The English Romantic poet, and the author of 'The Rime of the Ancient Mariner', he was born on 21 October 1772 in Ottery St. Mary, Devon, in the south-west of England. After leaving Jesus College, Cambridge, in 1794, he was briefly involved in an attempt to establish a Utopian colony in Pennsylvania, USA. This failed and he lived in Somerset, spending some time in Germany. In 1804 he went to Malta where he was appointed Acting Public Secretary, serving under Alexander Ball. Of Mdina, he wrote of the cotton weaving in the city which served to employ 'several hundred indigent females' as well as other people. He also wrote an account of an attack on a local person, believed to be Jewish, in the city and saw this as part of a general breakdown in law and order in May 1805. He saw this as a manifestation of some of the hatreds which surfaced from time to time in Maltese society. Coleridge returned to England two years later and soon after his return started increasing his use of opium. Although this was affecting him, he remained a major literary figure in England until his death. His connection with Malta was commemorated on a Maltese postage stamp issued on 3 May 1990.

References: Alethea Hayter, *A voyage in vain: Coleridge's journey to Malta in 1804*, London: Robin Clark Ltd, 1993; Barry Hough, and Howard Davis, *Coleridge's Laws: A Study of Coleridge in Malta*, Cambridge: Open Book Publishers, 2010; Donald Sultana, *Samuel Taylor Coleridge in Malta and Italy*, Oxford: Blackwell, 1969, reviewed by R J Rayson, *Melita Historica* vol 5, no 2 (1969), pp. 185–87.

CONNAUGHT HOSPITAL. *See* **Magisterial Palace**.

CONVENT CHAPEL OF ST PETER. This dates from the 1410s and underwent a major renovation in 1625. The altarpiece of the chapel was painted by Mattia Preti (1613–1699). From Calabria, Italy, a relative and student of Antonello de Messina, Preti came to Malta in 1661 and completed many paintings around the island. The painting in the Convent Chapel of St. Peter depicts St. Peter, St. Benedict and St. Scholastica.

References: Richard England and Conrad Thake, *Mdina: Citadel of Memory*, Malta: Atlantis, 1995, pp. 108–09; John Manduca, *Tourist Guide to City of Mdina*, Malta: Progress Press, 1975, p. 19.

DE COPIER, Marshal. A French Knight of the Order of St. John, in 1565 he was placed in charge of the cavalry based at Mdina during the **Great Siege**. Initially these were able to shadow the Turkish fleet and alert the Knights as to where the Turks were landing. The cavalry then retreated to Mdina from where they launched several sorties, some of which were very successful, in some cases taking prisoners, and in other instances they attacked the Turkish camp.

References: Ernle Bradford, *The Great Siege*, London: Hodder & Stoughton, 1967, p. 60, 65.

CORRADO. A Dominican, he was the bishop of Malta from 3 September 1371, taking over from Bishop **Antonio**, and was succeeded by Bishop **Antonio de Vulponno**.

CORSETO, ANTONIO (d. 1503). He was the bishop of Malta from 20 December 1501 until his death in September 1503.

CORTE CAPITANALE. This was originally a part of the **Magisterial Palace** and the location of the Courts of Justice presided over by the **Capitano della Verga** (Captain of the Rod). As a result over the entrance there is a balcony with figures representing Justice and Mercy on either side of it, along with the inscription 'Legibus et Armis', decorated with Doric and superimposed Corinthian pilasters. The flag of Malta and that of the Council of Europe fly on each side of the balcony. It is closed to the public except for the cells underneath which are now open as the **Mdina Dungeons**.

References: Can John Azzopardi, *Mdina, Rabat, Mosta*, Terni, Italy: Plurigraf, 1988, p. 12; Richard England and Conrad Thake, *Mdina: Citadel of Memory*, Malta: Atlantis, 1995, pp. 100–01; John Manduca, *Tourist Guide to City of Mdina*, Malta: Progress Press, 1975, p. 38; Edward Sammut, *The Monuments of Mdina*, Malta: Progress Press Co. Ltd, 1967, pp. 40–41.

COX, DENNIS HERBERT (1893–1980). A Briton who lived in Mdina, he was born on 1 March 1893 at Turlangton, Leicestershire, England, the son of Daniel Bordicott Cox and his wife Susan (née Vesey). He married Helen Lily Wilson, daughter of Edmund Keller Wilson and Ricarda (née Schemberi), and they had five daughters, the youngest, Irene, being born in Malta in 1922. Helen Cox, the mother, died on 28 April 1948 in Mdina, and Dennis Cox died on 1 October 1980 in Mdina.

CREMONA, PAUL (1946–). The archbishop of Malta from 2006 to 2014, he was born on 25 January 1946 in Valletta, the son of Joseph Cremona and Josephine (née Cauchi). Educated at the Valletta Montessori School and then at the Lyceum, in 1963 he joined the Dominican Order and then studied theology at St. Thomas Aquinas College in **Rabat**. Ordained priest on 22 March 1969, he went to Rome to study moral theology which he later taught at Rabat. The prior at the convent of Our Lady in the Grotto in Rabat from 1974 to 1980, he was the provincial of the Maltese Dominicans from 1981 to 1989, and then parish priest at Gwardamanga. He returned to Rabat as prior of Our Lady in the Grotto from 1997 to 2003. In 2006 he was appointed by Pope Benedict XVI as the archbishop of Malta. He resigned as Archbishop on 18 October 2014

References: Michael J. Schiavone, *Dictionary of Maltese Biographies*, Malta: pubblikazzjonijiet Indipendenza, 2009, vol 1, pp. 616–17.

CUBELS, DOMINGO (d. 1566). A member of the Sovereign Military Hospitaller Order of St. John of Jerusalem, he was the bishop of Malta from 10 December 1540, being ordained in 1541, and remained in office until his death on 22 November 1566. As a result, he was Bishop during the Turkish attack on the island in 1551, and also the Great Siege of 1565.

CUMBO, ANTONIO. The **Capitano della Verga** of Mdina, 1623–24, he appears to be the Antonio Cumbo who was the son of Salvo Cumbo and his wife Antonella (née Falsone).

– D –

D'ALAGONA, FRANCESCO. The **Capitano della Verga** of Mdina, 1571–73, 1578–79, and again from 1581–82, he was the son of Girolamo D'Alagona and his wife Donna Ventura Desguanez.

References: John Montalto, *The Nobles of Malta, 1530–1800*, Valletta: Midsea Books, 1979, p. 128 n9, 129 n36, 176, 224.

D'ALAGONA, D. GIROLAMO. The **Capitano della Verga** of Mdina, 1550–57, he was married Donna Ventura Desguanez, and their son was Francesco D'Alagona.

References: John Montalto, *The Nobles of Malta, 1530–1800*, Valletta: Midsea Books, 1979, p. 102, 105, 128 n9, 129 n36, 234.

D'AMICO INGUANEZ, GIO' FRANCESCO (d. 1790). The **Capitano della Verga** of Mdina, 1764–75, he was the second son of Claudio D'Amico Castelletti Inguanez and his wife Rosalea (née Moscati). He married Marchesa Asteria Testaferrata and was created 15th Baron of Djar-il-Bniet and Buqana. His older brother was archdeacon of the **Cathedral Church** in Mdina.

References: John Montalto, *The Nobles of Malta, 1530–1800*, Valletta: Midsea Books, 1979, pp. 27–29.

D'ARAGONA, GIOVANNI. The **Capitano della Verga** of Mdina, 1371–72, his family descended from the illegitimate children of King Frederick of Sicily.

DEBONO, JOSEPH PATRICK (1949–   ). Born on 17 March 1949, he spent 31 years representing to major Austrian pharmaceutical companies in the Libyan market. He is the current deputy vice-mayor of Mdina. Joseph Debono is married to Joanna Sant Cassia and they have two children: Andrea and Christian.

D'ESGUANEZ, ANTONIO (d 1457). The **Capitano della Verga** of Mdina in 1429, 1433–38, 1439–40, and 1442–54, he was the founder of the Inguanez family and hosted the visit of King Alfonso V of Aragon (Alfonso I of Sicily) when he stayed in Mdina in 1432. The adopted son and heir of Francesco

Gatto, he married Imperia, daughter of Francesco Gatto, who predeceased him. He also had a mistress Violante de Luna, and three illegitimate children. His Will which survives, shows the wealth of the family. As well as owning the family seat, **Casa Inguanez** in Mdina, and they also had a pharmacy, five taverns, nine shops and four houses, all in Mdina or **Rabat**, and also a galley and a number of slaves.

References: John Montalto, *The Nobles of Malta, 1530–1800*, Valletta: Midsea Books, 1979, pp. 14–15, 22–25.

D'ESGUANEZ, ANTONIO. He was the **Capitano della Verga** of Mdina, 1528–30.

D'ESGUANEZ, GERARDO. He was the **Capitano della Verga** of Mdina, 1440–42.

DE APAPIS, Don LORENZO (1501–1586). A clergyman, he became an acting notary at the age of 14, and in 1522 he was ordained priest. By 1546 he was the honorary canon at Mdina Cathedral but five years later when he was captured by the Turks whilst they were besieging Gozo in 1551. Taken away as a slave, he was later ransomed, and returned to Malta where he was involved in the enlarging of St. George's Church, Gozo. He followed the Galician rites and as a result in 1575 Inquisitor Dusina wanted him suspended. However this did not happen and Bishop Royas allowed him to maintain his post, later appointing him as Vicar General.

References: Michael J. Schiavone, *Dictionary of Maltese Biographies*, Malta: pubblikazzjonijiet Indipendenza, 2009, vol 1, p. 669.

DEL MONTE, PIETRO (1499–1572). He was the Grand Master of the Knights Hospitaller (Knights of Malta) from 1568 until his death in 1572. Born in Italy, the son of Francis and Margaret Ciocchi del Monte, Pietro's mother was the aunt of Pope Julius III (r. 1550–55). He was chosen to succeed **Jean de Vallette**, and had distinguished himself during the **Great Siege** of Malta in 1565 when he had the task of defending Senglea. He lost three ships in an engagement with the Corsair leader Ucialli in 1570, and hence was only able to loan three galleys for the Battle of Lepanto in the following year. They were put under the command of Gianandrea Doria and placed in one of the most dangerous positions during the battle, with very few survivors from two of them. However it was a great victory for the Christian Holy League and this reduced the likelihood of any attack on Malta. He constructed the Porta Del Monte which was demolished by the British in the nineteenth century and replaced by Porta Vittoria (Victoria Gate), Valletta. He died on 26 January 1572 at Valletta.

References: H.J.A. Sire, The Knights of Malta, New Haven: Yale University Press, 1994, pp. 74–75; George L. Williams, Papal Genealogy: the families and descendants of the Popes, Jefferson, NC: McFarland, 2004, p. 82.

DELLA CAVALLERIA, PAOLO (d. 1496). He was the bishop of Malta from 10 February 1491 to 30 March 1495 and then he was nominated as Bishop of Cefalù in northern Sicily. He remained in that position until his death in 1496.

DELLA ROVERE, RAFFAELE SANSONI RIARIO. He was the apostolic administrator of Malta from 23 May 1516 when Bernardino Cateniano retired, through to early 1520.

DEPASQUALE, ANNETTO (1938–2011). He was the auxiliary bishop of Malta from 1998 until his death in 2011. Born on 28 June 1938 at Qormi, he was educated at the Lyceum and then the Royal University of Malta, being ordained in 1962. An eminent theologian, he was professor in canon law at the faculty of theology at the University of Malta from 1990, having been a lecturer since 1968. He was the vicar general and deputy to Archbishop Joseph Mercieca from November 1989. Depasquale died on 29 November 2011.

References: Michael J. Schiavone, *Dictionary of Maltese Biographies*, Malta: pubblikazzjonijiet Indipendenza, 2009, vol 1, p. 711.

DE PIRO, GIUSEPPE (1877–1933). The founder of the Missionary Society of St. Paul, he was born on 2 November 1877 at Mdina, the seventh of the nine children of the Marquis Alexander de' Marchesi de Piro and Ursola Agius (née Caruana). After studying at the University of Malta and then the Pontifical Gregorian University, Rome, he was ordained on 15 March 1902 in Rome. Moving back to Malta, in 1910 from a small house in Mdina, he established the Missionary Society of St. Paul, appropriately named given St.

Paul's connections with Mdina. Its headquarters moved from one building in Mdina to another, and eventually in 1923, moved to the church of St. Agatha in nearby **Rabat**. With De Piro donating land adjacent to it, it was the Society's headquarters with De Piro heading it until his death on 17 September 1933.

References: J. Aquilina, 'Gallery of Distinguished Maltese: Mgr Giuseppe De Piro', *The Times* (8 November 1977); A. Galea, 'Mgr DePiro and the formation of the Young', *The Sunday Times* (4 June 2000); Michael J. Schiavone, *Dictionary of Maltese Biographies*, Malta: pubblikazzjonijiet Indipendenza, 2009, vol 1, pp. 713–14; Tony Sciberras, *Joseph de Piro (1877–1933)*, Parkville, Victoria, Australia: Missionary Society of St Paul, 2010; Joseph de Piro, www.camcpi.org/depiro.html.

DE PIRO, MARY THERESA (1946–). Mary de Piro was born in Valletta, Malta in 1946, the second daughter of Baron and Baroness de Piro d'Amico Inguanez. She first went to school at St Dorothy's Convent, situated in **Palazzo de Piro** within Mdina, before going on to study at the Institute of the Immaculate Conception at Badia a Ripoli, and the Accademia dei Belle Arti, both in Florence, Italy.

She has become an internationally renowned artist through exhibitions in London, Scotland, Italy and the United States as well as her native Malta. Her compositions vary in genre and are yet specific and recognisable in style. Commissions have included Malta landscapes, portraits and Sacred Art, including book covers, posters and Christmas cards. Her work can be found in private collections around the world, as well as in public institutions, businesses as well as the Malta government including the Central Bank.

Recently in London, she was chosen to represent Malta; first at a European Union (EU) sponsored exhibition of art, and secondly at the Italian Cultural Institute exhibition of art, from countries bordering the Mediterranean. She is currently preparing for a personal exhibition in 2014 at the recently renovated **Palazzo de Piro** in Mdina.

References: Michael J. Schiavone, *Dictionary of Maltese Biographies*, Malta: pubblikazzjonijiet Indipendenza, 2009, vol 1, pp. 714–15; Mary de Piro, http://www.marydepiro.com/.

DOMEIER, WILLIAM. He was a German physician who was a medical practitioner who gained his degree from Gottingen in 1784, and was in Malta for three years before settling in England where he became a Fellow of the Royal College of Physicians. He described his time in Malta in his book, *Malta in Observations on the climate, manners and amusements of Malta* (1810).

References: William Domeier, *Observations on the climate, manners and amusements of Malta*, London: Callow, 1810; Paul Xuereb, 'Malta in the 19th Century: A Selection of Visitors' Accounts', in *Images: Nineteenth Century Malta*, Valletta: Valletta Publishing Publication, 1989, p. 1–2.

DOMENICO. By tradition, he was the bishop of Malta from 8 May 1253, and took over from Bishop Riggerius and was succeeded by Bishop Jacobus in 1259.

– E –

EARTHQUAKE OF 1693. This earthquake was preceded by a foreshock at about 9 pm on 9 January 1693, with the quake itself taking place at 9 pm local time, on 11 January. The most powerful earthquake in Italian history, the epicentre was close to the east coast of Sicily with an estimated magnitude of 7.4 on the moment magnitude scale. The effect on Sicily was devastating with about two-thirds of the population of Catania killed. There was an initial withdrawal of the sea and when a tsunami followed, some galleys owned by the Knights of Malta which were in the harbour at Augusta were badly damaged.

The city of Mdina was badly affected by the earthquake which seriously damaged the **Cathedral Church**, forcing services to be held at Santa Maria della Porta (now **Chapel of St. Roque**) and there was also some damage to other buildings. The rebuilding led to a new architectural style which became known as the Sicilian Baroque.

There are a number of descriptions of the earthquake with Mario Antonio Bancati, a notary, being at the home of Grazia Cassar where he was drawing up her Will. He called it 'a distant rumbling noise as a chariot was heard coming from afar so that the house of Grazia first shook…'

References: Can John Azzopardi, *Mdina and the Earthquake of 1693*, Valletta: Heritage Books, c1993; Pauline Galea, 'Seismic history of the Maltese islands and considerations on seismic risk', *Annals of Geophysics* vol 50, no 6 (December 2007), pp. 725–40; Denis de Lucca, *Mdina: A History of Its Urban Space and Architecture*, Valletta: Said International, 1995, p. 71; D. H. Trump, *Malta: An Archaeological Guide*, London: Faber & Faber Ltd, 1972, p. 106.

EDUCATION. From Byzantine times, teaching in Mdina was very much the prerogative of the church, with boys attending classes run by the **Cathedral Church**. This continued in medieval times and gradually other small schools were established for boys and later for girls.

George Angas who visited Mdina in 1841 wrote, 'Among the boys, Mr S recognised one with whom he was well acquainted. He had formerly been at a Protestant school in Valetta (sic), but was removed here on his friends determining that he should become a priest. He appeared to be a lad of fine mind and good understanding, but he will probably lose all that he had acquired previously, as he is only taught the doctrines of the Popish faith with a little

St Nicholas College Mtarfa Primary

Hebrew. One of the priests belonging to the establishment showed us the sleeping apartments of the scholars, consisting of several long airy rooms, with a number of small beds arranged on each side. Every boy provides his own bedding, so that the furniture of the apartment is very various. Over most of the bedsteads was affixed either a small picture of the Virgin, or some favourite saint, to which they attach great importance. Several had Latin inscriptions upon them, and some were got up with a certain degree of childish taste, and were ornamented with small bows of ribbon.'

Some children in Mdina were educated at home, at least for the primary years, with others attending nearby schools. A girls' school was operated by the Sisters of St. Dorothy at **Banca Giuratale** from 1969; and from its establishment in 1987, many boys from Mdina have attended St. Nicholas College at Mtarfa.

References: George French Angas, *A ramble in Malta and Sicily in the Autumn of 1841*, London: Smith, Elder & Co, 1842, p. 50; Joseph J Camilleri, 'Early government schools in Malta', *Melita Historica* vol 5, no 3 (1970), pp. 259–68; Dominic V Scerri, *The Saga of Church Schools in Malta 1970–1986*, Valletta: Mut Publications, 2000.

ERARDI, STEFANO (1630–1716). A prominent Maltese painter, he was born in Valletta, the son of Mastro Sebastiano Erardi and Paulica (née Xerri). A painter, he had many commissions in churches in many parts of Malta. Among his more famous works are *The Annunciation* (1677) in the Carmelite Church in Mdina, and *Our Lady with the Child Jesus*, in Cathedral Church in Mdina.

References: J. Deono, *An inventory of Alessio Erardi's paintings and books*, s.n.: Malta, 1989; Edward Sammut, Art in Malta, np, 1954; Michael J. Schiavone, *Dictionary of Maltese Biographies*, Malta: pubblikazzjonijiet Indipendenza, 2009, vol 1, pp. 756–57. Portrait courtesy Michael J. Schiavone.

– F –

FALZON PALACE. *See* **Palazzo Falzon**.

FALZONE, AMBROGIO. He was the **Capitano della Verga** of Mdina, 1518–19, and 1523–24.

FALZONE, AMBROGIO. He was the **Capitano della Verga** of Mdina, 1597–98.

FALZONE, ANTONIO. He was the **Capitano della Verga** of Mdina, 1532–33.

FALZONE, GIACOME. The **Capitano della Verga** of Mdina, 1513–14, he was a notary in Mdina and the son of Antonio Falzone. He married Amata de Bernardo and they had several children, their eldest son Giovanni went into the church and became a Canon, and their second son **Matteo Falzone**, was created 1st Baron Falzone in 1521.

FALZONE, MATTEO. The **Capitano della Verga** of Mdina, 1534–36, 1540–42, 1557–63, and 1565–68, he was the son of **Giacome Falzone** and his wife Amata de Bernardo. In 1521 he was created 1st Baron Falzone. He married Paola Bondino and they had six children: Entiona, Antonella, Matteo (who inherited his father's title), Lucrezia, Caterina and Marietta. In 1565 he contributed to the massive thanksgiving service which took place after the defeat of the Turks.

References: John Montalto, *The Nobles of Malta, 1530–1800*, Valletta: Midsea Books, 1979, p. 102, 176.

FALZONE, MICHELE. The **Capitano della Verga** of Mdina, 1525–26, he was the son of Andrea Falsone, a notary in Mdina, and his wife Etagia de Bernardo. Michele Falzone married Margarita Caxaro. As vice-admiral of Malta in 1530, he held the formal dinner on the evening of 13 November 1530 after Grand Master **Philippe Villiers de L'Isle-Adam** formally arrived at Mdina and swore to uphold the privileges and liberties of the people.

References: Denis de Lucca, *Mdina: A History of Its Urban Space and Architecture*, Valletta: Said International, 1995, p. 43; John Montalto, *The Nobles of Malta, 1530–1800*,

Valletta: Midsea Books, 1979, p. 63.

FALZONE, PIETRO. The **Capitano della Verga** of Mdina, 1526–27, he was the son of Franco Falsone (sic) who had married his niece Agata Falsone, the daughter of Marchesino Falzone, 3rd Baron of Djar il-Chandul. Pietro inherited the title through his mother and became 4th Baron of Djar il-Chandul. He married Leonora Pache and they had several children with the title passing to the second child and oldest son, Leonardo, 5th Baron of Djar il-Chandul.

References: John Montalto, *The Nobles of Malta, 1530–1800*, Valletta: Midsea Books, 1979, p. 259.

FARRUGIA, JOSEPH M. (1868–1953). An author, he was born on 24 February 1868 at Vittoriosa, and then after studying at the Lyceum, he went on to the Mdina Seminary. In 1892 he was ordained a priest by Archbishop Gaetano Pace Forno, and always interested in history, he wrote much about the history of Malta, some of his works being published in Maltese, and others in English. He specialised in the history of Birgu, but also involved himself in social welfare issues. He died on 31 May 1953.

References: J.F. Darmanin, 'In Memoriam: Canon J.M. Farrugia (1868–1953)', *Melita Historica* vol 2, no 1 (1956); Michael J. Schiavone, *Dictionary of Maltese Biographies*, Malta: pubblikazzjonijiet Indipendenza, 2009, vol 1, p. 778.

FELICI, GIOVANNI DOMENICO. He was the **Capitano della Verga** of Mdina, 1624–25.

FERRIOLO, DIEGO. He was the **Capitano della Verga** of Mdina, 1635–36, and 1638–40.

FIRE BRIGADE. The fire brigade in Mdina operates as part of the Civil Protection Department (CPD), which in turn is under the Ministry for Justice and Home Affairs. The CPD was formed on 9 February 1989 and operates ten fire stations at seven locations with the Ta'Kandja Centre the closest to Mdina.

FITENI, SILVESTRO. The **Capitano della Verga** of Mdina, 1644–52, he was the son of Gio Antonio Fiteni, the holder of the fief of Budach (Budaq) and his wife Imperia Testaferrata. In 1646 he was created the Baron of Budach, the first title of nobility since the arrival of the Knights of St. John. As he had no family connections outside Malta, he was also the first Maltese to hold a direct noble title. He married Genova Passalacqua; they had no children. Silvestro Fiteni did have an illegitimate son with an African slave. The son, Giovanni, claimed the barony, and his older son, Silvestrino Fiteni (1667–1709) also made a claim for the title.

References: John Montalto, *The Nobles of Malta, 1530–1800*, Valletta: Midsea Books, 1979, p. 30, 89.

A tree just outside the walls of Mdina.
Photograph © allard1 / Fotolia.com

FLORA. There has long been a shortage of water in Mdina, and as a result houses had to be built with an underground cavern to allow them to collect rainwater during the winter. Many still do this. This shortage of water has meant that there are few gardens or plants within the old city of Mdina, although just outside it, separating Mdina from **Rabat**, are the **Howard Gardens** which have a wide range of different plants and trees. There was also a garden located below the Bastions, north of Mdina.

References: Anne Agius Ferrante, *No Strangers in the Silent City*, Valletta: Andrew Rupert Publishing, 1992, p. 29; S M Haslam, P D Sell and P A Wolsely, *A flora of the Maltese islands*, Msida: Malta University Press, 1977, reviewed by Edwin Lanfranco, *Melita Historica* vol 7, no 2 (1977), pp. 190–92; Hans Christian Weber & Bernd Kendzior, *Flora of the Maltese Islands: a field guide*, Weikersheim: Margraf, 2006.

DI FOIX, PIERRE (PIETRO) (1449–1490). A Franciscan, he was born on 7 February 1449 in Pau, France, the son of Gaston IV, Count of Foix, and his wife Eleanor of Navarre. This made him a nephew of King Louis XI of France. He was elected bishop of Vannes in 1476 and made a Cardinal Deacon by Pope Sixtus IV. From 14 May 1485 to 6 July 1489 he was the apostolic administrator of the see of Bayonne from 1484 until his death. He also brokered a peace agreement between King Charles VIII of France and Duke Francis II of Brittany. A close associate of King Ferdinand I of Naples, he was the apostolic administrator in Malta from 6 July 1489 until his death on 10 August 1490 in Rome. He was buried in St. Tryphon's Church which has since been demolished.

FONTENELLA TEA GARDEN. Located in **Triq is-Sur** – its official address is 1 Bastion Street – this tea garden offers a range of cakes, as well as pastries, baguettes and pizzas. From this tea garden there are spectacular views of the region and it is possible to see Mosta Dome, Naxxar and even Valletta. With a large array of homemade cakes, the tea garden is said to have some of the finest chocolate cakes and pastizzi in Malta. It also delivers cakes to nearby locations.

References: Carolyn Bain, *Malta & Gozo*, Footscray, Vic, Australia: Lonely Planet, 2004, p. 121; Fontanella Tea Garden, www.fontanellateagarden.com.

FOOTBALL. This remains a very popular sport all over Malta being introduced by the British in the mid-nineteenth century. A football association was formed in 1863 with the Malta Football Association (MFA) founded in 1900. All the football clubs draw from particular areas in Malta with **Rabat** Football Club popular with boys from Mdina, with games held on a football pitch at **Mdina Ditch**, just outside the city walls. On 26 March 2000, the Maltese postal authorities issued a stamp commemorating the 100th anniversary of the founding of the MFA.

In more recent times, the Mdina Knights Football Club has been the team for the Old City. They were founded in 2006 and officially recognised by the Malta Football Association in the same year, with their home ground being the Centenary Stadium at Ta'Qali. Playing in the Maltese Third Division, the club was formed by Gilbert Camilleri, Matthew Paris, Keith Galea and Sean Buhagiar. The current President of the Executive Committee is Joseph T. Vella. Their badge incorporates the silhouette of Mdina.

References: Carmel Baldacchino, *Maltese Footballers: Hundred of the Best*, Valletta: Progress Press, 2004; Joe H Griffiths, *A Football Saga: Fifty Years of Football in Malta*, Hamrum: Publishers Enterprises Group, 1985; Malta Football, www.maltafootball.com/; Mdina Knights, http://www.mdinaknightsfc.com/

FRENCH OCCUPATION. On 9 June 1798, the French fleet, on its way to Egypt under Napoleon Bonaparte, arrived off Valletta seeking fresh water. It had sailed from Toulon on 19 May and had 30,000 men under the command of General Napoleon Bonaparte. Anchoring off Valletta at 5.30 am, it made its request to Grand Master Ferdinand von Hompesch zu Bolheim who refused to allow them any water citing the Treaty of Utrecht by which only two foreign ships were allowed into the harbour at any one time. He was confident that the walls of the forts would stop the French as they had the Turks in 1565.

Napoleon Bonaparte was angered by this and ordered his ships to bombard Valletta. Two days later French soldiers started landing at various points around Malta. With the local militia pulling back to Valletta, the French quickly marched on Mdina as the symbolic capital of the island. Under General **Claude-Henri Belgrand de Vaubois**, they entered the city. Although the Maltese could have held out at Valletta, Hompesch decided not to do so and surrendered in return for lands and monies in France for the Knights of Malta. The surrender was signed on the French ship Orient. This allowed the French to then embark for

Egypt, leaving some 4,000 men under de Vaubois on the island of Malta. In Egypt between 1–3 August, the French suffered a humiliating defeat at the battle of the Nile. The Orient was destroyed during the battle and sank with much of the treasure of the Knights of Malta on board.

In Malta the French decided to establish a new revolutionary regime. This involved dismantling all the institutions of the Knights of Malta and disestablishing the Roman Catholic Church. The property of the latter was sequestrated and sold. In Mdina, the possessions of many churches including the **Carmelite Church and Convent** were offered for sale on Sunday 2 September 1798. The local people rose up in anger both at the sale, and that it was happening on a Sunday. When the French commander Masson, along with an officer and a soldier went to St. Paul's Church, **Rabat**, and started looting it, they were attacked and fled back into Mdina as a mob gathered. This led to the French fleeing into the **House of the Notary Bezzina** and the French officer Masson being thrown off the balcony of the house. Further Maltese insurgents managed to get into Mdina the following day and a massacre of all the French soldiers took place.

The outbreak in Mdina encouraged others elsewhere on the island to rise up against the French, and with help from some British ships and their crews, the French fled to the safety of Valletta and eventually, on 3 September 1800, surrendered after a long siege. The start of the French occupation was commemorated on a series of four Maltese postage stamps issued on 28 March 1998, with the uprising commemorated on another series of four stamps issued on 6 October 1999.

References: Alan Blondy, 'Malta and France 1789–1798: the art of communicating a crisis', in Victor Mallia-Milanes (ed), *Hospitaller Malta 1530–1798: studies on early modern Malta and the Order of St John of Jerusalem*, Msida: Mireva Publications, 1993, pp. 659–85; Dr Charles J Boffa, *The Saga of the French Occupation of Malta 1798–1800*, Valletta: Progress Press, 1998; Richard Cavendish, 'The French Surrender Malta', *History Today* vol 50, no 9 (September 2000), pp. 54–55; Didier Destremau, *Malta Tricolore: The Story of a French Malta, 1798–1964*, Malta: Midsea Books, 2005; Walter Ganado, Political parties in Malta following on the rising against the French, paper given at the Malta Historical Society, 4 December 1951, reviewed by Joseph Cassar-Pullicino, *Melita Historica* vol 1, no 1 (1952), p. 55; Christopher Hibbert, 'Bonaparte and the Knights of Malta', *History Today* vol 20, no 3 (March 1970), pp. 153–62; Denis de Lucca, *Mdina: A History of Its Urban Space and Architecture*, Valletta: Said International, 1995, pp. 115–17; William Zammit, 'Communicating a New Regime: The Maltese Printed Product during the French Occupation (1798–1800)', *History Week* (1999), pp. 1–52.

FRERE, JOHN HOOKHAM (1769–1846). An English diplomat and writer, he was born on 21 May 1769 in London, the son of John Frere, and Jane, daughter of John Hookham, a rich London merchant. Educated at Eton College, he proceeded to Caius College, Cambridge, where he became a good friend of George Canning. He served as a member of the British Parliament from 1796 to 1802, and was then posted to Lisbon as Envoy Extraordinary, and then went to Spain, Appointed to the Privy Council in 1805. Two years later he was appointed as head of the British mission to Berlin, and in the following year was the British representative to the Central Junta in Spain. He left Madrid ahead of the French and declining a peerage, went to Malta where he devoted himself to literature. He enjoyed the city of Mdina and some of the other Roman and medieval sites around the island. He died on 7 January 1846 at Villa Frère, at Pietà, west of Valletta.

References: Paul Cassar, 'John Hookham Frere in Malta (1821c–1846)', *Melita Historica* vol 9, no 1 (1984), pp. 49–73; Donald Sultana, *The journey of William Frere to Malta in 1832, preceded by a sketch of his life and of the Frere family, with particular reference to John Hookham Frere*, Malta: Progress Press, 1988.

– G –

GAFÀ, LORENZO (1638–1703). A baroque architect, he was born in 1638 at Vittoriosa (Birgu) and worked as a stone carver, his brother Melchiorre Cafà (1636–1667) was a sculptor. In 1661 he had already turned to architecture and was involved in the design of the choir of St. Philip, Zebbug, he then worked on a number of other churches, including St. Paul's at **Rabat** from 1664 to 1683; and the Sarria Church in Floriana in 1676. From 1668 to 1672 he worked on the **Carmelite Church** in Mdina, and after working on the Bishop's Palace (now **Archbishop's Palace**), he was involved in the design and then construction of St. Paul's **Cathedral Church**, Mdina after it sustained major damage in the 1693 earthquake. He also remodelled the Chapel of St. Agatha after it too had also been damaged in the **earthquake**. He was later involved in the design of St. Mary's church, Qrendi, and he died in 1703. Some of his sculptures appeared on a series of four postage stamps issued on 1 August 1967.

References: Mario Buhagiar, *Essays on the Knights and Art and Architecture in Malta 1500–1798*, Sta Venera, Malta: Midsea Books, 2009; Denis de Lucca, *Mdina: A History of Its Urban Space and Architecture*, Valletta: Said International, 1995, pp. 73–75; Quentin Hughes, *The building of Malta, during the period of the Knights of St. John*, London: A. Tiranti, 1967.

GAFFIERO, SALVATORE (SAVIOUR) (1828–1906). He was the auxiliary bishop of Malta from 1899 to 1906. Born on 8 March 1828 in Senglea, he was only twelve years old when he became the canon of his local collegiate church. Ordained priest on 20 December 1851, he joined the Oratorians Fathers of St. Philip Neri in Senglea and in 1875 was named canon of the **Cathedral Church** in Mdina. Ten years later, he was appointed vicar general by Bishop **Anton Buhagiar**, and then served as aide to Archbishop **Pietro Pace**. Nominated as titular bishop of Selymbria, he remained living in Floriana and served as auxiliary bishop of Malta until his death on 8 December 1906.

References: Michael J. Schiavone, *Dictionary of Maltese Biographies*, Malta: pubblikazzjonijiet Indipendenza, 2009, vol 2, p. 854.

Portrait by Edward Caruana Dingli, 1949.

GALEA, EMMANUEL (1891–1974). He was the auxiliary bishop of Malta from 1942 to 1974, being born on 10 March 1891 in Senglea. Ordained priest in 1915, in the following year he completed his doctorate in theology from the University of Malta, and in 1923 graduated with a doctorate in canon law from the Pontifical Gregorian University in Rome. The secretary general to Archbishop **Maurus Caruana**, and his successor Bishop (later Archbishop) **Michael Gonzi**. He died on 21 August 1974 and moves for his beatification stated on 24 June 2003.

References: Michael J. Schiavone, *Dictionary of Maltese Biographies*, Malta: pubblikazzjonijiet Indipendenza, 2009, vol 2, p. 864.

GALEA, JOSEPH (1912–1989). An historian, bibliophile and antiquarian, Chevalier Joseph Galea was born on 24 October 1912 in Valletta, the son of Emmanuel Galea and Vincenza (née Fenech). Educated at the Bishop's Seminary in Gozo, St. Aloysius College, and the Royal University of Malta 1930–34, he also studied history at General Western University, California. The Archives Assistant at the Royal Malta Library, remaining with the library until 1972, and involved in cataloguing the manuscripts at the **Cathedral Church**, he was active in a large number of history societies and organisations. One of his earlier works was 'A chronological series of the Bishops of Malta', published in the St. Paul's parish magazine, and a booklet on *Mdina: the Silent City 1798–1800* (1948). He married Paolina Vella on 3 February 1952 and they had a son, Patrick. They lived at Casa Viani, 5 Villegaignon St, Mdina, collecting many books and prints on Malta and the Order of St. John, as well as being keenly interested in fossil hunting. He died on 25 October 1989.

References: Joseph Galea, 'Malta under the Angevins', *Scientia* vol. 17 (1951); Joseph Galea, 'Malta and the Second World War: a bibliography', *Melita Historica* vol. 1, no 1 (1952); *Malta Who's Who 1964*, p. 98; *Malta Who's Who 1965*, pp. 127–28; *Malta Who's Who 1968*, pp. 183–84; *Malta Who's Who 1969/70*, p. 185; Michael J. Schiavone, *Dictionary of Maltese Biographies*, Malta: pubblikazzjonijiet Indipendenza, 2009, vol 2, pp. 873–74. Portrait courtesy Michael J. Schiavone.

GALEA, PIETRO PAOLO. The **Capitano della Verga** of Mdina, 1730–33, he was the Baron of San Marciano. He married Vincenza Ferriol who brought great wealth into his family including a palace in Valletta and a residence in Mdina.

References: John Montalto, *The Nobles of Malta, 1530–1800*, Valletta: Midsea Books, 1979, p. 241.

GARGAL, TOMÁS (1536–1614). A member of the Sovereign Military Hospitaller Order of St. John of Jerusalem, he was born in Catalonia, Spain. He was then the bishop of Malta from 11 August 1578 until his death on 10 June 1614.

GARZEZ, MARTIN (1526–1601). He was the Grand Master of the Knights Hospitaller (Knights of Malta) from 1595 to 1601. He had been born in Aragon in 1526 and was aged 69 when elected Grand Master to succeed **Hugues de Verdalle**. He had been involved in lessening the tensions between the Papacy and the Order of Malta which arose during the reign of **Jean de la Cassière**. To encourage new members he allowed some Swiss from non-noble families to become Knights so long as they were Catholic, not illegitimate, and their fathers had served as army or naval officers. Worried that the Turks might attack Malta again, he improved the defences of the island, and also that of Gozo organising the construction of the Garzes Tower in Gozo, but he died on 7 February 1601 before work started. In Mdina, he is best-remembered for trying to induce many citizens to stay in the old city by tax relief and other incentives.

References: Victor Mallia-Milanes, *Venice and Hospitaller Malta 1530–1798: aspects of a relationship*, Marsa: Publishers Enterprises Group, 1992; Alexander Sutherland, *The achievements of the Knights of Malta*, Edinburgh: Constable and Hurst, vol 2, 1831.

GATTO D'ESGUANEZ, ANTONIO. He was the **Capitano della Verga** of Mdina, 1493–99.

GATTO, FRANCESCO. A soldier, he was the **Capitano della Verga** of Mdina, 1403–06, and was possibly the same person who was **Capitano della Verga** of Mdina, 1431–33. A strong supporter of King Alfonso V of Aragon, the King granted him permission to place his coat of arms in Mdina alongside those of the King, and also exempted his family from paying some taxes. He had drawn up his Will in 1432 in which he named his heir as Imperia, his only daughter with his first wife Paola Castelli. He also left money to be held for his second wife Donna Constantia, but she was forbidden from remarrying.

References: John Montalto, *The Nobles of Malta, 1530–1800*, Valletta: Midsea Books, 1979, p. 17–18, 20–22, 24.

GAUCI, FRANCESCO. The **Capitano della Verga** of Mdina, 1799–1801, he was the son of Gio Nicolo Gauci-Apap (c1691–1767) and his wife Modesta Cuschieri Gatt. In 1762 he married Antonia Ducoss, and they had six children: Francesco; Pietro Paolo; Pasquale; Nicola; Maddelena; and Maria. In 1781 he was created the 1st (and last) Baron Gauci.

GENEALOGY. Because so many noble families of Malta have their family seats in Mdina, it is central to the genealogy of many Maltese. Details of many of them have been preserved and a large number of family trees are published online (www.maltagenealogy.com). There is also Mario Cassar's *The Surnames of the Maltese Islands* (2003).

Baptisms, marriages and burials were recorded in parish registers with those of Mdina (and also many other places in Malta) held in the **Cathedral Museum**. They go back to 1537 for St. John's Co-Cathedral in Valletta, and about 1550 for other places. Civil registration (for births, deaths and marriages) started in 1863, with records for Malta held at the Public Registry Office (L'Insinua), 197 Merchants Street, Valletta. It also holds Wills proven before 1863. For Wills from the last one hundred years, applicants should bring or include with any written application, a death certificate of the person concerned. In addition, there are census returns. The first was held in 1842, followed by censuses in 1851, 1861, 1871, 1881, 1891, 1901, 1911, 1921, 1931, 1948, 1957, 1967, 1977, 1987, 1997, and 2007. The earlier ones are held at the Public Library in Valletta.

Mdina featured in a 2013 Australian episode of the genealogical television series, *Who Do You Think You Are?* in which the Australian comedian Adam Hills had his ancestry traced back to his 11x great-grandfather Matteo Vassallo in fifteenth-century Mdina. During the programme, he visited the Notarial Archives, the **Palazzo Falzon**, and Birgu.

References: Mario Cassar, *The Surnames of the Maltese Islands: an etymological dictionary – the origin and meaning of over 1,100 entries*, Malta: Book Distributors Ltd, 2003; Charles A. Gauci, *The genealogy and heraldry of the noble families of Malta*, Marsa: Publishers Enterprises Group, 1991–92; Charles A. Gauci, *An illustrated collection of the coats of arms of Maltese families*, San Gwann: Publishers Enterprises, 1996; 'Malta', in Angus Baxter, *In Search of Your European Roots*, Baltimore, Maryland: Genealogical Publishing Company, 1994, pp. 181–82.

GERADA, EMMANUEL (1920–2011). He was the coadjutor archbishop of Malta from 1967 to 1973, being born on 18 May 1920 at Zejtun. Educated at the Lyceum, he proceeded to the Royal University of Malta and graduated BA in 1939, completing his theology degree two years later. Ordained priest on 1 August 1943, he went on to study at Nottingham University College in England, and in 1952 completed his doctorate in canon law at the Pontifical Gregorian University in Rome. Serving in India and then in Dublin, and later in Rwanda, he was consecrated as titular bishop of Nomentum in June 1967, and then auxiliary bishop of Malta. He served as papal nuncio in El Salvador and Guatemala and was a close friend of Archbishop Oscar Romero who was assassinated on 25 March 1980 while saying mass in San Salvador. Emmanuel Gerada died on 21 January 2011.

References: Warren G. Berg, *Historical Dictionary of Malta*, Lanham, Md.: The Scarecrow Press, 1995, pp. 52–53; Michael J. Schiavone, *Dictionary of Maltese Biographies*, Malta: pubblikazzjonijiet Indipendenza, 2009, vol 2, pp. 924–25.

GERMANS. Although Malta has been popular with German tourists since the 1970s, there has never been a large German community on the island. There was a German contingent amongst the Knights of Malta – these formed the Auberge of Germany. However they were not numerous and in 1783 were merged with the few English Knights to form the Anglo-Bavarian Langue. There are some carvings by Albrecht Dürer at St. Paul's Cathedral in Mdina, and three of these ('The Flight into Egypt', 'The Nativity of the Lord' and 'The Adoration of the Magi') appeared on a series of Maltese postage stamps issued on 10 November 2015, and there were some early German settlers. One of these families was the Hyzlers with Giuseppe Hyzler (1787–1858), a prominent artist, with some of his work being in the Church of St. Mary of Jesus in **Rabat**. And there is, of course, Ferdinand von Hempesch zu Bolheim who was the Grand Master of the Knights of Malta from 1797 to 1799. William Domeier was a German doctor who was in Malta in the 1800s, writing an

account of his stay. It was not until Manfred Moser became fascinated with Malta that a Maltese-German/German-Maltese dictionary was published in 2005.

References: E R Leopardi, 'Germans in Malta in the years 1565 – 1569', *Melita Historica* vol 4, no 2 (1965), pp. 117–27.

GHINUCCI, GIROLAMO (1480–1541). Born in Siena, he was a secretary to Pope Julius II. He was the apostolic administrator of Malta from the death of **Bonifacio Cateniano**, taking office on 10 September 1523, and holding it until 20 March 1538. He was in office in November 1530 when **Philippe Villiers de L'Isle-Adam** formally entered Mdina and swore to uphold and maintain the political liberties of Mdina. He stepped down on the appointment to bishop of **Tommaso Bosio**. A prominent theologian, he was involved in attacks on Martin Luther and actively took part in both the Fifth Council of the Lateran in 1512–17, with King Henry VIII of England briefly using his services as advisor and also running an embassy to Spain. From 1522 to 1535 he was also the Bishop of Worcester in England, being the last of the Italian absentee bishops to hold the see. He was succeeded by Hugh Latimer who was to be burned at the stake in 1555. Girolamo Ghinucci was created Cardinal on 21 May 1535 and died on 6 July 1541 in Rome.

References: Catherine Fletcher, *Our Man in Rome: Henry VIII and his Italian Ambassador*, London: Bodley Head, 2012, p. 26; Peter Gwyn, *The King's Cardinal: the rise and fall of Thomas Wolsey*, London: Pimlico, 1992, p. 155, 295.

GIURATI. *See* **Università Dei Giurati**.

GOLLCHER, OLOF FREDERICK (1889–1962). He was the owner of **Palazzo Falzon** and was from a Swedish family long resident in Malta. His grandfather, Olof Frederick Gollcher, had been born on 2 November 1829 at Stockholm, Sweden, the son of Johan Gustaf Gollcher and Maria Birgitta (née Wenstrom). He moved to Malta to run the company O.F. Gollcher & Sons, and in 1853 married Vincenza Bruno from a well-connected Maltese family. They had nine children, with Gustav being born on 26 December 1854. Gustav married Elisa Balbi, sister of Major H. Balbi, and their son, Olof Frederick Gollcher, was named after his grandfather. Moving to Mdina, he lived at the Palazzo Falzon with his wife Nella.

Born on 17 March 1889 in Valletta, Olof Gollcher was educated at Dulwich College, England, 1906–08, and in 1914 he joined the British Amy serving in World War I and was awarded the Medal of Montenegro. In the mid–1920s he was living in Rome, Italy. In 1927 he and his mother bought the Palazzo Falzon in Mdina. In 1936 he was created a Knight of Grace of the Grand Priory of the British Realm of the Venerable Order of the Hospital of St. John of Jerusalem. Awarded the OBA in 1937, in the following year he went to London and married Teresa 'Nella' Lucia Prior and they bought the rest of the Palazzo Falzon. He served in World War II and during the rest of his life remained a wealthy scholar and philanthropist. He died on 23 July 1962 aged 73, and was buried on 24 July 1962 at Ta'Braxia Cemetery.

References: *Dulwich College Register 1619–1926*, p. 433; *Dulwich College War Record 1914–1919*, p. 349; Anne Agius Ferrante, *No Strangers in the Silent City*, Valletta: Andrew Rupert Publishing, 1992, p. 25; Sir Harry Luke, *Malta: an account and an appreciation*, London: G.G. Harrap, 1960, p. 151.

GONZI, MICHAEL (1885–1984). The archbishop of Malta from 1943 to 1976, he was born on 13 May 1885 in Birgu, and studied at the University of Malta before going to Rome to continue his studies at the Pontifical Gregorian University, gaining a doctorate in canon law. He was ordained a priest in 1908 and returned to the University of Malta as a professor of sacred scripture and Hebrew. A co-founder of the Catholic Workers' Movement, he was elected to

Michael Gonzi, archbishop of Malta.
Painting by Edward Caruana Dingli.

the Senate for Labour in 1921. In the following year he became the private secretary to **Maurus Caruana**, the archbishop, and in 1924 was appointed as bishop of Gozo, becoming bishop of Malta in 1943. Because of the war, it was not until May 1944 that he rode into Mdina on a white mare, in the traditional style, formally to take possession of his archdiocese. A strong supporter of the British war effort, in the 1950s, he defended the Catholic Church against attacks from an increasingly secular population, and was an active member in the Second Vatican Council from 1962–65. He opposed the plan to integrate Malta with the British Isles – which would have seen Maltese representation in the British House of Commons – as he saw that this would diminish the power of the Church. In ill-health, he retired in 1976 and died on 22 January 1984. He was buried in Mdina **Cathedral**.

References: Warren G. Berg, *Historical Dictionary of Malta*, Lanham, Md.: The Scarecrow Press, 1995, pp. 55–56; Jeremy Boissevain, *Saints and Fireworks: Religion and Politics in Rural Malta*, London: The Athlone Press, 1965; Charles Buttiġieġ, *Mikiel Gonzi: Fifty years at the helm*, Klabb Kotba Maltin, 2015; D. Fenech, *The making of Archbishop Gonzi*, Malta: Union Press, 1976; M. Galea and E. Tonna, *L-arċisqof Gonzi*, Valletta: Associated News, 1984; Magnus Linklater, 'Vatican capitulates to priests on land reform', *The Sunday Times* (London) (16 May 1971); 'Mgr Gonzi, guardian of Malta morals dies at 98', *The Daily Telegraph* (23 January 1984); Michael J. Schiavone, *Dictionary of Maltese Biographies*, Malta: pubblikazzjonijiet Indipendenza, 2009, vol 2, pp. 939–40; S. C. Smith, 'Priests and politicians: Archbishop Michael Gonzi, Dom Mintoff, and the end of empire in Malta', *Journal of Mediterranean Studies*, vol. 23, no. 1 (2014), pp. 113–124; *Malta Who's Who 1969/70*, pp. 202–03.

GORI-MANCINI, GASPARE (1653–1727). Born in April 1653 at Rigomagno, he was ordained priest in the Sovereign Military Hospitaller

Order of St. John of Jerusalem on 25 March 1676. Appointed bishop of Malta on 1 June 1722, he was confirmed 7 June and remained bishop until his death on 16 July 1727.

GOURGION, GIOVANNI. The **Capitano della Verga** of Mdina, 1692–98, he was the son of Spirito Gourgion and his wife Antoina Ducoss who were married in 1643. In 1672 Giovanni married Anna Elena Muscat and their daughter Anna married Dr Gio Pio de Piro, 1st Baron of Budach (Budaq), 1st Marquis de Piro.

GREAT SIEGE (1565). In 1565 the Turks decided to capture Malta and sent an expeditionary force to the island. The administrative capital of Malta at that time was Birgu (now Vittorosia) and **Jean de la Valette** decided to concentrate his forces at Fort St. Elmo and Fort St. Angelo, recognising that both would have to withstand a siege with the Turks using their heavy cannons. As a result he sent his cavalry under **Marshal de Copier**, to Mdina but could spare few soldiers for the defence of the old city. As expected, the Turks landed at Marsasirocco Bay, and marched towards Birgu with the canons at Fort St. Elmo and Fort St. Aneglo firing their cannons on 18 May to alert the people in Mdina. The Turkish army, after it had disembarked, then passed Mdina although could easily have taken the city. However by tradition, a local nun had a vision that there should be a large procession to prevent this and all the citizens of Mdina dressed up and marched around the walls with Turkish scouts then reporting that the city was heavily defended.

The Turks then moved to attack Birgu with their main focus on capturing first Fort St. Elmo and then Fort St. Angelo. After subjecting Fort St. Elmo to a withering artillery barrage for four weeks, they managed to capture the fort and then turned their attention on Fort St. Angelo. During this period Mustapha, one of the Turkish commanders, decided to change his plan of attack. He contemplated the Turkish forces spending the winter on Malta and as a result felt that they should capture Mdina. However their attention at the time was focused on attacking Fort St. Angelo.

When the Turks had breached the walls and were launching an assault on Fort St. Angelo, some Maltese cavalry from Mdina rode into the lightly defended Turkish camp and sacked it, burning down the tents and destroying their supplies forcing the Turks to have to call off their attack. This proved crucial because without this distraction it is possible that Fort St. Angelo might have fallen, and the Turks would have been victorious.

A cannon in Mdina
Photograph by Robin Corfield.

For the Turks, they recognised that the cavalry from Mdina might continue to be a problem, and on 8 August they concealed some soldiers in Grand Master's Wood, some others in the village of Sebbug, and a third detachment near San Domingo. They sent some arquebusiers over to Mdina where, in plain view of the garrison, the Turks rounded up the cattle which they found grazing. This lured some of the soldiers under Captain Anastasio and Captain Lugny from the safety of Mdina. These chased the Turks who retreated, and then the Christians noted that another detachment of Turks was trying to cut them off. The Christians left the cattle and charged the Turks before heading back to Mdina. The garrison managed to kill 50 Turks, losing twelve of their number, and also 30 horses.

It seems that only when the Turks were about to withdraw from Malta, did they decide to attack Mdina sending over some of their men on 11 September. Francisco Balbi di Correggio surmises that the Turkish commanders probably wanted a victory to try to make up for their defeat elsewhere on Malta. Their timing was quite good as some 100 men from the Mdina garrison had just headed over to Birgu. However there were enough of the garrison left behind who were able to man the defences and armed with arquebuses, they saw off a minor Turkish attack. The Turks then withdrew from the island.

The defeat of the Turks became famous all over Europe and has been the subject of many books. The French philosopher Voltaire later commented, 'Nothing is better known than the siege of Malta'.

References: Joseph Attard, *The Knights of Malta*, San Gwann: Publishers Enterprises Group, 1992; Warren G. Berg, *Historical Dictionary of Malta*, Lanham, Md.: The Scarecrow Press, 1995, pp. 58–61; Ernle Bradford, *The Great Siege*, London: Hodder & Stoughton, 1967; Francisco Balbi di Correggio, *The Siege of Malta 1565*, translated by Ernle Bradford, London: The Folio Society, 1965, Harmondsworth: Penguin Books, 2003, p. 45, 151, 183–84; Simone Gismondi, *The 1565 Siege of the Knight of Malta at Fort St.*

Elmo, Florence: Edifir, 2008; T. H. McGuffie, 'The Great Siege of Malta 1565', *History Today* vol 15, no 8 (August 1965), pp. 539–48; Tony Rothman, 'The Great Siege of Malta', *History Today* vol 57, no 1 (January 2007), pp. 12–19.

GREEK'S GATE. This gate, known in Italian as Porta dei Greci, is located at the south-west entrance to the city. It is not certain how it gained its name. Traditionally it was because there was thought to be a Greek colony nearby, possibly southwest of Mdina, but some historians have doubted this was the case. After entering at the gate, a small square leads into St. Nicholas Street named after the patron saint of Greece. Slaves entering and leaving Mdina were not allowed to use the **Main Gate**, and as a result used the Greek's Gate. It was restored by Grand Master **António Manoel de Vilhena** (r. 1722–36), and on the gate are the coats off arms of both Vilhena, and also those of

Greek's Gate
Photograph JackF / Big Stock Photo

Emperor Charles V.

References: Can John Azzopardi, *Mdina, Rabat, Mosta*, Terni, Italy: Plurigraf, 1988, p. 37; Richard England and Conrad Thake, *Mdina: Citadel of Memory*, Malta: Atlantis, 1995, pp. 112–13; Denis de Lucca, *Mdina: A History of Its Urban Space and Architecture*, Valletta: Said International, 1995, p. 101; John Manduca, *Tourist Guide to City of Mdina*, Malta: Progress Press, 1975, p. 43.

GRIMA, ANNA M. (1958–). An artist, she was born on 16 February 1958 in Floriana and was educated at St. Dorothy's Convent in Mdina. When she was 24, she won a scholarship to study in Italy at the Academy of Fine Arts in Perugia. She then started designing clothes working with a Maltese fashion house, and also has had her paintings exhibited in galleries in Malta, France and Australia.

References: Michael J. Schiavone, *Dictionary of Maltese Biographies*, Malta: pubblikazzjonijiet Indipendenza, 2009, vol 2, pp. 971–72; Anna Grima, http://www.annagrima.com/.

GUALTIERI. By tradition, he was the bishop of Malta from 1091, and was appointed to the new **Cathedral** in Mdina when the Normans captured the island from the Arabs. According to early historians of Malta, he oversaw the initial building work of the Cathedral Church in Mdina. In recent years historians feel that the early accounts were inaccurate and that Gualtieri, if he existed, never had the title of 'bishop'.

DE GUEVARA, D. ANTONIO. The **Capitano della Verga** of Mdina, 1563–65, and 1568–70, he was in charge of Mdina in the run-up to and during the **Great Siege** of Malta, with the Turks initially deciding not to take Mdina, then changing their mind and planning an attack at the time of their fighting at Fort St. Angelo. The Maltese in Mdina, possibly realising that they might be assault, launched an attack of their own on the Turks. After the defeat of the Turks, he was one of the local nobles who contributed to a thanksgiving service in Mdina.

References: Ernle Bradford, *The Great Siege*, London: Hodder & Stoughton, 1967, p. 198; John Montalto, *The Nobles of Malta, 1530–1800*, Valletta: Midsea Books, 1979, p. 176.

DE GUEVARA, CARLO. The **Capitano della Verga** of Mdina, 1487–93, he was the fourth member of his family to hold this position.

DE GUEVARA, D. FERDINANDO. He was the **Capitano della Verga** of Mdina, 1574–78. In 1590 he sold his lands at Hain Cajat to Gregorio Xerri.

References: John Montalto, *The Nobles of Malta, 1530–1800*, Valletta: Midsea Books, 1979, p. 259–60.

DE GUEVARA, D. PIETRO. The **Capitano della Verga** of Mdina, 1595–97, and 1601–03, he was the son of Giovanni de Guevara, Baron di Ghajn Tuffieha, Gnien il Firen e Gattara, Castellano di Malta who died in 1511, aged 56, and his wife Margherita Cervantes. His grandfather was Giovanni De Guevara. He married Donna Enzione Inguanez and they had two sons, Antonio; and Ferdinand; and a daughter Isabella.

References: John Montalto, *The Nobles of Malta, 1530–1800*, Valletta: Midsea Books, 1979, p. 233.

DE GUEVARA, FERRANTE. The **Capitano della Verga** of Mdina, 1579–80, he was probably the Ferrari De Guevara who is mentioned on the Status Animarum for Mdina in 1561–62 – a list of the heads of each household in the city. It notes that Ferrari had a household of 14 people, which was, along with the households of Marco Inguanez and Francesco d'Alagona, the equal largest in Mdina.

References: John Montalto, *The Nobles of Malta, 1530–1800*, Valletta: Midsea Books, 1979, p. 224.

DE GUEVARA, GIOVANNI. The **Capitano della Verga** of Mdina, 1479–80, and 1500–06, he appears to have been the son of Don Diego De Guevara, the son of Don Ruy Lopez d'Avalos, Count of Ribadeo, Constable of Castile (1357–1421), and his second wife. He married Donna Paola Inguanez dei Baroni di Djar il-Bniet and they had several children including Matteo De Guevara. One of his grandsons was Pietro De Guevara who was the **Capitano della Verga** of Mdina, 1595–97, and 1601–03.

DE GUEVARA, MATTEO. The **Capitano della Verga** of Mdina, 1516–17, he was the son of Giovanni De Guevara. In 1516 or 1518 he married to Donna Perna Gatto Inguanez, 5th Baroness di Hemsija. They did not have children.

After his death, his widow was to marry three more times, with her second husband, whom she married in 1526 was Baron Cosimo Bellomo. In 1532 she married Baron Pietro Ortensio Spadafora; and her fourth husband was a noble from the Lafenca family.

References: John Montalto, *The Nobles of Malta, 1530–1800*, Valletta: Midsea Books, 1979, p. 239.

DE GUEVARA, TORRES. The **Capitano della Verga** of Mdina, 1481–82, he was the third member of his family to hold this title.

DE GUEVARA, TRISSANO. A juror in 1466, he was the **Capitano della Verga** of Mdina from 1468, and the first member of this family to hold this title.

GWANNI. By tradition, he was the bishop of Malta from 1113, he is said to have taken over from Bishop **Brialdo** and oversaw the construction work on the **Cathedral Church** in Mdina. There is the possibility that he may not have existed – and if he did, he certainly was not a bishop.

– H –

HAMILTON-ROSE, JOHN ARNOLD (1902–1971). An officer in the Royal Navy, he was born on 26 June 1902 in London, England, the son of Hamilton Rose and Elizabeth Louise Mary (née Rose), and was educated at Merchant Taylors School. He then joined the Royal Navy and was a Commander during World War II. After the war, he moved to Malta and in the 1960s, he was living at Beaulieu, 21 **Triq Villegaignon**, Mdina, later the home of **John Manduca**. He died on 1 February 1971 and was buried at Kalkara Naval Cemetery, Malta. His wife died on 4 June 1973 and was buried with him.

References: *Malta Who's Who 1964*, p. 111; *Malta Who's Who 1965*, p. 144; *Malta Who's Who 1968*, p. 211; *Malta Who's Who 1969/70*, p. 216.

HEALTH CARE. Because of its position along trading routes, there was always a problem with infections such as the plague being brought from other countries. After Venice started introducing quarantine controls in 1348, the Mdina municipality enforced its own quarantine measures. These were increased with the arrival of the Knights of St. John – they had a forty-day quarantine period enforced at Rhodes.

By the late fifteenth century there were a number of doctors known to be practising in Mdina. Glormu Callus had established a pharmacy business by 1491 and in 1519 it was being run by his son Antoni. There was, of course, **Guzeppi 'Matthew' Callus** later, and a prescription list from 1542 from the Santo Spirito Hospital in **Rabat** survives.

From the early seventeenth century, with the focus of Malta moving more to Valletta and neighbouring areas, the health care facilities in Mdina did not improve as much as those around the Grand Harbour, but with Rabat growing in importance, most medical facilities for people in Mdina came to be concentrated there. The plague in 1813 devastated the population of Malta causing the death of many people in Mdina. This forced improvements to the hygiene in the city. From 1908 until its closure in 1973, the Connaught Hospital operated in Mdina in what is now the **Magisterial Building**.

From the 1970s with large numbers of tourists coming to Malta, greater government income resulted in an expansion of the health care system, and there have been many studies of the health of Maltese including one in 1979–80 in which women in the western region of Malta, which included Mdina, were discovered to have the highest rates of breast cancer on the island.

References: Yana Mintoff Bland, 'Cancer in Malta: Trends in Mortality and Incidence Rates of Lung and Breast Cancer', Ronald G Sultana & Godfrey Baldacchino (eds), *Maltese Society: A Sociological Inquiry*, Msida: Mireva Publications, 1994, pp. 187–210 at p. 203; Vincent Borg, 'Medical practitioners in 16th century Malta', *History Week* (1981), pp. 82–85; Paul Cassar, 'British doctors and the study of medical and natural history of Malta in the nineteenth century', *Melita Historica* vol 3, no 4 (1963), pp. 33–41; Paul Cassar, *Medical History of Malta*, London: Wellcome Historical Medical Library, 1964, reviewed by Joseph Galea, *Melita Historica* vol 4, no 2 (1965), pp. 137–39; Stanley Fiorni, *Santo Spirito Hospital at Rabat, Malta: The Early Years to 1575*, Malta: Department of Information, Ministry of Health, 1989, reviewed by Godfrey Wettinger, *Melita Historica* vol 10, no 2 (1989), pp. 205–06; Joseph Galea, 'Before the motor ambulance came to Malta', *Melita Historica* vol 4, no 4 (1967), pp. 278–80; E. R. Leopardi, 'A Maltese district medical officer of the XVI century', *Melita Historica* vol 3, no 4 (1963), pp. 42–43; Paul Cassar, 'Malta's medical and social services under the Knights Hospitaller', in Victor Mallia-Milanes (ed), *Hospitaller Malta 1530–1798: studies on early modern Malta and the Order of St John of Jerusalem*, Msida: Mireva Publications, 1993, pp. 475–82; Fabian Mangion, 'Maltese islands devastated by a deadly epidemic 200 years ago', *The Times of Malta* (20 May 2013); Joseph Micallef, *The Plague of 1676: 11,300 deaths,* privately published, 1985; Charles Savona-Ventura, *Ancient and Medieval Medicine in Malta before 1600 AD*, San Gwann: Publishers Enterprises Group, 2004.

HENERICUS of CEFALÙ. A Franciscan, he was the bishop of Malta from 10 January 1334 to 1341, taking over from Bishop **Alduinus** and succeeded, in turn, by **Nicolaus Bonetti**.

HERALD'S LOGGIA. Located on **Pjazza San Pawl**, this building with its three semi-circular arches was where the Mdina City Herald (or Town Crier), known locally as the Banditore, stood and pronounced a 'Bando' (singular) or 'Bandi' (plural) – the proclamations, latest laws and decrees of the city governing body, the Università. Some of these dealt with local matters such as asking for all traders to bring their weights and measures to be checked, and also regulating the prices of goods being sold such as cheese, honey, pork or veal; for the washing of clothes in public fountains; of the disposal of garbage, One of the Bando which was read on 11 September 1472 announced a prohibition on the import of cattle from Gozo. Another on 30 September 1560 promised a reward of 100 scudi for any information which would lead to the arrest of the murderer of Fra Pietro de Revere, a knight from Provence who had recently been killed. The proclamation noted, 'if the informer is an accomplice, he will be paid only 50 scudi; in any case the informant's name would be kept secret'.

References: Richard England and Conrad Thake, *Mdina: Citadel of Memory*, Malta: Atlantis, 1995, pp. 98–99; John Manduca, *Tourist Guide to City of Mdina*, Malta: Progress Press, 1975, pp. 38–39; Edward Sammut, *The Monuments of Mdina*, Malta: Progress Press Co. Ltd, 1967, pp. 41–42.

DE HOMEDES Y COSCON, JUAN (c1477–1553). He was the Grand Master of the Knights Hospitaller (Knights of Malta) from 1536 until his death in 1552. A Spaniard from Aragon, he was elected in 1536 to succeed **Didier de Saint-Jaille** who had died on his way to Malta. His main task was to consolidate the position of the Knights in Malta by building new fortifications. In 1551, the Order of Malta lost its base at Tripoli in North Africa to the Ottomans led by Dragut (Turgut Reis) and Juan de Homedes y Coscon blamed Gaspard de Vallier, the Governor of Tripoli whom he arrested, defrocked and jailed. De Vallier was later rehabilitated by Jean de la Valette.

Homedes inherited the headquarters at Birgu, rather than Mdina, but felt it was vulnerable to attack and even after the completion of Castle St. Angelo, with developments in artillery, he felt that it was necessary to have another fort and started work on Fort St. Elmo. He had to face the Turks when, under Dragut, they attacked Malta in 1551 and lay siege to Mdina. Prior to this he had hired the Spanish military architect **Pietro Pardo** to study the defences of Mdina, and hence the city was able to withstand an attack, although would be helpless during a sustained siege.

Some of the French knights did not like Homedes and Giacomo Bosio relates some of the stories about him having been elected by intrigue, and then using his time as Grand Master to enrich himself and his family. Juan de Homedes y Coscon appears as a major character in Dorothy Dunnett's novel, *The Disorderly Knights* (1966). It portrays the Grand Master as being rather haughty but also miserly and cruel, and particularly biased towards the Spanish knights of the Order. He refuses to send any knights to help protect Mdina when it was under attack in 1551, but eventually consents to allow **Nicolas de Villegainon** to take with him six knights to help the beleaguered city.

Grand Master Homedes allowed four hundred Knights to go to North Africa as Emperor Charles V was keen to attack at Algiers. Seventy-five knights were killed or died from injuries or disease. This was very costly for the Order with Malta facing imminent attack. An attack on Zoara, west of Tripoli, in 1552 was more successful with the Knights taking the town but while they were plundering it, the Ottoman Turkish force counterattacked and killed 89 knights, another costly loss. Homedes died on 6 September 1553.

References: Dorothy Dunnett, *The Lymond Chronicles 3: The Disorderly Knights*, London: Cassell & Company, 1966, reprinted London: Penguin Books, 1999; Victor Mallia-Milanes & Louis J. Scerri, *An Uneasy Partnership: Malta 1530–1565*, Mdina: Midsea Books, 1985; Victor Mallia-Milanes, *Venice and Hospitaller Malta 1530–1798: aspects of a relationship*, Marsa: Publishers Enterprises Group, 1992; H.J.A. Sire, *The Knights of Malta*, New Haven: Yale University Press, 1994, pp. 63–68.

HOUSE OF NOTARY BEZZINA. When the French entered Mdina in 1798, they used this house, opposite the **Banca Giuratale** on **Triq Villegaignon** as their headquarters with **Pietro Antonio Bezzina** being a supporter of the French. When the Maltese rose up against the French on 2 September 1798, the crowds in the street surged into the house with General **Claude-Henri Vaubois** describing that 'we had to combat enraged lions'. The mob captured Citizen Colonel Masson and threw him to his death from the balcony of the house.

HOWARD GARDENS. This is located in the Main Bastion in Mdina and forms a natural barrier between Mdina and **Rabat**. The gardens were opened in 1924 and named after Joseph Howard who was the first Prime Minister of Malta, holding office from 1921 ti 1923. Located in the gardens is an old cross which is said to have been a gift from Count Roger from Normandy (Count of Sicily from 1071 to 1101), to celebrate the victory of Christianity over Islam in 1090. Elsewhere in the gardens are an orange garden, and a memorial to **World War II**.

References: Warren G. Berg, *Historical Dictionary of Malta*, Lanham, Md.: The Scarecrow Press, 1995, p. 65; Ivan Martin, 'Facelift at Mdina's Howard Garden must go', *Times of Malta* (14 March 2014).

– I –

INGUANEZ. *See also* **D'Esguanez**.

INGUANEZ STREET. *See* **Inguanez, Triq**.

INGUANEZ, TRIQ (Inguanez Street). This street, formerly called Long Street, runs across the southern part of Mdina from **Corte Capitanale** and the **Magisterial Palace**, through **Pjazza San Publiju** (St. Publius Square) to **Greek's Gate** Square.

INGUANEZ, ANTONIO. He was the **Capitano della Verga** of Mdina, 1548–50.

INGUANEZ, ANTONIO. The **Capitano della Verga** of Mdina, 1598–99, he was the Baron of Buqana and Djar il-Bniet.

INGUANEZ, ANTONIO GOFFREDO. From the famous Inguanez family, he was the **Capitano della Verga** of Mdina, 1538–40.

INGUANEZ, MARCANTONIO. The **Capitano della Verga** of Mdina, 1705–09, 1713–15, and 1721`–30, and 1740–61, he was the Baron of Buqana and Djar il-Bniet.

IS-SUR, TRIQ (Bastion(s) Street). This street runs along the north of the city from the Bastions Esplanade to what is now the **Cathedral Museum**. In medieval and early modern times it was one of the safest parts of the city and easily manned to prevent attack, with the south the most vulnerable point in any attack on Mdina. There is an interesting stone bridge connecting the first floor of one building with St. Dorothy's Convent. This was constructed in the twentieth century. **Palazzo de Piro** is located at 3 Triq Is-Sur. On 25 July and 31 July 1969, a 2–3 bedroom house in the street was advertised in *The Times* newspaper in London for sale for £19,000. In November 1970 Nigel Dennis lived at 7 The Bastions, with Georgina O'Connell, widow of Dr O' Connell, living there in November 1973 when her only son John Philip, was married to Madeleine, the eldest daughter of the Most Noble Baron and Baroness de Piro d'Amico Inguanez.

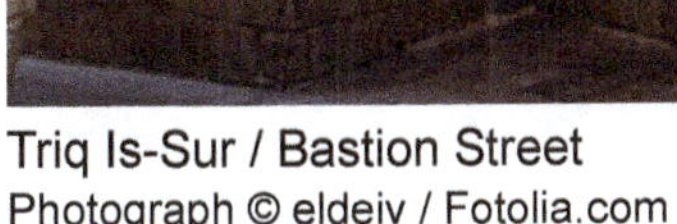

Triq Is-Sur / Bastion Street
Photograph © eldeiv / Fotolia.com

Triq Is-Sur / Bastion Street
Photograph © mariontxa / Fotolia.com

References: Richard England and Conrad Thake, *Mdina: Citadel of Memory*, Malta: Atlantis, 1995, pp. 76–79.

– J –

JACOBUS. By tradition, he was the bishop of Malta from 27 May 1259, taking over from Bishop **Domenico** at the **Cathedral Church** in Mdina, and was, in turn, succeeded by Bishop **Marinus**.

JACOBUS of MALTA 'JAMES' (c.1230–1298/9). The bishop of Malta from 1274 until 1297, he was the first bishop to be born in Malta. As a young man he joined the Franciscans and probably served in Sicily. He was presented to Pope Gregory X by the Malta **Cathedral** Chapter to become the next bishop of Malta and this was approved in 1274 by the Angevin King Manfred of Sicily (1258–1266). However eight years later Malta passed to the Kings of Aragon with James II taking over Sicily. In 1297 King Frederick II of Sicily (r. 1296–1337) exiled Bishop Jacobus from Malta and in the following year he was an administrator of a diocese in southern Italy. He died before 8 May 1299.

References: Michael J. Schiavone, *Dictionary of Maltese Biographies*, Malta: pubblikazzjonijiet Indipendenza, 2009, vol 2, p. 1022.

JAIME. He was the bishop of Malta from 21 December 1445, succeeding **Senatore di Noto**, and was, in turn, succeeded by **Antonio de Alagona**.

JEWISH COMMUNITY. There was a large Jewish community in medieval Malta and a synagogue built during the fourteenth century was located in St. Saviour Street, opposite the **Carmelite Church**. It has been estimated that up to a third of the population of the city might have been Jewish. In 1492 King Ferdinand of Aragon and Queen Isabella of Castile ordered the expulsion of all Jews from their lands which included Malta. Some Jewish people later returned and **Samuel Taylor Coleridge** wrote a report on an attack in 1805 on somebody whom he believed was Jewish.

References: Warren G. Berg, *Historical Dictionary of Malta*, Lanham, Md.: The Scarecrow Press, 1995, p. 70; Richard England and Conrad Thake, *Mdina: Citadel of Memory*, Malta: Atlantis, 1995, p. 10; 'Malta', Encyclopedia Judaica vol 11, p. 831; John Manduca, *Tourist Guide to City of Mdina*, Malta: Progress Press, 1975, p. 29; Godfrey Wettinger, *The Jews of Malta in the late Middle Ages*, Valletta: Midsea Books, 1985, reviewed by Joseph Cassar-Pullicino, *Melita Historica* vol 9, no 2 (1985), pp. 186–89.

JOCOBUS (GIACOMO). He was the bishop of Malta from 7 June 1346 until around 1356, and was succeeded by Bishop **Mario Corrado**.

JOHANNES I (GIOVANNI I). He was the bishop of Malta from 1167 to 1169, being based at the **Cathedral Church** in Mdina. Regarded as wise, he was consulted by kings of Sicily. The first of the list of bishops of Malta cited by early modern historians for whom there is external evidence he existed, although he may have been the major Christian figure in Malta, it seems unlikely that he was actually a bishop.

References: Ugo Falcando, Graham A. Loud & Thomas Wiedemann, *A History of the Tyrants of Sicily by Hugo Falcandus 1153–69*, Manchester: Manchester University Press, 1998, p. 173; Jeremy Johns, *Arabic Administration in Norman Sicily: The Royal Diwan*, Cambridge: Cambridge University Press, 2002, p. 93.

JOHANNES II (GIOVANNI II). By tradition, he was the bishop of Malta from 1211–24, he was at the **Cathedral Church** in Mdina at a time when the Normans were consolidating their rule in Malta and had introduced Latin as the language of government.

JOHN (JOHANNES) NORMANDUS. By tradition, he was the Bishop of Malta from 1268, he took over from Bishop **Marinus** and was only in office at the **Cathedral Church** in Mdina for about two years.

JULIANUS (GIULIANO). The bishop of Malta from around 533 or 553, he was at the old Christian Cathedral (on the site of the **Cathedral Church**) in Mdina when the Byzantine general Belisarius captured Malta.

– K –

'KNIGHTS OF MALTA'. This is the name of the museum located in **Casa Magazzini** (*qv*).

KOSTANTINU. The bishop of Malta from 501, he was at the old Christian Cathedral (on the site of the **Cathedral Church**) in Mdina during the latter period when the Vandals controlled Malta.

Mdina.
Painting by Robin Corfield.

– L –

LABINI, VINCENZO, of BITONTO (1735–1807). A member of the Sovereign Military Hospitaller Order of St. John of Jerusalem (S.M.H.O.), he was born on 28 April 1735 at Bituntin, joined the S.M.H.O. and was ordained priest on 23 September 1758. He appointed the bishop of Malta from 19 June 1780, and ordained on 25 June. Remaining in office until his death on 30 April 1807, he was the first titular bishop of Rhodes from 3 March 1797. Labini was bishop during the French Occupation and then the initial establishment of British rule.

References: Michael Galea, *The life and times of Vincenzo Labini, Bishop of Malta,* Malta: np, 1980.

LEAR, EDWARD (1812–1888). An English writer and illustrator, famous for his eccentric poetry, he was born on 12 May 1812 near London, the twentieth of the twenty-one children of Jeremiah Lear and his wife Ann Clark (née Skerrett). Ill as a young boy, he was largely educated at home and started work as an ornithological draftsman. From 1837 to 1848 he spent most of his time living in Rome, after which he travelled to Greece via Malta. He returned to Malta on his way back to Italy, and went to Malta for a third time in 1866. In spite of three visits, he was unimpressed with the island but did paint *A distant view of Mdina.* This watercolour over pencil, previously owned by Franklin

Lushington, was sold by the Fine Art Society, London, in 1947 and then re-sold at auction by Sotheby's on 6 June 2007 for £10,800 (estimate £5,000–7,000). In the 1870s he moved to live at Sanremo, in northern Italy, and died on 29 January 1888.

References: Susan Chitty, *That Singular Person Called Lear*, London: Weidenfeld & Nicolson, 1988; Emanuel Fiorentino, 'Edward Lear in Malta', *History Week* (1984), pp. 33–40; Peter Levi, *Edward Lear: a biography*, London: Macmillan, 1995; Vivien Noakes, *Edward Lear*, London: Fontana/Collins, 1979.

LEPIDOPTERY. British butterfly hunters were prominent throughout Europe late in the nineteenth century and early twentieth century. Some of their collections and also later accumulations are exhibited at the National Museum of Natural History (formerly the **Magisterial Palace**) in Mdina. One of the most prominent lepidopterists in Malta is Paul Michael Sammut (1945-   ), who has published much on the subject. In June 2002 the Maltese postal authorities issued a series of 16 stamps each with a different butterfly or moth found in Malta.

References: P.M. Sammut, 'A systematic and synonymic list of the Lepidoptera of the Maltese Islands', *Neve Entomologische Nachrichten* vol 13 (1984), pp. 1–124; A. Valletta, 'A century of butterfly hunting in Malta', *The Link* No 10 (1953), pp. 4–7, reviewed by Joseph Cassar-Pullichino, in *Melita Historica* vol 1, no 3 (1954), pp. 186–87.

DE L'ISLE-ADAM, PHILIPPE VILLIERS (1464–1534). The Grand Master of the Knights Hospitaller (Knights of Malta) from 1521 until his death in 1534, he was born in 1464 and was from an important French noble family. This was the same family as Jean de Villiers, the Grand Master from 1284 to 1291, who was in office at the time of the fall of Acre, and was the uncle of

Philippe de L'Isle Adam
Drawing by Gordon Home

Anne de Montmorency, the Constable of France under King Francis I and Henry II. In 1510 De L'Isle-Adam had fought at the battle of Laiazzo, and had become the Prior of the Langue of Auvergne, being elected the 44th Grand Master of the Order of St. John of Jerusalem in 1521. When his predecessor, Fabrizio del Carretto died, it was thought that the Portuguese knight and the Chancellor of the Order, Amdré do Amaral, would succeed but instead De L'Isle-Adam was elected instead, in spite of the fact he was not present at the election. He did arrive soon afterwards and his main task was to prepare Rhodes which was under imminent threat.

De L'Isle-Adam was in command of the Order during the siege of Rhodes in 1522 when Sultan Suleiman the Magnificent led his troops in an attack on the island; and also when 600 knights and 4,500 soldiers held off Turkish forces of 100,000 for half a year. Eventually Grand Master Philippe Villiers de l'Isle-Adam was forced to negotiate and eventually agreed to leave with the surviving knights. On 1 January 1523, L'Isle-Adam led the knights to the harbour and left for Crete. It was a decision he regretted for the rest of his life, and he tried hard to persuade the Venetians to help retake Rhodes from the Turks. After a short period at Kandi in Crete, the Knights moved to Messina, Sicily; then to Viterbo in Central Italy. There they received the offer of the island of Malta, and the majority of the Chapter General of the Knights Hospitaller voted to accept this. However with the plague threatening, they moved to Nice, France and were there from 1527 to March 1530 when the Emperor Charles V formally ceded the islands of Malta and Gozo to the Order. However he did not grant them the right to mint their own money.

Philippe Villiers de l'Isle-Adam moved to Malta and on the morning of 13 November 1530, and decided to make his formal entry into Mdina.

It was a Sunday and the Grand Master and his knights left Birgu in the early morning and on their way to Mdina were met by about 500 armed Maltese riding their donkeys. Along the route, nobles and clergy joined the group and proceeded to the Augustinian Priory at **Rabat**. There the Grand Master changed his robes and walked to the Great Gate of Mdina – located to the east of the current **Main Gate**. There he was met by the governor of the city and the nobles and in front of them publically swore to maintain the rights and the ancient privileges of the nobles and all the Maltese people, including the promise made in 1427 by Alonso V of Aragon 'the Magnanimous' in which no part of the islands could be removed from the royal demense without the consent of the people. He then established his headquarters in Mdina.

His arrival in Mdina is celebrated in a famous painting by the French eighteenth century artist Chevalier Antoine de Favray (1706–1792) – it now hangs in the Palace at Valletta, and was reproduced on a 1943 Maltese postage stamp, part of a definitive series. However with the Knights having a strong fleet, his plan was for Birgu to be the capital but this needed to be fortified. With the construction of Fort St. Angelo, the Knights then had a base. He started renewing the **city walls** at Mdina and the Spanish military engineer **Pietro Pardo** was called in to help in strengthen the defences at Mdina, done largely during the reign of one of de l'Isle-Adam successors, **Juan de Homedes**. De L'Isle-Adam died on 21 August 1534 in Mdina, still saddened by the loss of Rhodes, but his legacy was to tie the Knights Hospitaller to Malta. He was succeeded by **Piero de Ponte**. He was buried at St. John's Conventual Church (now St. John's Co-Cathedral), Valletta; and was commemorated on a Maltese postage stamp issued on 26 February 1999.

References: Michael Galea, *Grand Master Philippe Villiers de l'Isle-Adam 1521–1534*, SanGwann: Publishers Enterprises Group, 1997; Victor Mallia-Milanes & Louis J. Scerri, *An Uneasy Partnership: Malta 1530–1565*, Mdina: Midsea Books, 1985; Victor Mallia-Milanes, *Venice and Hospitaller Malta 1530–1798: aspects of a relationship*, Marsa: Publishers Enterprises Group, 1992; John Montalto, *The Nobles of Malta, 1530–1800*, Valletta: Midsea Books, 1979, p. 63; H.J.A. Sire, *The Knights of Malta*, New Haven: Yale University Press, 1994.

LUCILLU (LUCILLO). The bishop of Malta from 592 to 599, he was at the old Christian Cathedral (on the site of the **Cathedral Church**) in Mdina when Malta was controlled by the Byzantines. Although appointed by Pope Gregory I (r. 590–604), Lucillu fell foul of the Papacy and in September 598 Gregory wrote a letter to John, archbishop of Syracuse, urging that Lucillu be dismissed as he had been found guilty of misconduct.

References: Jeffrey Richards, *Consul of God: The Life and Times of Gregory the Great*, London: Routledge & Kegan Paul, 1980, pp. 155–56.

– M –

MACEDONIA, GIACINTO. He was the **Capitano della Verga** of Mdina, 1668–69, and 1675–77.

The Magisterial Palace
Photograph Anibal Trejo / Big Stock Photo

MAGISTERIAL PALACE. Located in **Pjazza San Publiju** (St. Publius Square), it was constructed in about 1730 by the Grand Master **António Manoel de Vilhena** (r. 1722–36), and has had a large number of uses over the years and is often known as the Palacio Vilhena (Vilhena Palace), the Connaught Hospital (1908–73) and Natural History Museum (or National Museum of Natural History, from 1973). It is located to the east of the **Main Gate**, and close to the location of the original gate to the city. During renovation work on the palace in 1962, some heavy Roman masonry was uncovered and this is believed to be part of the original city walls. Amongst the debris was also some Middle Bronze Age pottery.

The current palace dates from c1454 when it was built to serve as the centre of the local government of **Università**, being the headquarters of the

The entrance to the Magisterial Palace
Photograph © Robert Lerich / Fotolia.com

Capitano della Verga (Captains of the Rod) who presided over the local assembly. He was allowed a number of bodyguards to live in the palace which was then the Chiramonte Castle. Under Grand Master **Philippe Villiers de L'Isle-Adam** it was remodelled into a palace. However in the **earthquake** of 1693, the palace was badly damaged and 20 years later, António de Vilhena remodelled it and embellished it considerably. This saw the construction of a new French Parisian Baroque building designed by **Charles François De Mondion**, with the entire structure screened by a wall with its own decorated gateway adorned with his coat of arms, with lions on both sides. It makes use of the French design of Philibert de l'Orme with columns not continuous but broken at regular intervals. There is a bronze relief of Vilhena above the entrance fashioned by the local sculptor Pietro Paolo Troisi.

One of the halls within the palace is decorated with six escutcheons of the holders of the office of the Captain of the Rod, although they operated from a new palazzo in **Triq Villegaignon**. In the basement there were a number of cells in what is now the **Mdina Dungeons**.

During the cholera outbreak of 1837, patients were treated in the building. In 1860 the British army used it as a temporary sanatorium. In 1908 the building was transformed into a hospital and when King Edward

The gate to the Magisterial Palace
Photograph © eldeiv / Fotolia.com

The inner courtyard at the Magisterial Palace.
Photograph © R J Lerich / Big Stock Photo.

VII visited the island on 22 April 1909, he officially named it the Connaught Hospital after his brother the Duke of Connaught. The hospital continued to operate from the building until 1956 when it closed down. For many years the building remained unused but on 22 June 1973, refurbished, it was reopened as the National Museum of Natural History. This allowed for the display of many items which had remained in storage since being put in crates for safety during **World War II**. On 15 February 1980 the building featured on one of a series of four Maltese postage stamps commemorating the work of UNESCO in Malta.

The museum contains exhibits relating to the geology of Malta, prehistoric life and also stuffed animals. Of particular interest are the teeth of the ancient shark *Carchaodo megaladon aggasiz* which have an edge of 18 cm (7.1 inches), the overall shark having been some 25m (82 feet) long and flourishing about 30 million years ago. There is also the pickled remains of a 16 kg (35.3 lbs) squid which was found at Xemxija in St. Paul's Bay in the north-east. Other exhibits include a tusk of a pygmy elephant, the item previously owned by Giovanni Francesco Abela. There are also the teeth of a pygmy hippopotamus, and the lower jaw bone of a giant dormouse. Some of the halls are dedicated to **ornithology** and **lepidoptery**. The L. Mizzi Hall has a large display of minerals which were part of the collection of Lewis Mizzi. The George Zammit Maempel Halls explain the geology of Malta. The museum is open daily, except for public holidays. On 24 May 2013, the museum was opened in the evening by Heritage Malta to highlight the collection, as part of the European Night of Museums.

References: 'A night at the Museum', *The Times of Malta* (20 May 2013); Can John Azzopardi, *Mdina, Rabat, Mosta*, Terni, Italy: Plurigraf, 1988, p. 9–11; Carolyn Bain, *Malta & Gozo*, Footscray, Vic, Australia: Lonely Planet, 2004, p. 119; John J. Borg, *The National Museum of Natural History*, Sta Venera: Heritage Books in association with Heritage Malta, 2007; Paul Cassar, *Medical History of Malta*, London: Wellcome Historical Medical Library, 1964, pp. 221–23; Richard England and Conrad Thake, *Mdina: Citadel of Memory*, Malta: Atlantis, 1995, pp. 36–39; John Manduca, *Tourist Guide to City of Mdina*, Malta: Progress Press, 1975, pp. 15–17; Edward Sammut, *The Monuments of Mdina*, Malta: Progress Press Co. Ltd, 1967, pp. 14–16; D H Trump, *Malta: An Archaeological Guide*, London: Faber & Faber Ltd, 1972, pp. 41–52 & 104; Neil Wilson, *Malta*, Melbourne: Lonely Planet Publications, 2000, p. 130; George Zammit-Maempel, *An Outline of Maltese Geology & Guide to the Geology Hall of the National Museum of Natural History, Mdina, Malta*, Valletta: Progress Press, 1977.

MAIN GATE. Sometimes also called the Mdina Gate, this is the main entrance to the city of Mdina, and is one of the best-known sites for tourists many of whom enter the city through the gate. It is located in the south-east of the city. The earlier gate, fashioned by the Arabs, was slightly to the east of the current gate, with access across a drawbridge over a moat. That gate was decorated with the arms of the Inguanez family being installed by order of King Alfonso V of Aragon (r. 1416–58) to commemorate Antonio Inguanez who put down a rebellion in 1428. It was through this gate that **Philippe Villiers de L'Isle-Adam** entered the city promising to maintain and uphold the rights and privileges of the nobility before they were handed the keys of the city. It was also through this gate that the Christian cavalry sallied forth during the **Great Siege** of Malta in 1565, attacking the Turks on several occasions.

The Main Gate at night.
Photograph © esinel_888 / Fotolia.com

In 1724, the current gate was installed by the Grand Master **António Manoel de Vilhena** whose arms are located above the gate. It was designed by **Charles François de Mondion**, with the stone carvings by Gerolamo Fabri and his sons. To reach it there is a relatively narrow stone bridge which has at the entrance of the bridge, two lions which are the escutcheon (supporters) in Vilhena's coat of arms. The arms of the Inguanez family were moved to the new gate, and above the gate, on the inside, there is a bas relief made from stone which includes images of **St. Paul**, **St. Publius** and St. Agatha, the patron saints of the island and the protectors of the city. There is also the coat of arms of Mdina.

When the French arrived in the city in 1798, they removed the arms of the Inguanez family and replaced it with a 'statue of liberty' to commemorate the

The Main Gate
Photograph © McCarthys_PhotoWorks / Fotolia.com

French Revolution. The Inguanez family arms was later restored. However in 1886 the Inguanez family arms were replaced by the British Governor, General Sir Lintorn Simmons. The Roman headless marble statue which used to be located in the wall of the entrance is now at the Museum of Roman Antiquities in **Rabat**. The main gate has appeared on a large number of postcards and in 1956 appeared on the one shilling postage stamp issued as part of a definitive set.

References: Can John Azzopardi, *Mdina, Rabat, Mosta*, Terni, Italy: Plurigraf, 1988, p. 8; Dominic Cutajar, *Malta: A Presentation in Colour*, Valletta: MJ Publications, 1986, p. 26; Richard England and Conrad Thake, *Mdina: Citadel of Memory*, Malta: Atlantis, 1995, pp. 32–33; John Manduca, *Tourist Guide to City of Mdina*, Malta: Progress Press, 1975, p. 14; Edward Sammut, *The Monuments of Mdina*, Malta: Progress Press Co. Ltd, 1967, pp. 11–12.

MAITLAND, THOMAS (1760–1824). The British Governor from 1813 to 1824, he was born on 10 March 1760 probably at the family residence near Edinburgh, the son of James Maitland, the 7th Earl of Lauderdale. He was commissioned into the Edinburgh Light Horse soon after he was born, but only took up the commission in 1778. He later transferred to the 72nd Foot

and then the 62nd Foot, being promoted to Major and gazetted Lieutenant Colonel in 1794, then promoted to full Colonel and eventually Brigadier-General. The Governor of Ceylon (now Sri Lanka) from 1805 to 1811, he was then posted to Malta where he gained the nickname as 'King Tom'. He was also High Commissioner of the Ionian Islands from 1815–23. There was going to be an advisory council in Malta but Maitland when he was appointed governor said he would not accept this. He enjoyed his time in Malta and did visit Mdina on occasions. However he started to drink heavily and died on 17 January 1824 at Floriana, being buried four days later at Valletta. His long funeral procession was painted by Giuseppe Preca.

References: H. M. Chichester, 'Maitland, Sir Thomas (1760–1824)', revised by Roger T. Stearn, *Oxford Dictionary of National Biography*, Oxford University Press, 2004; Cyril Willis Dixon, *The Colonial Administrations of Sir Thomas Maitland*, London: Longmans, Green and Company, 1939; Tom Hedley, *Duello: The Story of How Silvio Silvestri swayed the outcome of the power game over the future of Malta before the Congress of Europe danced in Vienna in 1814*, Valletta: Progress Press, 1977; Walter Frewen Lord, *Sir Thomas Maitland: the Mastery of the Mediterranean*, London: T. Fisher Unwin, 1897; Nicholas de Piro, *The International Dictionary of Artists who Painted Malta*, Valletta: Audio Visual Centre Limited, 2003, p. 374–75.

MAMO, FRANCESCO. The **Capitano della Verga** of Mdina, 1627–29, he was the son of Nicolo Mamo, and was named after his grandfather, Francesco.

MANDUCA, ANTONIO. The **Capitano della Verga** of Mdina, 1533–34, 1536–38, and 1542–45, he was later brought before the local tribunal on charges relating to heresy but managed to escape Malta.

References: John Montalto, *The Nobles of Malta, 1530–1800*, Valletta: Midsea Books, 1979, p. 192.

MANDUCA, JOHN A. (1927–). An author, he was born on 14 August 1927 in Mdina, son of Philip dei Conti Manduca and Emma (née Pullicino) and educated at St. Edward's College at Birgu. In 1945 he joined

Allied Newspapers Limited and then worked as the parliamentary and then deputy editor of *The Times of Malta* from 1953. He was also the Malta correspondent of the British newspapers, *The Daily Telegraph* and *The Sunday Telegraph* from 1946 to 1962. In 1962 he joined the Broadcasting Authority and in the following year joined Malta Television Service Ltd, being the director and manager from 1968–71. From 1971 until his retirement in 1976, he was the Managing Director of the Rediffusion Group of Companies, and also a member of the board of governors of St. Edward's College from 1966 to 1975, and then again from 1991 to 1998, being Chairman for the last three years. From 1987 to 1990 he was Malta's High Commissioner to London, and also Ambassador to Norway, Sweden and Denmark, and then Ambassador to Ireland. A keen author, in 1967 he wrote a best-selling *Tourist Guide to Malta and Gozo*, which went through seven editions. In 1975 he was the author of the *Tourist Guide to City of Mdina*. Living at Beaulieu, Pjazza tas-Sur (Bastion Square), Mdina, he was also the editor of *Mdina: the old city in Malta* (1991). In November 2003 he received the Gold Award for his service to Malta.

References: *Malta's Who's Who 1987*, p. 115; John Manduca, *Tourist Guide to City of Mdina*, Malta: Progress Press, 1975; John Manduca, *Mdina: the old city in Malta*, Valletta: Midsea Publications Ltd, 1991, a supplement of Heritage; Michael J. Schiavone, *Dictionary of Maltese Biographies*, Malta: pubblikazzjonijiet Indipendenza, 2009, vol 2, pp. 1092–93.

MANDUCA, SALVATORE. The **Capitano della Verga** of Mdina, 1761–64, he styled himself as Count Manduca although this was never a registered title until he was formally appointed by Grand Master Ferdinand von Hompesch. He opposed the French invasion, and was one of the two people elected to lead the people in the fighting against the French.

References: John Montalto, *The Nobles of Malta, 1530–1800*, Valletta: Midsea Books, 1979, p. 45, 122, 355.

MARINUS (MARINO) di SORRENTO. By tradition, he was the bishop of Malta in 1267, he was only in office at the **Cathedral Church** in Mdina for a year. After he died, by tradition, **Johannes Normandus** took over as bishop.

MARIO CORRADO. A Dominican, he was the bishop of Malta from 1356, taking over from Bishop **Jocobus**, and being succeeded, in turn, by Bishop **Antonio** in 1370.

References: Anthony Luttrell, 'The Benedictines and Malta 1363–1371', *Papers of the British School at Rome* vol 50 (1982), pp. 146–65.

MATTEI, FERDINANDO (1761–1829). The bishop of Malta from 1807 until his death, he was born on 24 July 1761 at Senglea. In 1793 he was appointed canon coadjutor to the dean of the **Cathedral** Chapter in Mdina, then promoted to dean in 1804. During the **French Occupation** of Valletta in 1799, he managed to escape the city, and in 1805 was appointed titular Bishop of Paphos in Cyprus. After the death of **Vincenzo Labini**, the bishop of Malta, the British government claimed the right to choose his successor but the Holy See argued that the nomination had to be made by the King of Sicily, and then presented to the Holy See. This took place with Mattei nominated on 18 September 1807 by King Ferdinand IV of Sicily, and this was agreed to by the Holy See. Mattei's period as Bishop was one of consolidation for the Roman Catholic Church in Malta after the upheavals which had taken place with the arrival and departure of the French, and the start of British rule. He died on 14 July 1829. His major legacy is the raising of the status of St. John's in Valletta to become St. John's Co-Cathedral. Although the seat of the bishop remained in Mdina, from Bishop Mattei to the present day St. John's Co-Cathedral was an alternative see.

References: Warren G. Berg, *Historical Dictionary of Malta*, Lanham, Md.: The Scarecrow Press, 1995, pp. 77–78; Michael J. Schiavone, *Dictionary of Maltese Biographies*, Malta: pubblikazzjonijiet Indipendenza, 2009, vol 2, pp. 1109–10.

DI MAZARA, GIOVANNI. The **Capitano della Verga** of Mdina, 1517–18, 1520–21, and 1524–25, he was probably the Giovanni Mazara who was the son of Cataldo Mazara and Comizia (née Celetri).

DI MAZARA, (PIETRO) GIOVANNI. The **Capitano della Verga** of Mdina, 1458–60, 1467–68, 1471–73, 1474–75, and from 1476–77, he was the 10th Baron di Ghajn Rihani and Delimara, succeeding to the title from his nephew Peri Giovanni Mazzara.

References: John Montalto, *The Nobles of Malta, 1530–1800*, Valletta: Midsea Books, 1979, p. 168.

DI MAZARA, SIMONE. The **Capitano della Verga** of Mdina, 1473–74, from 1477, and again 1486–87, he was the son of **Giovanni Mazzara**, the 8th Baron of Ghajn Rihani and Delimara, and his wife Elena Mirabella. The great-grandson of Giacomo Mazzara, he was named after his grandfather Simone, a soldier. Simone di Mazara married Donna Margharita de Nava and they had two children.

A cobbled street in Mdina.
Photograph © lupideloop / Fotolia.com

MDINA DEFENCE SYNDROME. This was a medical condition in which a sufferer ends up helpless and lost. It derives its name from Mdina because of the narrow streets of the city which have seemingly indistinguishable features. In spite of its small size, tourists regularly become lost in Mdina, and this is supposed to be similar to the medical condition.

References: Saviour Chircop, 'As We Sit Together, Should We Use the Phone? A Research Agenda for the Study of Media in Malta', in Ronald G Sultana & Godfrey Baldacchino (eds), *Maltese Society: A Sociological Inquiry*, Msida: Mireva Publications, 1994, p. 360.

MDINA DITCH. This is the ditch which is on the outside of the city walls from **Greek's Gate**, past the **Main Gate**, to the **Xara Palace**. Originally constructed to help protect the city from attack, it was later used for locating

Mdina Ditch Gardens
Photograph willmac / Big Stock Photo

a **football** ground and a tennis court. However with archaeologists locating the remains of a medieval tower, and plans to protect the Vilhena bastion, the European Union offered to fund 85% of the €6.2m project to turn Mdina Ditch into a recreational space covered in turf, and with many trees and fountains. This project was unveiled by George Pullicino, the prime minister and resources minister when he visited Mdina Ditch on 12 January 2011.

References: 'Mdina Ditch to become recreation area', *The Times of Malta* (12 January 2011).

MDINA DUNGEONS. These are located just inside the **Main Gate** to Mdina, and are under the **Corte Capitanale**, adjoining the **Magisterial Palace**. Prisoners were ordered to be detained there by the **Captani della Verga** (Captains of the Rod) and other civic officials. Count Cabrera of Modica in Sicily was imprisoned there after he fled from Gozo. The most famous person held in them was Mikiel Anton Vassali (1764–1829). A linguist and the compiler of a Maltese-Italian dictionary, he was also a political agitator conspiring with, amongst others, the Jacobites in the hope that they might wrest the islands from the control of the Knights of Malta.

The dungeons are now open to the public and there are a number of displays showing various methods of torture and execution, accompanied by a soundtrack of screams, groaning and gasping. Some of the events 'celebrated' in the museum include the torture and killing of Teodorius, the nephew of the Byzantine Emperor Heraclius. He was exiled to Malta where he was killed. There is also an exhibit showing the Arabs executing people by burying them under large stones. Torture was formally abolished by the British in 1813. The museum which is credited as 'Malta's only dark walk attraction' and is open from 10 am to 4.30 pm every day.

References: Anne Agius Ferrante, *No Strangers in the Silent City*, Valletta: Andrew Rupert Publishing, 1992, p. 51; Carolyn Bain, *Malta & Gozo*, Footscray, Vic, Australia: Lonely Planet, 2004, p. 119; Mdina Dungeons, www.dungeonsmalta.com.

MDINA EXPERIENCE. Located at 7 Mesquita Square, this is the name given to a 25-minute audio-visual show in a building on Misrah Mesquita. It shows the history of the city from ancient times through the Roman period, and the rule of the Arabs, Normans, Spaniards and the Knights. It starts every half hour from 10.30 am to 4 pm on weekdays, and from 10.30 am to 2 pm on Saturdays.

References: Carolyn Bain, *Malta & Gozo*, Footscray, Vic, Australia: Lonely Planet, 2004, p. 119.

Mdina glass
Photograph by Robin Corfield

A variety of products produced by Mdina glass with some keys commemorating the opening of the Sheraton Hotel in Malta, 1967.

MDINA GLASSWORKS. Located off **Pjazza San Publiju** (St. Publius Square), just inside the **Main Gate** of Mdina, this famous glassworks has produced elegant glassworks since 1968 including paperweights, bottles and a range of other products. They are all individually made and visitors are allowed to watch them being hand-blown and crafted in a variety of colours. They have been exported to Italy from 1971, and in 1975 when Joseph Said – a glassmaker since 1968 – became the production manager, production increased but without compromising quality. There were significant exports to Germany from 1976 and to Japan from 1983. They have long been collected by connoisseurs around the world. In 1996 former US President Jimmy Carter and his wife visited Mdina Glass.

References: Mark Hill, Michael Harris and Graham Rae, Michael Harris: *Mdina glass & Isle of Wight studio glass*, London: Mark Hill Publ., 2006; Ruth Jordan, 'Mediterranean colours in Maltese Glass', *The Daily Telegraph* (9 July 1969), p. 15; Mdina Glasss, www.mdinaglass.com.mt.

MDINA KNIGHTS FOOTBALL CLUB. *See* **Football**.

MDINA REHABILITATION PROJECT. Established under the Ministry for Resources and Infrastructure, this project has the aim of improving Mdina and preserving its history. In July 2002 it presented an application for the paving of all streets in Mdina with hard stone from Sicily. Some seven weeks later, it was controversially involved in replacing information signs which had been removed after they had been installed during the evening of 19 July 2002 during the celebration of the feast of **Our Lady of Mount Carmel**.

Charging a cannon during the Medieval Mdina Festival, 19 April 2009.
Photograph willmac / Big Stock Photo.

MEDIEVAL MDINA FESTIVAL. This is a festival which has taken place each year in April or May since 2008, although there was an earlier festival on 14–15 April 2004. It celebrates medieval life with people dressed in medieval and early renaissance costume marching through the city. The sbandieratori (flag throwers) lead the procession, and there are displays of jousting, and falconry, as well as a human chess game, and art exhibitions. During the festival held in 2012, the two re-enactment groups, Anakron and Show of

Knight sword-fight during the Medieval Mdina Festival, 10 April 2010. Photograph willmac / Big Stock Photo.

A blacksmith during the Medieval Mdina Festival, 13 April 2013. Photograph willmac / Big Stock Photo.

Arms so impressed the film director Ray Mizzi that he decided to shoot his next film in Mdina (see **popular culture**). The festivals have taken place on 18–19 April 2009, 9–11 April 2010, 7–8 May 2011, 14–15 April 2012, 6–7 April 2013 and 3–4 May 2014. The next one is scheduled for 6–7 April 2015.

MEDINA. Located at 7 Triq is-Salib Imqaddes, this restaurant is located in a medieval townhouse and is regarded as one of the most romantic venues in Mdina. In a garden-courtyard, alfresco dining is popular, with dining in the building which is warmed by open fireplaces.

References: Carolyn Bain, *Malta & Gozo*, Footscray, Vic, Australia: Lonely Planet, 2004, p. 121.

MERCIECA, JOSEPH (1928–). The archbishop of Malta from 1976 to 2007, he was born on 11 November 1928 at Gozo and went to the Gozo Seminary and then proceeded to the Pontifical Gregorian University. He was ordained priest on 8 March 1952, then returned to Gozo where he taught theology and canon law at his old seminary, 1959–69 and then became a judge at the Sacred Roman Rota in 1969. In 1974 he was appointed Auxiliary Bishop and also the titular Bishop of Gemelle in Numidia, North Africa. This appointment surprised Archbishop **Mikiel Gonzi** who had not heard of him at that time, however they developed a good working relationship. Raised to vicar general, he was nominated as metropolitan archbishop of Malta on 12 December 1976 and enthroned the same day. He hosted visits to Malta from Pope John Paul II on 25–27 May 1990, and 8–9 May 2001, as well as a stopover in Luqa. On 11 November 2003, on reaching the age of 75, Bishop Joseph Mercieca tendered his resignation and this was accepted in January 2007.

References: Warren G. Berg, *Historical Dictionary of Malta*, Lanham, Md.: The Scarecrow Press, 1995, pp. 85–86; Charles Buttiġieġ, *Ilkoll Aħwa Fi Kristu – Memorji*, Klabb Kotba Maltin, 2014; 'Mintoff tells Pope to remove archbishop', *The Daily Telegraph* (10 August 1982); Michael J. Schiavone, *Dictionary of Maltese Biographies*, Malta: pubblikazzjonijiet Indipendenza, 2009, vol 2, pp. 1121–22 (which lists his day of birth as 12 November).

MESQUITA SQUARE. This square is located off Triq Mesquita, and in medieval and early modern times, the local militia would train there. It was also the location of the market held in Mdina from medieval times until the late nineteenth or early twentieth century.

References: Richard England and Conrad Thake, *Mdina: Citadel of Memory*, Malta: Atlantis, 1995, pp. 50–51.

MICALLEF, GIO' BATTA. He was the **Capitano della Verga** of Mdina, 1653–54, and 1656–58.

MISRAĦ IL-KUNSILL ĊITTÀ NOTABILE (Notabile City Council Square). This square in Mdina is located in the south-eastern corner of the city.

MNARJA (or **IMNARJA**) **RACES**. This annual event takes place in Mdina and **Rabat** each year on 29 June, on the feast of St. Peter and St. Paul, although some trace it back to the pagan Roman feast of Luminaria ('the illumination'). Initially the event was celebrated near St. Paul's Grotto, but since 1613 has been held at the **Cathedral Church** in Mdina. It involved a race which saw competitions involving horses, men, boys and slaves in different races with the winner the first to reach the square in front of Mdina called Saqqaja. An oil on canvas painting by Antoine de Favray (1706–1798) captures the scene in the eighteenth century.

References: Sir Harry Luke, *Malta: an account and an appreciation*, London: Corgi, 1968, p. 30; John Montalto, *The Nobles of Malta, 1530–1800*, Valletta: Midsea Books, 1979, p. 74; Nicholas de Piro, *The International Dictionary of Artists who Painted Malta*, Valletta: Audio Visual Centre Limited, 2003, p. 176–78.

DE MOLINA Y ARAGONÉS, MIGUEL JERÓNIMO (1638–1698). Born in October 1638 at Castel d'Emposta, he was ordained a priest of the Sovereign Military Hospitaller Order of St. John of Jerusalem, 5 March 1662. He was appointed bishop of Malta on 16 April 1678, ordained on 24 April, and remained in office until 25 May 1682 when he was nominated as bishop of Llerida, a position he held until his death on 31 August 1698.

MOMPALAO, ALESSANDRO. The **Capitano della Verga** of Mdina, 1677–78, he was the son of Dr Pietro Mompalao and his wife Claudia (née Castelletti). He married Margarita Busuttil, and after her death, in 1690 married Natalizia Briffa, and they had one daughter, Geronima. The great-grandson of his brother Pietro, was also called Alessandro Mompalao, and this Alessandro Mompalao was created Baron di Frigenuini in 1737.

References: John Montalto, *The Nobles of Malta, 1530–1800*, Valletta: Midsea Books, 1979, p. 38.

MOMPALAO, CALCERANO. The **Capitano della Verga** of Mdina, 1700–02, he was the son of **Pietro Mompalao** and his wife Caterina de Lorenzo. In 1682 he married Agata Balzano, and their son **Pietro** became an Hereditary Knight of the Holy Roman Empire through a title he inherited from his mother. It was Pietro's fourth son Alessandro Mompalao who was created the Baron di Frigenuini in 1737. Calcerano Mompalao's second wife was Anna Perdicomati Bologna, and they had a daughter, Antonio, and a son Gio Batta.

References: John Montalto, *The Nobles of Malta, 1530–1800*, Valletta: Midsea Books, 1979, p. 171.

MOMPALAO, PIETRO. The **Capitano della Verga** of Mdina, 1673–75, and 1682–84, he was the son of Dr Pietro Mompalao and his wife Claudia (née Castelletti). The younger brother of Alessandro Mompalao, he married Caterina de Lorenzo and they had a son, **Calcerano Mompalao**.

References: John Montalto, *The Nobles of Malta, 1530–1800*, Valletta: Midsea Books, 1979, p. 254 n77.

MOMPALAO, PIETRO. The **Capitano della Verga** of Mdina, 1717–21, he was the son of **Calcerano Mompalao** and his first wife Agata Balzano. Through his mother, he inherited the title of Hereditary Knight of the Holy Roman Empire. His fourth son was **Alessandro Mompalao** who was created the Baron di Frigenuini in 1737.

DE MONDION, CHARLES FRANÇOIS (1681–1733). A French military engineer and Baroque architect, he arrived in Malta in 1715 under Grand Master Ramon Perellos y Roccaful, and worked as a deputy to Rene Jacob de Tigne, the senior military engineer in Malta at that time. In 1722 with the elevation of **Antonio Manoel de Vilhena** to be Grand Master, de Mondion was able to work on many of de Vilhena's ambitious building projects. This saw a new 'masterplan' drawn up for the city with many changes. These included improving the walls of Mdina, the design of the City Gate (**Main Gate**), and the design of the Magisterial Palace. Elsewhere in Malta, he worked on Fort Manoel to help protect Marsamxett Harbour. He died on 25 December 1733 and was buried in the crypt of the Chapel of St. Anthony of Padova, at Fort Manoel.

References: Denis De Lucca, 'French military engineers in Malta during the 17th and 18th centuries', *Melita Historica* vol 8, no 1 (1980), pp. 23–33; Denis de Lucca, *Mdina: A History of Its Urban Space and Architecture*, Valletta: Said International, 1995, pp. 90–109; Denis De Lucca, Mondion: the achievement of a French military engineer working in Malta in the early eighteenth century, Malta: Midsea Books, 2003.

MONEY. Over the centuries, many foreign currencies have been used in Mdina, from Phoenician and Carthaginian coins, Greek and Roman coins, and later a variety of European ones. The currency in use during medieval times was the scudi with one scudo having the same value as 20 tani, which in turn had the same value as 240 grani. The Knights of Malta had wanted the right to mint their own coins but when the grant of the Maltese islands was issued by Emperor Charles V it did not mention this, much to the disappointment of Grand Master **Philippe Villiers de L'Isle-Adam**. The British then started using their currency from 1825 to 1972, with £1 having the same value as 20 shillings, or 240 pence. The Maltese lira or pound dates from 1972 (10 mils making 1 cent, and 100c making one lira – £1 or Lm1), which resulted in Malta remaining within the Sterling area, allowing British tourists to visit in large numbers in the 1970s when there were severe currency restrictions on Britons taking money overseas. There are some coins in a number of museums in Mdina, but the most extensive collection on display to the public is at the National Museum in Valletta.

References: Joseph C Sammut, 'Coinage in Malta', *Treasures of Malta* vol 12, no 2 (No 35) (Easter 2006), p. 35–41; Michael A Sant, 'The first minting of fiduciary copper coinage in Malta: 1565 or 1566?', *Melita Historica* vol 5, no 4 (1971), pp. 277–81; D H Trump, *Malta: An Archaeological Guide*, London: Faber & Faber Ltd, 1972, p. 52.

MONSON, WILLIAM JOHN (1796–1862). A British visitor and medical adviser, he was born on 14 May 1796 at Negapatam (now Nagapattinam), India, the son of Colonel William Monson, who was later a Member of the British Parliament for Lincoln, and his wife Ann (née Debonaire). He went to Malta in 1813 and his description includes much on the medical conditions on the island which was facing a plague epidemic. In 1828 he married Eliza, daughter of Edmund Larken, and they had six sons and three daughters. He became the 6th Baron Monson in 1841 after the death of his cousin, Frederick, the 5th Baron Monson. He died on 17 December 1862 at the Great Western Hotel, Paddington, London.

References: Burke's *Peerage and Baronetage*; William Monson, *Extracts from a journal,*

Maltese money in 1829.

London: Rodwell & Martin, 1820; Paul Xuereb, 'Malta in the 19th Century: A Selection of Visitors' Accounts', in *Images: Nineteenth Century Malta*, Valletta: Valletta Publishing Publication, 1989, p. 3–4.

MONTAGNES, SALVATORE 'SALVO'. The **Capitano della Verga** of Mdina, 1580–81, he was the 2nd Sinore de Recona, the grandson of Fernando Montagu from Spain, and son of Aloiseo Montagu and his wife Margherta de Bandino. In 1561 in Mdina Salvo Montagnes married Giovanna Xerri. After her death, he married Imperia Vella in 1583 in Mdina, and they had two daughters, and a son, Aloiseo, who later inherited his father's title.

References: John Montalto, *The Nobles of Malta, 1530–1800*, Valletta: Midsea Books, 1979, p. 176.

MOSCATI. *See* **Muscat**.

MTARFA CLOCK TOWER. This is located some 2 km north-west of Mdina in the township of Mtarfa. It was built in 1895 by the British – Mtarfa being the location of their military base, and it became a well-known local landmark. However in April 2006 it broke down and became an issue in the local elections over whether money should be spent to repair it. In the end it was left to local enthusiasts and the clock is now working again.

MURINA, GUGLILMO. The **Capitano della Verga** of Mdina from 1372, he was granted the fiefdom of Bucane. He was married to Elvira de Baroni de Osa and they had seven daughters: Margherita, Ursula, Caterina, Johanna, Eleanore, and Anna. He also had an illegitimate son Guglielmo Murina, a soldier who served in the forces of Aragon in the Eastern Mediterranean.

MUSCAT (or **MOSCATI**), **ANTONIO**. The **Capitano della Verga** of Mdina, 1715–17, he was the third son of Emmanele Moscati and his wife Margarita (née Sceberras). In 1711 he married Scolastica Falsone, and they had a son Ignazio, 1st Count of Bahrja; and four dauhters: Geronima, Rosales, Elizabetta, and Teresa.

MUSCAT (or **MOSCATI**), **GIO' DOMENICO**. The **Capitano della Verga** of Mdina, 1660–62, and 1669–71, he was the son of Dr Filippo Moscato and his wife Caterina Gauci whom he married in 1623. Dr Gio Domenico Muscat married Eufemia Tonna Pontremoli in 1649 and they had seven children:

Filippo, later a canon in the church; Carlo, also later a canon; Perino, later a monk; Emanuele; Tomaso, later a monk; Vincenzo; and Elena.

MUSCAT, GIUSEPPE. The **Capitano della Verga** of Mdina, 1815–18, he was in charge of the council of the city at the end of the Napoleonic Wars, and at the start of British rule, he was the last person to hold the title of **Capitano della Verga**.

References: Tom Hedley, *Duello: The Story of How Silvio Silvestri swayed the outcome of the power game over the future of Malta before the Congress of Europe danced in Vienna in 1814*, Valletta: Progress Press, 1977.

MUSCAT, JOSEPH A. (1915–1999). A medical doctor, he was born on 9 September 1915 in Mdina, and educated at St. Aloysius College and the Royal University of Malta, graduating as a doctor in June 1940. He practised for many years and specialised in sports medicine, his contribution in this field was recognised in 1989 by the award of the International Trophy of the International Olympic Committee. He died on 28 August 1999, and in 2008 he was inducted into the Hall of Fame by the Malta Olympic Committee.

References: Michael J. Schiavone, *Dictionary of Maltese Biographies*, Malta: pubblikazzjonijiet Indipendenza, 2009, vol 2, pp. 1222–23. Portrait courtesy Michael J. Schiavone.

MUSIC. There has long been a tradition of music in Malta with a number of instruments which are unique to the island. These include the flejguta (whistle flute), the zummara (reed pipe), the zaqq (bagpipes), the zafzafa (friction drum), and the tambor (tambourine).

Since the building of the **Cathedral** in Mdina in 1090 there has been a long tradition of church music with a number of prominent musicians working in the city. This included a significant number of artists and copyists who worked at Mdina Cathedral between 1527 and 1538, with the cathedral archives housing a rich collection of late medieval and early renaissance music.

The baroque traditions of music from the seventeenth and eighteenth centuries have also resulted in the cathedral archives holding much material from this era. **Francesco Azopardi** (1748–1809) was the organist at Mdina Cathedral from 1774, and in 1787 took over as maestro di cappella at the cathedral when Benignon Zerafa resigned. His contribution was commemorated on a Maltese postage stamp issued on 13 October 2004. Nicholas Isouard probably studied under Azopardi, and Pietro Paolo Bugeja certainly studied under Azopardi. The latter was appointed the next maestro di cappella when Azopardi died. **Emanuele Bartoli** who was a tenor at Mdina Cathedral from 1883 until the 1910s, was born in Mdina.

References: John Azzopardi, *Nicolo Isouard de Malte*, Mdina: Friends of the Cathedral Museum, 1991; Franco Bruni, *The Vella composers: Dr Giuseppe (1827–1912) and his sons Alberto (1861–1931), Luigi (1868–1950) and Paolo (1873–1948): biographical notes and a complete catalogue of their works at the Cathedral Museum, Mdina, Malta*, Collegeville, Minn.: Hill Monastic Manuscript Library, 1997; Franco Bruni, '17th century music prints at Mdina', *Early Music* vol 27, no 3 (August 1999), pp. 467–79; Lino Bugeja, 'Mdina Cathedral's musical tradition', *The Times of Malta* (28 April 2013); Franco Bruni, *La cappella musicale della cattedrale di Malta nei diciassettesimo e dicottesimo secolo,* Villeneuve d'Ascq: Presses universitaires du Septentrion, 2000; Franco Bruni, *Musica e musicisti alla cattedrale di Malta nei secoli XVI-XVII*, Valletta: Malta University Press, 2001; Stanley Fiorini, 'Church music and musicians in late mediaeval Malta', *Melita Historica* vol 10, No 1 (1988), pp. 1–12; Sylvia Moore, 'Malta' in Grove's *Dictionary of Music and Musicians* vol 11, pp. 589–90; Matteo Sansone, 'Italian Baroque music in Malta: a madrigal from the music archives of the Cathedral Museum in Mdina', *California Italian Studies Journal* vol 1, no 1 (2010), pp. 1–11.

Photograph by Robin Corfield, 1975.

– N –

DE NASIS, PAOLO. The **Capitano della Verga** of Mdina, 1462–66, he was the sixth child of Simone de Nasis, a member of the Università de Giurati in 1434 and again in 1456, and his wife Paola (de Falzone). He married Isabella Vella Navarra; they had no children. His older brother Pino was the father of Paolo de Nasis, the **Capitano della Verga** of Mdina, 1531–32.

DE NASIS, PAOLO. The son of Pino de Nasis and Antonella (née Caxaro), and nephew of **Paolo de Nassis**, the **Capitano della Verga** of Mdina, 1462–66, his father had been a member of the Università de Giurati in 1475, and on 13 November 1530 Paolo was the senior member of the Università de Giurati, and part of the official party who welcomed Grand Master **Philippe Villiers de L'Isle-Adam** to Mdina, formally handing him two symbolic keys to the city, after which the doors to Mdina were opened to him. He was **Capitano della Verga** of Mdina, 1531–32. Paolo married Francesco Falsone Vaccaro and they had two children, Santoro de Nasis who became a Canon in the Cathedral Church, dying in 1580; and Perio de Nasis.

References: John Montalto, *The Nobles of Malta, 1530–1800*, Valletta: Midsea Books, 1979, p. 63.

NATIONAL ARCHIVES OF MALTA. The National Archives of Malta have been located at **Rabat**, close to Mdina, since 1994. It was formally established in 1971 when a Committee on the Preservation of Public Records was formed by Guze' Cassar Pullicino. The public records held at Casa Leone were opened to the public in 1972 and moved to the Grand Master's Palace in Valletta, placed under Michael Ellul. In the late 1980s, the archives were held in three separate locations, and in January 1986 there were plans to establish a single headquarters with most papers still in Valletta. In September 1987 some of the old court records were moved to the **Banca Giuratale** in Mdina, the transfer completed in October 1988. Many other records were moved to a disused hospital building in Rabat, with most records moved there on 28

July 1989. On 28 May 1994 Ugo Mifsud Bonnici, the fifth President of Malta, presided over the opening of the National Archives building at Rabat. The Legal Documentation Section remained in Mdina in the Banca Giuratale, with a branch office located in Gozo.

References: The National Archives of Malta, https://secure2.gov.mt/nationalarchives/logger.aspx.

NATURAL HISTORY MUSEUM. *See* **Magisterial Palace**.

The National Library of Malta in the 1910s.

NATIONAL LIBRARY OF MALTA. This dates back to 1555 and the original collection came from Claude de la Sengle requesting all the Knights of Malta to leave their collections of books to the Order when they died. The largest collection of books in early modern times was from Louis Guérin de Tencin, the Bailiff Grand Cross of the Order who died died in 1766. It included within it the collection of Cardinal Joaquin Portocarrero who had in 1760 and whose books had then been purchased by de Tencin. This resulted in the library being briefly called the Bibliotheca Tanseana. Many French books were sent there in the early years of eighteenth century.

In 1776 this repository became a public library (Bibliotheca Publica) and Stefano Ittar, a Polish-born architect living in Italy, moved to Malta to design the current building which is in Valletta. With the French invasion, the establishment of the archives was put on hold, and it was only in 1812 that the library was formally opened by Sir Hildebrand Oakes, the British Civil Commissioner. Since 1925 it has been the legal deposit and copyright library for Malta, and includes the archives from the Università dei Giurati of Mdina. It is open from Monday to Saturday from 8.15 am to 1.15 pm, except for in winter when it remains open on weekdays to 5 pm.

References: Warren G. Berg, *Historical Dictionary of Malta*, Lanham, Md.: The Scarecrow Press, 1995, pp. 90–91; National Library of Malta, http://www.libraries.gov.mt/nlm/index.htm.

NATIONAL MUSEUM OF ARCHAEOLOGY. This is housed in the former Auberge de Provence in Republic Street Valletta and was opened as the National Museum in 1958. In 1974, many of the paintings were moved to the National Museum of Fine Arts. The National Museum of Archaeology holds a large number of items found all over Malta including some from archaeological digs in and around Mdina. It is maintained by Heritage Malta.

References: Carolyn Bain, *Malta & Gozo*, Footscray, Vic, Australia: Lonely Planet, 2004, p. 66; Sharon Sultana, *The National Museum of Archaeology*, Sta Venera: Heritage Books, 2006; D H Trump, *Malta: An Archaeological Guide*, London: Faber & Faber Ltd, 1972, p. 41–52.

NATIONAL MUSEUM OF FINE ARTS. This museum, located in South Street, Valletta, is the major museum in Malta for the visual arts and is managed by Heritage Malta. It is located in a building which had been the private home of Ramon de Sousa y Silva, a wealthy Portuguese Knight of Malta, and was briefly the home of Louis Charles of Orleans, Comte de Beaujolais. In the 1920s it was Admiralty House used by the Commander-in-Chief of the British Mediterranean Fleet, with the building becoming the National Museum of Fine Arts in 1974. It holds a number of important artworks including the national collection of art of Malta with a number of works featuring Mdina, and works by **Edward Lear** and others.

References: Carolyn Bain, *Malta & Gozo*, Footscray, Vic, Australia: Lonely Planet, 2004, p. 66; *The National Museum of Fine Arts: a brief guide*, Valletta: Midsea Books Ltd, nd.

NATIONAL MUSEUM OF NATURAL HISTORY. *See* **Magisterial Palace**.

DE NAVA, ALFONSO. The **Capitano della Verga** of Mdina, 1570–71, and 1582–84, he was the son of Petruccio de Nava and his wife Isabella (née Calava). He married Diane de la Roche, daughter of Cav. Fra Flotte de la Roche, Knight of Malta and Annica Peralta, and they had two children: Vincenza de Nava and Paola de Nava, both of whom died in infancy.

References: John Montalto, *The Nobles of Malta, 1530–1800*, Valletta: Midsea Books, 1979, p. 69.

DE NAVA, GIOVANNI. The **Capitano della Verga** of Mdina, 1527–28, he was the son of Perone de Nava and his wife Imperia (née Lavagna). He married Eva de Perrollo and they had three children: Inguaterra, Giovanni and Betta.

References: John Montalto, *The Nobles of Malta, 1530–1800*, Valletta: Midsea Books, 1979, p. 18, 20, 141, 143, 318 n4.

DE NAVA, GIUSEPPE. The **Capitano della Verga** of Mdina, 1573–74, he was the son of Giovanni de Nava and his wife Paolo Falsone. He married Francesca Inguanez in 1541, and they had one child, Vincenza. In 1551 he sold half of his land at Marnisi to Salvatore Cumbo.

References: John Montalto, *The Nobles of Malta, 1530–1800*, Valletta: Midsea Books, 1979, p. 233, 259.

DE NAVA, INGUATERRA. The **Capitano della Verga** of Mdina, 1519–20, he was the son of Giovanni de Nava and his wife Imperia de la Xabica. He was the holder of land at Montahlib, Salamuni and Diarezara, and married Imperia de Nava. They did not have any children.

NAVARRA, UGOLINO. The **Capitano della Verga** of Mdina, 1587–90, he was the son of Paolo Navarra and his wife Cornela Mannara. In 1572 he married Isabella Cassia and they had two children: Cornelia; and Paolo. He bought the territory of Bahria from Giovanni de Guevara.

References: John Montalto, *The Nobles of Malta, 1530–1800*, Valletta: Midsea Books, 1979, p. 259.

NELSON, HORATIO (1758–1805). The famous British Admiral, he was born on 29 September 1758 at Burnham Thorpe, Norfolk, England, the sixth of the eleven children of Rev Edmund Nelson. Educated at Paston Grammar School, North Walsham, and King Edward VI's Grammar School, Norwich, he joined the Royal Navy and was a Midshipman serving initially on the HMS *Raisonnable*. He then served on the HMS *Carcass* which sailed close to the North Pole; and was later serving in the East Indies and then in the West Indies during the American War of Independence. With the start of the French Revolutionary Wars, he served in the Mediterranean, and was involved in some of the fighting during the French invasion of Italy. Being involved in the British victory at the battle of Cape St. Vincent, in 1798 with the French having

taken Malta, Nelson captured Malta which became a British colony and important naval base. Five years later, on 21 October 1805 he spectacularly led the British to victory at the battle of Trafalgar but died as victory was secured. In an interesting twist, some parts of the television series Hornblower, starring Ioan Gruffudd as Horatio Hornblower, were filmed at Mdina with the **Main Gate** being easily recognisable.

References: Roger Knight, *The Pursuit of Victory: The Life and Achievement of Horatio Nelson*, London: Allen Lane, 2005; Christopher Hibbert, *Nelson: A Personal History*, London: Viking, 1994; Brian N Tarpey, *Nelson at Malta*, Milton Keynes: Brifma Associates, 1994; Brian N Tarpey, *Nelson's marines at Malta*, Milton Keynes: Brifma Associates, 1995.

NEWSPAPERS. Because of its small population and size, there has never been a newspaper in Mdina. The best-known newspaper in Malta is *The Times* (formerly *The Times of Malta*). Founded by Lord **Strickland** and then run by his daughter Mabel, the newspaper is the oldest paper in Malta still being published and remains the newspaper 'of the record', with a daily circulation of some 37,000. It had started as *Il-Progress* in Maltese, an evening newspaper, with an English supplement. However there was so much demand for an English-language newspaper that *The Times of Malta* was first published on 7 August 1935. It is now called *The Times*. The other main English-language newspaper in Malta is *The Malta Independent*. The two other daily newspapers are: *L-Orizzong* ('The Horizon'), founded in 1962, and with a circulation of 25,000 in 2002, and associated with the Malta Labour Party; and *In-Nazzjon*, founded in 1970 with a circulation of 20,000 in 2003, and connected to the Maltese National Party. There are also a number of weekly newspapers. All of these are available in Mdina.

References: A F Sapienza, *A checklist of Maltese periodicals and newspapers*, Msida: Malta University Publications, 1977; Ninette Camilleri & Romaine Petrochino, *Supplement to a Checklist of Maltese Periodicals and Newspapers Covering the Tears 1974–1989*, Msida: Malta University Publications, 1990.

NICOLAUS (NICCOLÒ). By tradition, he was the bishop of Malta from 1304 to 1322, living next to the **Cathedral Church** in Mdina. It is now clear that the Cathedral Church was being built by the 1320s.

NORMAN HOUSE. *See* **Palazzo Falzon**.

NOTABILE CITY COUNCIL SQUARE. *See* **Misraħ il-Kunsill Ċittà Notabile**.

DI NOTO, SENATORE. He was the bishop of Malta from 13 February 1432 until his death, being succeeded in December 1445 by Bishop **Jaime**.

NOVELS. Despite of the wide possibilities for the setting of stories, including on the life of **St. Paul**, relatively few novels have been set in Mdina. Dorothy Dunnett's novel, *The Disorderly Knights* (London: G.P. Putnam, 1966) involves some members of a Scottish family going to Malta where they meet with the Grand Master **Juan de Homedes** and are present during the Turkish attack on Malta in 1551. This story included much on Mdina but there are only passing references in novels set during the **Great Siege** such as David W. Ball's *Ironfire: a novel of the Knights of Malta and the last battle of the Crusades* (New York: Delacorte Press, 2004). Simon Scarrow's *Sword & Scimitar* (London: Headline, 2012) makes mention of the final Ottoman attack on Mdina (p. 543f). More on Mdina appears in James H. Jackson's *Blood Rock* (London: John Murray, 2007). An exception to this is Tim Willocks's *The Religion* (London: Jonathan Cape, 2006). Although savaged by some reviewers, notably Rachel Aspden in *The Observer*, who was shocked by the level of violence in the book, it is an historical novel set during a vicious conflict. It focuses on a disgraced Maltese noblewoman living in Sicily working with a 'notorious adventurer and arms merchant' called Mattias

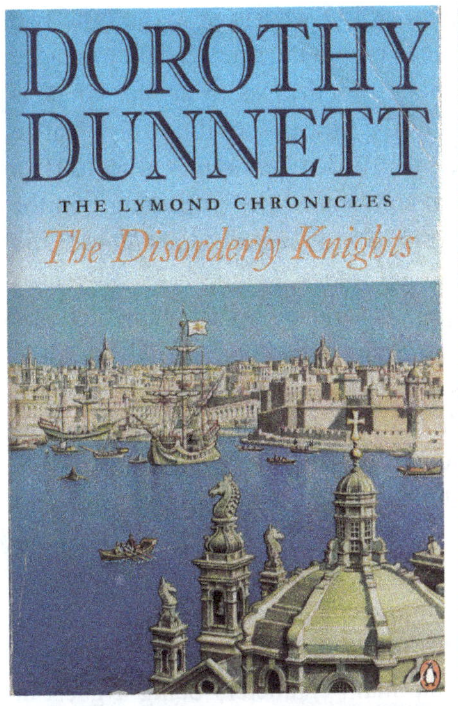
DOROTHY DUNNETT
THE LYMOND CHRONICLES
The Disorderly Knights

TIM WILLOCKS
THE RELIGION

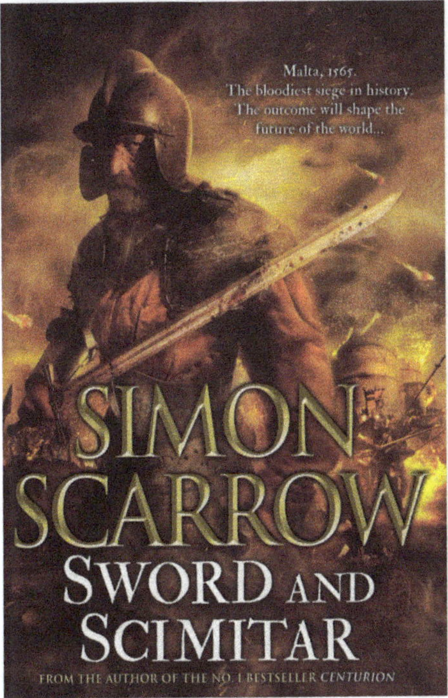
Malta, 1565.
The bloodiest siege in history.
The outcome will shape the
future of the world...
SIMON SCARROW
SWORD AND SCIMITAR
FROM THE AUTHOR OF THE NO. 1 BESTSELLER CENTURION

Edward J Kelly
The Mdina Touch

Tannhauser, seeking to trace her illegitimate son who is in Malta. The two travel to Malta in 1565 as the Ottoman siege is about to start, and they manage to reach Mdina where information is sought from the Casa Manduca which is easily recognisable as one of the homes of the Maltese nobility which can be found in Mdina. The story now has a sequel, *Twelve Children of Paris* (2013).

Mdina does not feature much – although sometimes in passing – in the various novels set in the Napoleonic Wars. C.S. Forester's *Hornblower and the Atropos* (London: Michael Joseph, 1953) does include brief references to Malta, with C. Northcote Parkinson, in his series of books on the fictional Richard Delancey, covering the siege of Valletta in *Touch & Go* (London: John Murray, 1977). Patrick O'Brian's *Treason's Harbour* (London: Collins, 1983) includes more details on Malta in the 1790s, but neither of his heroes, Jack Aubrey nor Dr. Stephen Maturin, visit Mdina, nor does the indefatigable Thomas Kydd who goes to Valletta in Julian Stockwin's *Command* (London: Hodder & Stoughton, 2006).

Set during World War II is Mark Mills's *The Information Officer – Malta, 1942 – one man to catch a killer – to save an island* (London: HarperCollins Publishers, 2009), although the story begins in London in 1951, it quickly reverts to wartime Malta with one of the main characters being a guest at the Xara Palace Hotel which had been requisitioned by the Royal Air Force (p. 189f, 230f, and 357f).

For Mdina in more recent times, Alethia Hunt, *Mystery in Mdina* (London: Robert Hale, 1982) is a mystery story set in a hotel in the city with the fictional Alethea Hunt, her sister Liz and Paul Fenton catching up with each other after 20 years. Alan Tucker's (or Victor Fenech's), *Let Now Mdina Sleep* (Leicester: Aardvark Press, 2003) is also set in Mdina. J. Edward Kelly's *The Mdina Touch* (Lulu.com, 2007) focuses on the fictional Steve Parker who is in Mdina where he has to face a hidden enemy with occult powers gained from the Knights Templar.

References: Rachel Aspden, 'All's small in love and war', *The Observer* (6 August 2006); Tim Willocks, *The Religion*, London: Jonathan Cape, 2006, pp. 211f, 413f, 612f.

Photograph by Robin Corfield, 1975.

– O –

OGERIUS. He was the bishop of Malta from 27 October 1343 until around 1346, being succeeded by Bishop **Jocobus**.

ORNITHOLOGY. There has been much interest by Britons and others into the birdlife of Malta with observations conducted all over the island including around Mdina. However with the number of hunters in southern Italy and in Malta, there are relatively few birds in Malta, although some do manage to survive and can be seen nesting in some walls and cavities in Mdina and elsewhere. There is an extensive collection of stuffed birds in the National Museum of Natural History, located in the **Magisterial Palace**. One of the most prominent Maltese ornithologists of the nineteenth century was Antonio Schembri (1813–1872). On 22 June 2001 the Maltese postal authorities issued a series of 16 stamps each showing birds of Malta.

References: David A Bannerman and Joseph A Vella-Gaffiero, *Birds of the Maltese archipelago*, Valletta: Museums Department, 1976, reviewed by Giovanni Mangion, *Melita Historica* vol 7, no 1 (1976), pp. 98–99; J Sultana, C Gauci and M Beaman, *A guide to the birds of Malta*, Valletta: Malta Ornithological Society, 1975, reviewed by Giovanni Mangion, *Melita Historica* vol 7, no 1 (1976), pp. 98–99; new edition, 1982; Joe Sultana and Charles Gauci, *A new guide to the birds of Malta*, Valletta: Ornithological Society, 1982.

OUR LADY OF MOUNT CARMEL. This statue is located in **Triq Villegaignon** and dates from the early nineteenth century. It shows Our Lady of Mount Carmel nursing the infant Jesus. As well as being an important local landmark, each year on 16 July, the feast day of Our Lady of Mount Carmel, there is a race from the **Benedictine Nunnery** in Triq Villagaignon to **Pjazza tas-Sur** (Bastion Square).

References: Richard England and Conrad Thake, *Mdina: Citadel of Memory*, Malta: Atlantis, 1995, pp. 62–63.

– P –

DE PACE, ANDREA. A Franciscan, he was the bishop of Malta from 1408 until the following year when he was nominated as bishop of Catania, Sicily, a post he held until 1411 as a rival to Mauro Cali.

PACE, PIETRO (1831–1914). He was the bishop of Malta from 11 February 1889 until his death on 29 July 1914. Born on 9 April 1831 at Victoria, Gozo, he went to Rome to study from the age of 14 and served as a private tutor to the Orsini family. With their help he was granted an audience with Pope Pius IX and urged that Gozo become a separate diocese. Ordained priest on 17 December 1853, he completed a doctorate in theology, canon law and civil law from La Sapienza University, and returned to Malta becoming a canon at the **Cathedral Church** in Mdina. On 12 March 1877 he was appointed bishop of Gozo, ordained on 8 April, and installed on 2 July. Appointed bishop of Malta, he was also the titular archbishop of Rhodes. He urged for a regular ferry service between Malta and Gozo, and died on 29 July 1914. The only Roman Catholic clergyman at the time of his death to have received the KCVO, he was buried in Gozo Cathedral.

References: Michael J. Schiavone, *Dictionary of Maltese Biographies*, Malta: pubblikazzjonijiet Indipendenza, 2009, vol 2, p. 1265; *The Times* (30 July 1914), p. 10.

PACE FORNO, GAETANO (1807–1874). The bishop of Malta from 1857 until his death, he was born on 5 September 1807 (or 5 June 1809) at **Rabat**, Gozo, the son of Francesco Pace, a lawyer, and Luica dei Baroni Forno. Joining the Augustinians on 20 July 1824, he was ordained priest on 22 September 1832 in Naples, and after many years in Italy, returned to Malta and in 1848 opened a school for boys in Valletta. There were moves to establish a bishopric of Gozo, and prominent people on that island sought him out to see if he would take up the offer. He was coadjutor bishop of Malta and titular bishop of Hebron on 25 September 1857, and was appointed bishop of Malta (the first Augustinian to hold that position). Pace Forno was consecrated on 4 October 1857 in Rome, and succeeding as bishop of Malta on 3 December. He served on the First Vatican Council and remained bishop until his death on 22 July 1874.

References: Michael J. Schiavone, *Dictionary of Maltese Biographies*, Malta: pubblikazzjonijiet Indipendenza, 2009, vol 2, p. 1269.

PALACIO VILHENA. *See* **Magisterial Palace**.

PALAZZO BONICI. Located in Mdina close to the **Benedictine Monastery,** this is the family seat of the Barons Bonici of Qlejja.

References: Anne Agius Ferrante, *No Strangers in the Silent City*, Valletta: Andrew Rupert Publishing, 1992, p. 73.

PALAZZO COSTANZO. Located in Villegaignon Street, this is a Baroque palace formerly the family seat of the Costanzo. The Palazzo Costanzo Restaurant and Cafeteria was located there in 1996. It is now the location of the Medieval Times exhibition which has 15 scenes showing life in medieval times in Malta with the explanations in a variety of languages including English.

PALAZZO DE PIRO. The family seat of the De Piro family located at 3 Triq Is-Sur, it was originally three separate houses, the oldest part dating back to the early sixteenth century and was designed by the architect Girolamo Cassar (c1520–1589/92). Remodelled and extended, in 1868, Marquis Alexander de' Marchesi de Piro d'Amico Inguanez and his wife Ursola (or Orsola) Agius (née Caruana) moved there soon after they married. They brought up their seven sons and two daughters – including their seventh child, Giuseppe de Piro. The house was extensively remodelled in the nineteenth century, and it was later used by as a part of St. Dorothy's Convent school. In 2005, the Metropolitan Cathedral Chapter (which is responsible for maintaining the Mdina Cathedral and the Cathedral Museum) purchased the house and has undertaken extensive restoration work on it.There is now a museum of tools in the Palazzo.

References: Palazzo de Piro, www.palazzodepiro.com; 'A rather unique museum opens in Mdina', *Malta Independent* (18 August 2014).

PALAZZO FALZON. Located in **Triq Villegaignon**, this dates from the thirteenth century and for many years was known as the 'Norman House'.

Palazzo Falzon
Photograph © schneiderpics / Fotolia.com

It was built in around 1495 for Vice Admiral Falzon of Aragon, and was one of the best-kept houses in Mdina, as well as being the best preserved late medieval house in the whole of Malta. Grand Master **Philippe Villiers de L'Isle-Adam** was entertained in the house, and stayed there at night during his first visit to the city in 1530. The home of Captain **Olof Frederick Gollcher** OBS (1889–1962), it was opened to the public as a museum dislaying its period furniture, renaissance painting and exquisite old Maltese silver. It also includes displays of a large array of weapons including many early modern swords, chain mail and helmets. It was renovated and reopened in 2007 and exhibits the collection of Gollcher including paintings, furniture, ceramics and silver, and a medal from **Alof de Wignacourt** dating from 1607, and a 1791 Robert Robin Fob Watch. There is also a painting by Mattia Preti (1613–1699), *Lucretia Stabbing Herself*.

The Palazzo Falzon featured in an Australian 2013 episode of the genealogical television series, *Who Do You Think You Are?* with the Australian comedian Adam Hills having his ancestry traced back to Matteo Vassallo in fifteenth-century Mdina. Some of the silver which had originally been held in the Palazzo Falzon was taken to Britain by its owner who retired to England

and offered it for sale on 21 May 2013 by auction by Rowley's Fine Art and Antiques, held at Tattersalls, Newmarket.

References: Aldo Azzopardi, *Malta and its islands*, Luqa: Plurigraf, nd, p. 123; Can John Azzopardi, *Mdina, Rabat, Mosta*, Terni, Italy: Plurigraf, 1988, p. 32–33; Mario Buhagiar, 'The Palazzo Falsone at Mdina', *Treasures of Malta* vol 12, no 2 (No 35) (Easter 2006), p. 15–18; Richard England and Conrad Thake, *Mdina: Citadel of Memory*, Malta: Atlantis, 1995, pp. 70–73; 'Maltese Silver collection could make more than €8,000 at auction', *The Times of Malta* (13 May 2013); John Manduca, *Tourist Guide to City of Mdina*, Malta: Progress Press, 1975, pp. 29–30; 'Palazzo Falson – Historic House Museum', *Treasures of Malta* vol 13, no 1 (No 37) (Christmas 2006), p. 13; *Rowley's Fine Art and Antiques, Sale Catalogue, 21 May 2013*, lots 326–332; Edward Sammut, *The Monuments of Mdina*, Malta: Progress Press Co. Ltd, 1967, p. 33 & 35.

PALAZZO GATTO MURINA. Located in Gatto-Murina Street, this residence was built in 1350 for Francesco Gatto, and is well-known for its fine architecture with its impressive double windows and sculptured hoodmoulds, some modelled on their counterparts in Sicily. Commander Robert Tatton Bower, Royal Navy, and May Carribea Strickland, moved there from London in May 1967. One of their daughters, Monica Juanita Bower, married Bernard Peter, son of Lieutenant-Colonel Count Peter de Salis, on 5 August 1967. Another daughter, Veronica Mary Bower married Commander John Slocock of the Royal Navy, in March 1968. The Palazzo is the location of the audio-visual presentation, *Tales of the Silent City,* for tourists and other visitors to the city, and which can be seen on the top floor of the building.

References: Richard England and Conrad Thake, *Mdina: Citadel of Memory*, Malta: Atlantis, 1995, pp. 48–49; John Manduca, *Tourist Guide to City of Mdina*, Malta: Progress Press, 1975, p. 43; *The Times* (26 May 1967), p. 12.

PALAZZO GOURGION. *See* **Casa Gourgion**.

PALAZZO SANTA SOFIA. Located on **Triq Villeaignon**, it is said to be the oldest surviving building in Malta, and remains one of the best-preserved medieval buildings in the city. A plaque on the wall dates it to 1233 although some historians have queried whether this date is accurate. It was only one storey tall until 1938 when the second floor was added.

References: Richard England and Conrad Thake, *Mdina: Citadel of Memory*, Malta: Atlantis, 1995, pp. 54–57; *Images: Nineteenth Century Malta*, Valletta: Valletta Publishing Publication, 1989; John Manduca, *Tourist Guide to City of Mdina*, Malta: Progress Press, 1975, p. 27.

Palazzo Santa Sofia in the nineteenth century.

PARDO, PIETRO. He was a Spanish military engineer who came to Malta in the early 1530s to give advice to Grand Master **Juan de Homedes** to help prepare the defences of Mdina. It was his work that helped to save the city in 1551 from falling to the Turks during their first major assault on Malta, fourteen years before the Great Siege.

DE PARISIO, RAIMONDO. The **Capitano della Verga** of Mdina, 1466–67, he was the son of Bartolomeo Parisi and his wife Anna de Licara. His grandfather Raimondo Parisi was a tax collector in Malta for the King of Sicily, with Raimondo later working as a secretary for King Alfonso of Sicily. He married Isabella la Rocca and they had a daughter Beatrice, and a son Dionisio. Beatrice married Milte Ferrante Paglia, a juror in Mdina, and a member of the Università Dei Giurati. Dionisio later served as secretary to the king.

DI PATERNO', CARLO. He was the **Capitano della Verga** of Mdina, 1454–55. His family, originally from Aragon, were also prominent in Catania, Sicily, and Carlo di Paterno was the seventh child of Nicholas, Baron of

Floresta, a nobleman from Catania.

PATERNÒ, GIOVANNI (d. 1511). A Benedictine, he was the bishop of Malta from 8 January 1479 to 6 July 1489, being nominated as archbishop of Palermo. He remained in that position until his death on 24 January 1511.

DE PAULE, ANTOINE (c1551–1636). The Grand Master of the Knights Hospitaller (Knights of Malta) from 1623 to 1636, he was elected after the sudden death of Luis Mendes de Vasconcellos. He built a third magisterial residence, Sant'Antonio and in 1631 he called the Chapter-General of the Order of Malta – the last time it was called for 145 years. He worked on improving the fortifications at Floriana, and he died on 9 June 1636 in Malta. He was succeeded by Giovanni Paolo Lascaris.

References: H.J.A. Sire, *The Knights of Malta*, New Haven: Yale University Press, 1994, pp. 77–78.

DI PELLEGRINO, GIACOMO. The **Capitano della Verga** of Mdina from 1365, he was the son of Luca de Perregrino (sic) and his wife Antonia de Barone di Spadafora, and was descended from an illegitimate son of Conrad IV, Duke of Swabia, King of Sicily and Germany from 1235 to 1254. In 1360 Giacomo was created Baron of Ghajn Tewzin; and in 1361, Giacomo was created Baron of Ghajn Qajjed, Benwarrad, Chabelbelach, Gnien is-Sultan, la Hafe, Jardino di lo Re, Viridarium Magnum e di Ghajn Tuffieha. In 1362 he married Margherita d'Aragona, the illegitimate daughter of King Frederick III of Sicily (r. 1295–1337). His wife survived him and when she died in 1418 she left much of her fortune to the Carmelite Order in Malta, and also for the holding of masses, as well as liberating her husband's slave.

References: John Montalto, *The Nobles of Malta, 1530–1800*, Valletta: Midsea Books, 1979, p. 152, 165.

DE PELLEGRINO, PAOLO. He was the **Capitano della Verga** of Mdina, 1428–29.

PELLERANI, GIOVANNI CARMELO (1702–1783). A member of the Sovereign Military Hospitaller Order of St. John of Jerusalem, he was born on

6 February 1702 at Mazarien, and ordained priest on 3 March 1726. He was appointed bishop of Malta on 28 May 1770 and ordained on 25 August 1770, holding office until 18 March 1780. He was also vice-chancellor of the island of Rhodes, and titular bishop of Rhodes from 19 June 1780. In August 1772 some of his officials were attacked by sailors from the Order of St. John and Pellerani then had two of them arrested. However other knights opposed this and broke into the prison and freed them, causing simmering resentment for some years. He died on 18 April 1783.

References: Dennis Angelo Castillo, *The Maltese Cross: A Strategic History of Malta,* Westport, Conn.: Praeger Security International, 2005, p. 93.

PEROWNE, STEWART (1901–1989). A British diplomat and historian, he was a resident of Mdina during the mid–1930s. Born on 17 June 1901 at Hallow, Worcestershire, England, his grandfather and later his father were both Bishops of Worcester. Educated at Haileybury College 1915–20, and Corpus Christi College, Cambridge, he served in the Palestine Government Education Service and was Assistant Secretary in Malta from 1934 until 1937, living in Mdina during that time. His brother, Leslie Arthur Perowne (1906–1997) visited him in Mdina – he was later Head of Music at the British Broadcasting Corporation. He also designed postage stamps for Malta in 1938, and in the following year wrote, *Notes on Three Tablets in the 'Ta Giesu' Church, Rabat, Malta*. Later serving in Aden, Baghdad, Barbados and then Cyrenaica, Stewart Perowne was married to the British explorer and travel writer Freya Stark from 1947 to 1952. Perowne wrote a large number of books including *The siege within the walls: Malta 1940–1943* (1970); and *The Journeys of St. Paul* (1973). In his later holidays in Malta, he stayed at the **Xara Palace Hotel** in Mdina. He died on 10 May 1989 in Charing Cross Hospital, London.

References: Anne Agius Ferrante, *No Strangers in the Silent City*, Valletta: Andrew Rupert Publishing, 1992, p. 25; E.C. Hodgkin, 'Perowne, Stewart Henry (1901–1989)', *Oxford Dictionary of National Biography*, Oxford University Press, 2004; Sir Harry Luke, *Malta: an account and an appreciation*, London: G.G. Harrap, 1960, p. 151; Stewart Perowne, *The siege within the walls: Malta 1940–1943*, London: Hodder & Stoughton, 1970; Stewart

Perowne, *The Journeys of St. Paul*, London: Hamlyn, 1973; *Who's Who 1979*, p. 1960.

PERTICOMATI, FRANCESCO. The **Capitano della Verga** of Mdina, 1633–35, he was the son of Giovannetto Perdicomati from Rhodes who arrived in Malta with the knights in 1530 as a young man. In 1576 he married Leonora Cagliola, the illegitimate daughter of Agistino Cagiola, a Knight of St. John, and Maddalena Zammit. After Leonora's death, he married Vincenza Bologna in 1635 and they had two children: Leonora, and Pietro.

PERTICOMATI BOLOGNA, ANTONIO. He was the **Capitano della Verga** of Mdina, 1698–1700.

PHOENICIAN AND PUNIC MDINA. The Phoenicians reached Malta in about 1000 BC and used it as an outpost calling the island Maleth or Malat meaning 'safe haven'. They established their headquarters at Mdina, and from the start of the eighth century there appears to have been trade with Greece although Anthony Bonanno argued in 1983 that there is no evidence that there was a Greek colony in Malta. The Carthaginians took control of the island and were the major maritime power in that part of the Mediterranean until their defeat in the First Punic War in 241 BC. At the start of the Second Punic War in 218 BC, the Romans took control of the island from the Carthaginians.

References: Anthony Bonanno, 'The tradition of an ancient Greek colony in Malta', *Hyphen* vol 4, no 1 (1983), pp. 1–17; Anthony Bonanno, 'Malta's role in the Phoenician Greek and Etruscan trade in the western Mediterranean', *Melita Historica* vol 10, no 3 (1990), pp. 209–24; Tancred C. Gouder, 'Malta and the Phoenicians', *Annual Report of the Lombard Bank (Malta) Ltd*, 1991, pp. 3–20; 'Malta and the Phoenician world', *Journal of Maltese Studies* vol 3, no 2, part 1 (1993), pp. 170–290; George A Said-Zammit, 'The Punic tombs of the Maltese islands', *History Week* (1993), pp. 67–80; George A Said-Zammit, 'The Phoenician and Punic Necropolis of Rabat Malta', *Melita Historica* vol 13, no 2 (2001), pp. 127–46.

PHOTOGRAPHY. There have been photographers taking pictures of Malta since Rev George Wilson Bridges started taking photos after he arrived on the island on 2 March 1846. James Robertson and Felice Beato left an assistant in Malta in 1856, and soon the iconic image of Malta was that of the walled city of Mdina. The light made photography relatively straightforward and from the late nineteenth century many visitors to Malta – often heading to Egypt or another destination – started photographing Mdina with images of the city appearing on many postcards.

Pjazza San Pawl.
Photograph © robert lerich / Fotolia.com

References: Carmelina Grech, *Old Photographs of Malta*, Stroud, UK: Sutton Publishing, 1999.

PIERRERA, STAFANO. The **Capitano della Verga** of Mdina, 1456–57, he was from the fief della Garia which had been granted to him and his descendants in 1448. A representative of the Università Dei Giurati in 1456, he married Clovely Vassallo and they had a son Martiano.

PJAZZA SAN PAWL (St Paul's Square). This is located close to the geographical centre of the city of Mdina. It takes its name from the **Cathedral Church** dedicated to **St. Paul**. This is said to have been built over the Roman headquarters where Publius (later **St. Publius**) lived. He was the host of Paul of Tarsus (later St. Paul) after he (Paul) was shipwrecked on Malta and brought to the city of Melita (now Mdina). The Cathedral Church is on the eastern side of the square, with the **Banca Giuratale** on the southeast corner.

References: John Manduca, *Tourist Guide to City of Mdina*, Malta: Progress Press, 1975, pp. 20–21.

PJAZZA SAN PUBLIJU (St Publius Square). This square is located just inside the **Main Gate** to Mdina. It is named after **St. Publius**, the Roman governor of Malta who hosted Paul of Tarsus (later **St. Paul**) – Paul cured Publius's father of dysentery. The Main Gate is on the southern side of the square, with the **Tower of the Standard** (now the location of the Mdina **Police** Station) on the left, and the **Magisterial Palace** (now the venue of the National Museum of Natural History on the eastern side. **Triq Inguanez** runs along the northern side of the square.

PJAZZA TAL-ARĊISQOF (Archbishop Square). Sometimes appearing on maps as 'Bishop Square', it is located to the south of the **Cathedral** with the **Archbishop's Palace** being on the east side of the square, and the **Cathedral Museum** on the south side of the square.

PJAZZA TAS-SUR (Bastion Square). In the north of Mdina, it was the location of the Benedictine Abbey of Santa Scholastica founded in 1494 but the nuns moved to a Convent in Vittoriosa in 1604. Part of that abbey is now the house Beaulieu which was owned by **John Hamilton-Rose**, and then by **John Manduca**.

References: Richard England and Conrad Thake, *Mdina: Citadel of Memory*, Malta: Atlantis, 1995, pp. 74–75; John Manduca, *Tourist Guide to City of Mdina*, Malta: Progress Press, 1975, p. 30.

PJAZZETTA BEATA MARIJA ADEODATA PISANI (Blessed Maria Adeodata Pisani Square). This square is on the eastern corner of **Triq Villegaignon** and **Triq Inguanez**.

PLATAMONTE, FRANCESCO. He was the **Capitano della Verga** of Mdina, 1438–39.

POINTE DE VUE GUESTHOUSE AND RESTAURANT. This is one of the only two places to stay for visitors to Mdina (the other is the **Xara Palace**), and was originally converted into a tavern in 1898; the building itself dating from the seventeenth century. It is located just inside the **Main Gate** and has a restaurant which offers many Maltese specialities including rabbit, lamb, fish and also pizzas.

References: *1000x European Hotels*, Berlin: Braun, 2008, p. 973; Carolyn Bain, *Malta & Gozo*, Footscray, Vic, Australia: Lonely Planet, 2004, p. 120; http://mol.net.mt/point.

POLICE. The police force in Malta was created by the British who had to restore order after the surrender and flight of the French. This was established on a formal basis under the governorship of Sir **Thomas Maitland** in 1814 with the executive police directed by the inspector general of police who took orders from the Governor, and after self-government, from the Minister for Justice and the Police. This makes the Malta Police Force (MPF) one of the oldest in continuous lineage in Europe. There was also the Judicial Police which was headed by magistrates. The police force has currently some 1,732 members with 106 civilian employees. The only police station in Mdina is located in the **Tower of the Standard**. During **World War II**, Magistrate Willie Soler is recorded as having held some of his sessions in the station.

References: Edward Attard, *A History of the Malta Police 1800–1964*, Malta: Progress Publishers, 2003; Roy D. Ingleton, *Police of the World*, London: Ian Allan Ltd, 1979, pp. 114–15; Laurence Mizzi, *The People's War: Malta 1940/43*, Valletta: Progress Press, 2002, p. 276.

DE PONTE, PIERO (1462–1535). He was the Grand Master of the Knights Hospitaller (Knights of Malta) from 1534 until his death in 1535. Originally from Asti in northern Italy, his family were from Casal-Gros and Lombriax. Joining the Order of St. John of Jerusalem, he became governor of the island of Langò (now Cos) after the fall of Rhodes. He was still there when, in 1534, he was elected to succeed **Philippe Villiers de l'Isle-Adam** as the 45th Grand Master of the Order of Malta. He immediately travelled to Malta and died on 18 November 1535, only 15 months after his election. He was initially buried in the Chapel of Our Lady of Victories at Fort St. Angelo, Birgu, with his body later reinterred in the crypt of St. John's Co-Cathedral, Valletta.

References: Victor Mallia-Milanes & Louis J. Scerri, *An Uneasy Partnership: Malta 1530–1565*, Mdina: Midsea Books, 1985.

POPULAR CULTURE. Because of its location on a hill, its fortifications and its narrow alleys, Mdina was used for a number of films including in Anthony Horowitz's 'Alex Roder series' where Mdina is the scene of an ambush when British intelligence operatives from MI6 try to retrieve John Rider, Alex's father. Mdina was also used for the filming of the first series of HBO's *Game of Thrones* where it is the fictional capital city of King's Landing. It is also the capital of the clan Lasombra in World of Darkness produced by White Wolf Publishing. More famously one of the squares was used for a scene of a carnival in *Gladiator* (2000). In mid-2013, the film *Adormidera*, directed by Ray Mizzi, was shot in Mdina. Set in the thirteenth century, this is about five soldiers returning home after a war, and face different problems. The film had its premiere on 28 September, and went on general release on 2 October.

References: 'Director Ray Mizzi to release full feature film in October', *Malta Independent* (20 August 2013).

PORTELLI, ANGELO (1852–1927). The auxiliary bishop of Malta from 1914 to 1927, he was born on 24 April 1852 as Francis Xavier Portelli, and joined the Dominican Order when he was 16, taking the name Angelo. Studying theology at the St. Thomas Aquinas College, **Rabat**, he was ordained

priest in 1874, and completed his doctorate in theology two years later. Lecturing at St. Thomas Aquinas College, he was the parish priest of Porto Salvo, Valletta from 1896 to 1902. On 14 May 1911 he was consecrated as titular bishop of Selinonte, and auxiliary to the bishop of Malta. Working with Bishop **Pietro Pace**, he became the apostolic administrator when Bishop Pace died in 1914. He himself died on 19 June 1927.

References: Michael J. Schiavone, *Dictionary of Maltese Biographies*, Malta: pubblikazzjonijiet Indipendenza, 2009, vol 2, p. 1303.

DE PORTOCARRERO, DIEGO. He was the **Capitano della Verga** of Mdina, 1413–14.

POSTAL SERVICES. Malta has long been a clearing-house for letters in the Mediterranean long before the establishment of the postal services. Letters were transferred from one ship to another, and under French Occupation an ink-stamp with 'Malte' designated letters which passed through the island. In 1847 the whole system was overhauled with the General Post Office located in Valletta. Being a British colony, British stamps (first issued in 1840) could be used, and there are surviving covers which show that stamps from France, Italy, Egypt and India were used until 1 December 1860 when the first Maltese postage stamp was issued. By 2010 some 1,500 stamps had been issued in Malta.

The first post office for Mdina was the Notabile Branch Post Office which was initially authorised to sell stamps from 1 October 1891 as a postal agency and it was upgraded to become a branch post office on 15 November 1897 being moved to Strada San Paolo, Rabat. There was one collection and one delivery each day, with the handstamp / postmark being 'Notabile'. In around September 1937 the post office moved to 10 Museum Road, Rabat, facing the south-west wall of the city. In September 1954 the post office was closed for repairs, and a new temporary post office was established in a school building in St. Peter and St. Paul Square.

From 1960 a handstamp 'Mdina' was used, and the post office at 10 Museum Road, Rabat, was designated as the Mdina Branch Post Office. This post office was formally closed on 9 March 1974, but it seems likely that the last stamps sold, and the last letters franked were on the previous day, 8 March.

Relatively few stamps include Mdina in the design. The first was the two shilling stamp issued in the definitive series in 1926–27, also having the same value in the 1938–43 definitive series, with an engraving from Antoine Favray's painting of Grand Master **Philippe Villiers de L'Isle-Adam** entering Mdina featuring for the 2½d value. The **Main Gate** to Mdina was the one shilling value for the 1956–57 definitive series.

The Sovereign Military Order of Malta (S.M.O.M.), a Roman Catholic Order based in Rome, Italy, also issues its own stamps. The S.M.O.M. has bilateral postal agreements with 50 countries but most philatelists regard the stamps as cinderellas. Because of its history, the S.M.O.M. has issued a number of stamps which cover aspects of Maltese history including heraldry, paintings and some reproductions from antique maps, but none covering Mdina.

References: 'An issue is born: Malta 1956–57', *Gibbons Stamp Monthly* vol 30, no 5 (January 1957), pp. 50–53; vol 30, no 6 (February 1957), pp. 64–66; vol 30, no 7 (March 1957), pp. 76–77; Nick Halewood, 'Queen Elizabeth Definitives part 11 – Malta 1956–57 and 1963–64', *Gibbons Stamp Monthly* vol 29, no 1 (June 1998), pp. 86–89; David Horry, 'The postmarks of Malta and Gozo within the King George VI period, 1937–1956', *Gibbons Stamp Monthly* (July 2012), pp. 122–24; James A. Mackay, *Malta – The story of Malta and her stamps*, London: Philatelic Publishers, 1966; 'Malta', in *International Encyclopedia of Stamps* vol 4, pp. 1182–89; R. E. Martin (ed), *Malta: The Stamps and Postal History 1576–1960*, London: Malta Study Circle, 1980, pp. 373–75; Edward B. Proud, *The Postal History of Malta*, Heathfield: Proud-Bailey Co Ltd, 1999, pp. 269–73; John Woolford, 'Malta: The George Cross Island', *Gibbons Stamp Monthly* vol 29, no 11 (April 1999), pp. 64–67; Godwin Said (ed), *S.M.O.M. Stamp and Coin Catalogue 1996*, Valletta: Said International Ltd, 1996; A. J. Sefi, *The Postage Stamps of Malta*, London: D. Field, 1913; *Village Postmarks Malta*, Watford Heath, UK: Malta Study Circle, 1975.

PUJADES, JUAN. He was the bishop of Malta from 21 January 1512 until his death later that year.

PULLICINO, Sir PHILIP (1885–1960). A prominent Maltese lawyer and judge, he was born on 21 November 1885 in Mdina, the son of Judge

Giovanni Pullicino and his wife Giorgina, dauighter of Judge Pasquale Mifsud. He was educated at St. Aloysius College and the University of Malta, graduating with a law degree in 1907 and then being called to the Bar. Appointed an advocate for the poor in 1918, he was a judge in 1928–29, and was then treasury counsel and public prosecutor from 1929, being knighted in 1934. The attorney general from 1937 to 1941, he was also an official member of the Council of Government in 1939, and also a legal adviser to HM Forces and the treasury solicitor's agent 1934–55. He married Maude, daughter of Colonel Achilles Samut, and they had six sons and five daughters. He died on 16 July 1960. One of his daughters is **Anne Agius-Ferrante**.

References: Michael J. Schiavone, *Dictionary of Maltese Biographies*, Malta: pubblikazzjonijiet Indipendenza, 2009, vol 2, p. 1344; *Who Was Who 1951–1960*, p. 896. Portrait courtesy Michael J. Schiavone.

– R –

RABAT. This is a village just outside Mdina, in an area that was part of the Roman settlement of Melita (Mdina). Its name derives from the Arab word for 'suburb' and it is the location of a number of important amenities that also serve the people in Mdina. Of historical interest are St. Paul's Catacomb and also the **Roman** Villa discovered in 1881 and which is now the site of the museum. During times of attack such as in 1551 and again in 1565, the people in Rabat fled into Mdina behind the safety of the city walls. In 1658, the **Carmelite Church and Convent** moved from Rabat to Mdina, although the Dominican Monastery (1466) and the Augustinian Friary (1571) remained in Rabat. Rabat has a population of 7,064 (March 2011).

References: Can John Azzopardi, *Mdina, Rabat, Mosta*, Terni, Italy: Plurigraf, 1988, p. 38–57; Carolyn Bain, *Malta & Gozo*, Footscray, Vic, Australia: Lonely Planet, 2004, pp. 121–22; John Manduca, *Tourist Guide to City of Mdina*, Malta: Progress Press, 1975, pp. 44–47.

RADIO. There are many radio stations in Malta and because of the city's location, reception for all of them is good in Mdina. All radio stations in Malta are supervised and regulated by the Malta Broadcasting Authority which was established in 1961 to oversee both radio and television.

References: Francis Zammit Dimech, *The Untruth Game: Broadcasting Under Labour*, Valletta: Progress Press, 1986.

RAILWAYS. A small railway line operated in Malta between 1883 and 1931 connecting the army barracks at Mtarfa, past Mdina, and Valletta. For the people of Mdina, a third gate in the city walls was created along Magazines Street, on the western walls. Because it was so small, it was soon nicknamed 'the hole in the wall'. During World War II, the Italian leader Benito Mussolini famously announced that the Italian air force had destroyed the entire railway system in Malta which had, in fact, not been operating for nine years. The railway station was bought by a local businessman and in 1986 was restored and opened as a restaurant called the Old Railway Station. Drinks can be ordered at the old ticket office, and dining takes place on the platform. There is a large model train engine and photographs of the railways in Malta.

References: Warren G. Berg, *Historical Dictionary of Malta*, Lanham, Md.: The Scarecrow Press, 1995, pp. 80–81; Josef Bonnici & Michael Cassar, *The Malta Railway*, Malta: The

Notabile Railway Station Malta.

Authors/Gutenberg Press, 1988; Bernard L. Rigby, *The Malta Railway*, Lingfield, UK: Oakwood Press, 1970, reprinted 2004, 2008.

DE RIBERA, PIETRO. The **Capitano della Verga** of Mdina, 1482–84, in 1486 he was an ambassador. He married onna Anna di Antiocha and they had two daughters, Beatrice and Catalina.

RICCARI, GIULIO. He was the **Capitano della Verga** of Mdina from 1399.

RINALDUS. By tradition, he was the bishop of Malta from 1122. He took over from Bishop **Gwanni** and saw the continuation of the construction of the Cathedral Church in Mdina. However recent historians argue that he was part of a list of Norman 'bishops' invented by early modern historians. The story of the Muslim plot to kill the Christians in Malta – traditionally dated to 1127 – may also have been an invention of early modern writers. Roger II of Sicily did sent soldiers into Malta in 1127 to ensure the strengthening of Norman rule over the island.

DE ROHAN-POLDUC, EMANUEL (1725–1797). He was the Grand Master of the Knights Hospitaller (Knights of Malta) from 1775 until his death in 1797. Born on 18 April 1725 at La Mancha, Spain, he was from an influential French noble family, and was at the Court at Parma and then in London, before being appointed the Order's Ambassador to Emperor Francis I of Austria. He succeeded Francisco Ximenes de Texada who had been unpopular. During his reign, Grand Master de Rohan improved the defences of Malta with St. Lucian's Tower was renamed for Rohan. He died on 14 July 1797 at Valletta, and was buried at St. John's Co-Cathedral.

References: Michael Galea, *Grand Master Emanuel de Rohan 1775–1797*, Valletta: privately published, 1996; Frank Ventura, 'Grand Master De Rohan's astronomical observatory', *Melita Historica* vol 10, no 3 (1990), pp. 245–55.

ROJAS DE PORTALRUBIO, MARTÍN (1512–1577). A member of the Sovereign Military Hospitaller Order of St. John of Jerusalem, he was born in Toledo, Spain, and was the bishop of Malta from 5 November 1572, ordained on 9 November, and remained in office until his death on 19 March 1577. It was during his time as bishop that St. John's Co-Cathedral in Valletta was constructed but this was not the residence of the bishop of Malta until the 1820s when the bishops (and later archbishops) maintained their principal residences at Mdina, and another at Valletta.

ROMAN MDINA. The Romans took control of Malta in 218 BC during the Second Punic War, and it is recorded that Hamilcar, son of Gisco, had a Carthaginian garrison of some 2,000 soldiers and it was he who surrendered Malta to the Romans. However it was not until 21 BC that they started to enlarge the settlement at Mdina which was three times the size of the present city. The main city on the island is described in the works of Cicero, Livy and Diodorus who spoke of the stately buildings. The Greek geographer Ptolemy (AD c90–168) also mentions that there were four centres on the island, one of which was the city of Melita from which the island gained its name. As recently as 1647, the Maltese historian Giovanni Francesco Abela (1582–1655) mentioned the Roman marble columns and statues in the streets and a surviving temple dedicated to Apollo. The Museum of Roman Antiquities in **Rabat**, constructed in the 1920s, holds many of the Roman artefacts discovered in Mdina.

Cicero mentions a few prominent Maltese with whom he had some connections. Given the importance of Mdina during Roman times, it is possible that they might have hailed from the city. Diodorus Melitensis – Diodorus 'the Maltese' had moved to Sicily where he became involved in a dispute with Caius Verres, the unscrupulous governor who was later charged with his actions against the Sicilians. There was also Aristotelis Melitensis (Aulus

Licinius), another friend of Cicero. The clash between Cicero and Verres is described by Cicero in his *Orations*, and forms the basis of Robert Harris's novel, *Imperium* (2006). It is recorded that in AD 535 Malta passed to the Byzantine Empire.

Some of the filming of *Gladiator* (2000) was shot at Fort Riscasoli (formerly St. Elmo Barracks), with one scene being shot in a square in Mdina.

References: Thomas Ashby & G. McN. Rushforth, 'Roman Malta', *The Journal of Roman Studies* vol 5 (1915), pp. 23–30; Anthony Bonanno, *Roman Malta: the archaeological heritage of the Maltese Islands*, Valletta: World Confederation of Salesian Past Pupils of Don Bosco, 1992; Tancred Gouder, *The mosaic pavements in the Museum of Roman Antiquities at Rabat, Malta*, Malta: Department of Museums, 1983; Diana Landau (ed.), *Gladiator: The Making of the Ridley Scott Epic*, New York: Newmarket Press, 2000, pp. 76–89; Denis de Lucca, *Mdina: A History of Its Urban Space and Architecture*, Valletta: Said International, 1995, Chapter 1; Neil Wilson, *Malta*, Melbourne: Lonely Planet Publications, 2000, pp. 130–31.

RUGGERIUS (RUGGERIO) of CEFALÙ. By tradition, he was the bishop of Malta in 1251, being at the **Cathedral Church** in Mdina for his short time as bishop.

RULL, BARTOLOMEO (1691–1769). Born at Pollensa, Spain, he was an ordained priest of the Sovereign Military Hospitaller Order of St. John of Jerusalem, on 6 March 1718. He was appointed the bishop of Malta on 19 December 1757, ordained on 7 May 1758, and installed on 27 June of that year, remaining in office until his death on 19 February 1769. He was also Grand Prior of the Order of St. John.

– S –

ST. AGATHA'S CHAPEL. Located on **Triq Villegaignon**, it was built in 1417 but was damaged during the **earthquake** of 1693, and rebuilt in 1694 with **Lorenzo Gafà** drawing up a slightly different design. It commemorates St. Agatha, one of the three patron saints of Mdina. According to legend, she fled to Malta from Sicily during a period of persecution by the Romans under their Emperor (Trajan) Decius – and also to escape the advances of the **Roman** governor of Sicily. She may have sought refuge in the catacombs in **Rabat**. Certainly she returned to Sicily where she was thrown into prison and tortured, with her breasts cut off with shears. The current chapel has an altarpiece designed by Giuseppe D'Arena in the seventeenth century. A special mass is held on 5 February each year commemorating the day on which St. Agatha died.

References: Richard England and Conrad Thake, *Mdina: Citadel of Memory*, Malta: Atlantis, 1995, pp. 42–43; John Manduca, *Tourist Guide to City of Mdina*, Malta: Progress Press, 1975, p. 17; Edward Sammut, *The Monuments of Mdina*, Malta: Progress Press Co. Ltd, 1967, p. 18.

DE SAINT-JAILLE, DIDIER (d. 1536). He was the Grand Master of the Knights Hospitaller (Knights of Malta) being elected in 1535 to succeed **Piero de Ponte**. He immediately made his way to Malta but died in 1536 before he reached the island. He was succeeded by **Juan de Homedes y Coscon**.

References: Victor Mallia-Milanes & Louis J. Scerri, *An Uneasy Partnership: Malta 1530–1565*, Mdina: Midsea Books, 1985.

ST. LUKE. One of the Four Evangelists and the author of the Gospel According to St. Luke, as well as Acts of the Apostles, by tradition he was a physician from Antioch, although many modern scholars doubt this. He was certainly a good friend of the Apostle Paul (later **St. Paul**), and may have been on Paul's ship that wrecked off the coast of Malta as he later wrote, 'And when we came to Rome …' (Acts 28:16). By tradition he died aged 84 in about AD 150 in the city of Thebes in Greece. A painting of the

St. Agatha's Chapel
Photograph © robert lerich / Fotolia.com

Virgin Mary reputedly by St. Luke is held at the **Cathedral Church** in Mdina.

ST. NICHOLAS' CHAPEL. This chapel, located on St. Nicholas Street, close to **Greek's Gate**, was originally built in 1550 and then rebuilt in 1692 just before the **earthquake** of 1693. This area was not a part of the renewal program of the city by **Manoel de Vilhena**. It has long been somewhat dilapidated and used as a storage space by the **Cathedral**.

References: Richard England and Conrad Thake, *Mdina: Citadel of Memory*, Malta: Atlantis, 1995, pp. 106–07; John Manduca, *Tourist Guide to City of Mdina*, Malta: Progress Press, 1975, p. 43.

ST. NICHOLAS COLLEGE, MTARFA. This is one of the major state secondary schools for children from Mdina. The building was originally the Mtarfa Royal Artillery and Naval Hospital for which the foundation stone was laid by General Sir Leslie Rundle, the Governor of Malta, on 6 January 1915. It was formally opened in 1920 although it was in use before this. It closed in 1978 and a boys' secondary school opened in 1987 and has also been named after Sir Terri Zammit (1864–1935), a prominent scientific researcher. It has about 380 boys, aged between eleven and 15.

References: St. Nicholas College, http://schoolnet.gov.mt/mtarfasecondary/.

ST. PAUL. The Apostle Paul, famously converted to Christianity on the road to Damascus in Syria, became a prominent preacher and early Christian missionary. He travelled extensively around the eastern Mediterranean,

St. Paul on the Cathedral Church, Mdina.
Photograph © JackF / Fotolia.com

and wrote a number of letters to Christians in some of the important cities. However in AD 57 he was arrested in Jerusalem and held in prison for two years. A **Roman** citizen, he appealed for judgement by the Roman Emperor and this saw him taken to Rome.

Journeying by sea, and possibly travelling with Luke (later **St. Luke**), his boat was shipwrecked on Malta. By tradition when he arrived on Malta, he and other survivors from the shipwreck built a bonfire to warm themselves. Paul picked up a bundle of sticks and threw them onto the fire – but this included, by accident, a snake which bit Paul. Paul suffered no ill-effects and this was regarded as his first miracle on the island. Paul and his companions then went to Mdina where they met with Publius (later **St. Publius**), the Roman governor – although some recent archaeologists have suggested that it might have been at the Roman villa uncovered near Bugibba where the seventeenth century church, San Pawl Milqi (St. Paul Welcomed) is located.

St. Paul in Malta from *Picture Stories from the Bible* (Leicester, UK, 1943).

PAUL HEALS MANY; IS SHOWERED WITH GIFTS WHEN HE SAILS.

Acts 28:9-21

The father of Publius was suffering from fever and dysentery, and he was cured by Paul with the result that Publius converted to Christianity. Paul then left for Rome where he remained for most of the rest of his life, and killed in Rome in about AD 67, during the persecution by the Emperor Nero.

References: Warren G. Berg, *Historical Dictionary of Malta*, Lanham, Md.: The Scarecrow Press, 1995, pp. 99–100; Mario Buhagiar, 'St. Paul's Shipwreck and Early Christianity in Malta', *The Catholic Historical Review* vol 93, No. 1 (January 2007), pp. 1–16; H.V. Morton, *In the Steps of St. Paul*, London: Rich & Cowan, 1936, pp. 377–82; Malcolm Muggeridge and Alec Vidler, *Paul – Envoy Extraordinary*, London: William Collins, 1972; George H. Musgrave, *Friendly Refuge: a study of St. Paul's Shipwreck and His Stay in Malta*, Heathfield, Sussex, UK: Heathfield Publications, 1979; R. Martin Pope, *On Roman Road with St. Paul*, London: Epworth Press, 1939, p. 126; Robert Farrugia Randon, John Azzopardi & Joseph Joseph Calleja, *St. Paul: His Life, The shipwreck Tradition and Culture in Malta and Elsewhere*, Malta: privately published, 2000; Jean Scott Rogers, *In Search of Paul*, London: Arthur Barker, 1964; Justo Pérez de Urbel, *Saint Paul: The Apostle of the Gentiles*, London: Elek Books, 1958, pp. 350–52.

ST. PAUL OUTSIDE THE WALLS. This church known in Italian as 'San Paolo fuor le Mura' is also known as the Collegiate Church of St. Paul in **Rabat**. By tradition it dates back to about AD 60 when Paul (later **St. Paul**) was on the island of Malta and started converting people in the grotto which became a part of St. Paul's Catacombs. Although outside the current city of Mdina, it was within what had been the Roman city – with the earliest written record of the Church dating back to 1372.

References: John Azzopardi, 'St. Paul Outside the Walls at Rabat, Malta', *Treasures of Malta* vol 9, no 1 (No 25) (Christmas 2002), p. 43–49.

ST. PAUL SQUARE. *See* **Pjazza San Pawl**.

ST. PAUL STREET. *See* **San Pawl, Triq**.

SAN PAWL, TRIQ (St Paul Street). This street is in Mdina off **Pjazza San Pawl**. In 1960 the only public **telephone** box in the city was located in this street.

ST. PUBLIUS (33-c.125). The first Maltese Saint, he was the **Roman** chief of the island. After Paul of Tarsus (later **St. Paul**) was shipwrecked on the island, he was brought to Publius who, by tradition, lived in Mdina, his father suffering from dysentery. There, according to the Acts of the Apostles:

In the same quarters were possessions of the chief man of the island, whose name was Publius; who received us, and lodged us three days courteously. And it came to pass, that the father of Publius lay sick of a fever and of a bloody flux: to whom Paul entered in, and prayed, and laid his hands on him, and healed him. So when this was done, others also, which had diseases in the island, came, and were healed: Who also honoured us with many honours; and when we departed, they laded us with such things as were necessary. [Acts xxviii 7–10].

After Paul left, Publius embraced Christianity and Malta became Christian and celebrates the fact that it was the first nation in the world to become Christian. By tradition Publius was the bishop of Malta from 60 to 67, and then moved to Greece where, at a great age, he was martyred in Athens, Greece, in AD c.125, during the persecutions of Emperor Hadrian. He is a patron saint of Malta, as well as the town of Floriana, and 21 January is his feast day. He is the eponym of **Pjazza San Publiju** in Mdina. A large Roman villa and farm was found on the hillside above Burmarrad, some 2 kms south of Bugibba, and 6 kms from Mdina. Some historians have argued that this may have been the residence of Publius and where he met and entertained Paul – not at Mdina.

References: H.V. Morton, *In the Steps of St. Paul*, London: Rich & Cowan, 1936, p. 380.

ST. PUBLIUS SQUARE. *See* **Pjazza San Publiju**.

ST. ROCH STREET. *See* **Santu Rokku, Triq**.

SANTU ROKKU, TRIQ (St Roch Street). This street runs from **Triq Villegaignon** eastwards until **Triq is-Sur** (Bastion/s Street). It gives its name to the **Chapel of St. Roque**, with the **Cathedral Church** also being located on this street.

SAMMUT, EDWARD (1912–1984). An historian, he was born on 14 April 1912 in Valletta and educated at St. Aloysius College and then the Royal University of Malta. Going to Rome in 1938 to study at the University of Rome, he returned to Malta at the outbreak of World War II, and was conscripted into the Royal Malta Artillery. After the war he began practising law and served in Malta, and then in Benghazi, Libya. Back in Malta he became the art correspondent and also the parliamentary reporter for the *Times of Malta*. His interest in local history saw him write a large number of articles and in 1960 completed *The Monuments of Mdina*. In 1976 he completed his MA thesis in History, *The Life and Works of Melchior Gafà*, at the University of Malta. He died on 17 December 1984.

References: *Dr Edward Sammut (1912–1984): ad memoriam, with a bibliography of his writings*, Mdina: Friends of the Cathedral Museum, 1985; Edward Sammut, *The Monuments of Mdina: the ancient capital of Malta and its treasures*, Valletta: Progress Press Co Ltd, 1960, reviewed by Joseph Cassar-Pullicino, *Melita Historica* vol 3, no 1 (1960), pp. 70; Michael J. Schiavone, *Dictionary of Maltese Biographies*, Malta: pubblikazzjonijiet Indipendenza, 2009, vol 2, pp. 1389–90. Portrait courtesy Michael J. Schiavone.

SANT, GIOVANNI FRANCESCO. He was a treasurer of the commission established by the French in 1798 to run Malta during their occupation of the island. He was then the **Capitano della Verga** of Mdina, 1801–14, having been ennobled by Grand Master Ferdinand von Hompesch. He was appointed Presidente della Congregazione delle Povere Inferme for twelve years up to the first decade of British rule.

References: John Montalto, *The Nobles of Malta, 1530–1800*, Valletta: Midsea Books, 1979, p. 35, 113 n85, 119, 351, 353.

SANT, PUBLIO MARIA DEI CONTI (1779–1864). The bishop of Malta from November 1847 until his retirement on 3 December 1857, he was born on 26 August 1779 in Valletta, the son of Conte Gio Francesco Sant, the Capitano di Verga, and his wife Baroness Clara Felecita Bonnici Cassia. Educated at the Monza Imperial College in Milan, he returned to Malta and was ordained priest on 21 December 1805. Four years later he was appointed as canon of the Cathedral Chapter and then on 1 October 1817 was appointed the titular bishop of Larada. On 28 June 1818 in the **Cathedral Church** in Mdina he was consecrated bishop of Larada by Bishop Ferdinando Mattei. After the separation of the Bishopric of Malta from the Metropolitan of Palermo in 1831, Publius Sant was made honorary vicar general of the diocese of Malta, succeeding Bishop **Francesco Saverio Caruana** in 1847. Less than a year after becoming bishop, then with the approval of the Holy See, he was able to declare the Virgin Mary as the special patron saint of Malta. In ill-health, he retired in December 1857 and died on 29 October 1864, and was buried at Mdina Cathedral.

References: Michael J. Schiavone, *Dictionary of Maltese Biographies*, Malta: pubblikazzjonijiet Indipendenza, 2009, vol 2, p. 1408. Portrait courtesy Michael J. Schiavone.

SANT CASSIA, PAUL (1954–). An anthropologist, he was born on 24 October 1954 at Mdina, and educated at St. Aloysius College and the University of Malta, before proceeding to England to continue his studies at Christ's College, Cambridge. During his time at Cambridge he was a research fellow and a consultant to the Australian Institute of Multicultural Affairs. In 1986 he was appointed director of studies in social anthropology at Selwyn College, Cambridge, and director of studies in anthropology at Trinity College, 1986–91; and also assistant curator at the University Museum of Archaeology and Anthropology in Cambridge. A Reader in anthropology at Durham University, he is head of the department of anthropological sciences and chairman of the Mediterranean Institute, University of Malta. He has written extensively on anthropology in Cyprus.

References: Paul Sant Cassia, *Bodies of Evidence: Burial, Memory and the Recovery of Missing Persons in Cyprus*, Oxford: Berghahn, 2005; Paul Sant Cassia, 'Tradition, Tourism and Memory in Malta', *The Journal of the Royal Anthropological Institute* vol 5, No. 2 (June 1999), pp. 247–63; Paul Sant Cassia, 'Guarding Each Other's Dead, Mourning One's Own: The Problem of Missing Persons and Missing Pasts in Cyprus', in D. Theodossopoulos (ed), *When Greeks think about Turks*, London & New York: Routledge, 2007, pp. 111–28; Michael J. Schiavone, *Dictionary of Maltese Biographies*, Malta: pubblikazzjonijiet Indipendenza, 2009, vol 2, pp. 1409–10.

SANT-MANDUCA, PETER DEI CONTI (1966–). A member of the Nationalist Party, he is the current Mayor of Mdina, holding this position from 2003, succeeding **Mario Galea Testaerrata**. He was born on 15 January 1966 at St. Julians, the older son of Giovanni Maria Sant-Manduca and his wife Louisette Bonnici-Mallia. Peter grew up in Mdina and was educated at St. Joseph's School, De La Salle College and St. Aloysious College, completing a degree from the National Industrial council for the Flour Milling Industry. In 1988 he became a director and senior partner of the St. Publius flour mills, and in the following year he qualified as a miller. In 1991 he became managing director and senior partner of San Pedro International Ltd, and in the following year became the senior partner of Mdina Bastions Ltd, and in 1996 became senior partner of Mdina Holdings Ltd. In 2000 he was elected to Mdina council, and was elected mayor in 2003, re-elected in 2006, and re-elected again in 2009. From 2003 to 2008 he was the deputy chairman of the Mdina Rehabilitation Committee. He is married to Alexandra (née Apap Bologna), and they have two daughters: Alexia and Christina.

DI SANTA COLOMBA, FRANCESCO. He was the **Capitano della Verga** of Mdina, 1406–08.

SAULI, BANDINELLO (d. 1518). Born in c1494 at Genoa, he was from the son of Pasquale Sauli and Mariola Giustiniana Longhi. He was the bishop of Malta from 5 October 1506 to 1509 when he was nominated as bishop of Gerace, a post he held until 19 November 1517. On 10 March 1511 he was made cardinal deacon by Pope Julius II and participated in the papal conclave of 1513 that elected Pope Leo X. He died on 29 March 1518 at Monterotondo, and was buried at Santa Maria in Trastevere.

SCERRI. *See also* **Xerri**.

SCERRI, CAMILLE. Born in c.1962, and a schoolteacher at St. Nicholas College, Mgarr Primary, she was elected to the Mdina local council in 2009 for the Nationalist Party. She is married with one son.

SCIBERRAS TESTAERRATA, D. PASQUALE (1735–1812). The **Capitano della Verga** of Mdina, 1775–97, he was the Baron of Castel Cicciano. The son of Michele Sceberras and Clara Testaferrata, in 1755 he married Lucrezia Dorrell. This made him the brother-in-law of Gio Francesco Dorrell who was involved in a major investigation into the establishment in Freemasonry in Malta.

References: John Montalto, *The Nobles of Malta, 1530–1800*, Valletta: Midsea Books, 1979, p. 344.

SCICLUNA, CARMELO (1800–1888). He was the bishop of Malta from

15 March 1875 until his death on 12 July 1888. Born on 3 August 1800 in Qormi, he studied for the priesthood and was educated at the University of Malta. Ordained on 18 December 1824, he served under Bishop **Francis Caruana** and was nominated as canon of the Cathedral Chapter, and later as vicar general. On 11 April 1875 he was consecrated bishop at St. John's Co-Cathedral, and made his formal solemn entry into the **Cathedral Church** in Mdina on 7 June of the same year. Named as a count by Pope Pius IX in July, he died on 12 July 1888.

References: Michael J. Schiavone, *Dictionary of Maltese Biographies*, Malta: pubblikazzjonijiet Indipendenza, 2009, vol 2, p. 1458. Portrait courtesy Michael J. Schiavone.

SCICLUNA, CHARLES JUDE (1959–). The Archbishop of Malta, he was born on 15 May 1959 in Toronto, Canada, his parents being Maltese. They moved to Qormi, Malta, when he was eleven months old, and he went to school and attended the major seminary there. Studying civil law at the University of Malta, he graduated in 1984 and was ordained a priest on 11 July 1986. He then studied at the Pontifical Gregorian University in Rome, graduating with the Doctorate in Canon Law in 1991.

Returning to Malta, he was Professor of Pastoral Theology and Canon Law at the local Faculty of Theology and Vice-Rector of the Major Seminary of the Archdiocese. He was also involved in parochial work for the parishes of St. Gregory the Great in Sliema, and Transfiguration in Iklin, as well as being chaplain to the Convent of St. Catherine. He was named as the auxiliary bishop of Malta in October 2012, and was ordained on 24 November. On 25 February 2015 his appointment as Archbishop of Malta was announced, and he was installed on 21 March.

Photograph by NickGeorge1993, Wikipedia Commons.

SCOUT MOVEMENT. Because of the small population of Mdina, there has never been a Boy Scout troop based in the city. Boys from Mdina have long been members of the **Rabat** Troop which dates back to 15 September 1913 when the Malta Boy Scouts Association was formally registered at the Imperial Scout Headquarters in London. At that time there were 20 boys in the troop – it is not known whether any of the initial members were from Mdina. Many scouts from all over Malta have, obviously, been to Mdina, as have visiting scouts from other countries when in Malta for Jamborees or exchanges. When Sir Robert Baden-Powell arrived in Malta in February 1933, he, his wife, and their daughter Heather all went to Mdina, with the Baden-Powells returning for another official visit to Mdina in April 1934. Robert Baden-Powell had been posted to Malta as military secretary and senior aide-de-camp to his uncle Sir Henry Smyth from 1890 to 1893. Yet another official visit by Baden-Powell in 1937 is commemorated on a Maltese postage stamp issued in 2007 on the 100th anniversary of the establishment of scouting in Malta. The boys from the Rabat Troop lead the **Mnarja** procession each June.

References: Tim Jeal, *Baden-Powell*, London: Hutchinson, 1989, pp. 143–48; J. A. Mizzi, *Scouting in Malta: An Illustrated History*, Malta: The Author, 1989, p. 40, 143, 152.

DE LA SENGLE, CLAUDE (1494–1557). He was the Grand Master of the Knights Hospitaller (Knights of Malta) from 1553 until his death in 1557. Originally from France, he fought against Dragut in the Mediterranean, serving at Djerba and Tripoli. When he was appointed Grand Master of the Order of Malta, succeeding **Juan de Homedes y Coscon**, he continued the work of his predecessor in strengthening the defences in Malta. He expanded Fort St. Michel and completed the work on Fort St. Elmo to help protect Malta from naval attack. He also developed Senglea which was named after him, and which still uses his coat of arms. Claude de la Sengle died on 18 August 1557 at Mdina, and was buried in the chapel of Fort St. Angelo. He was succeeded by **Jean de la Valette**. His heart was later buried in the Church of the Annunciation at **Rabat**.

References: Victor Mallia-Milanes & Louis J. Scerri, *An Uneasy Partnership: Malta 1530–1565*, Mdina: Midsea Books, 1985; Victor Mallia-Milanes, *Venice and Hospitaller Malta 1530–1798: aspects of a relationship*, Marsa: Publishers Enterprises Group, 1992; H.J.A. Sire, *The Knights of Malta*, New Haven: Yale University Press, 1994, p. 68.

DE SEPÚLVEDA, JUAN. The bishop of Tui, Spain, from 27 June 1505, he was then bishop of Malta from 14 July 1514 until his retirement in 1516. He was then appointed the titular archbishop of Corinh.

DE SERRANO, RUGGIERO. The **Capitano della Verga** of Mdina, 1418–21, he was the second son of Angelo Serano and his wife Perna Merlo. His older brother Tomassina was a juror in 1405 and again in 1416. Ruggiero de Serrano married Clara Sillato and they had a son Giacomo, and two daughters Antonia and Lara. Antonio married Giacomo la Rocca who was the ambassador of the Università Dei Giurati in 1438.

SIEGE OF 1551. In 1551, the Turks under Dragut attacked Malta some 14 years before the **Great Siege** of 1565, bu with a much smaller force than the later attack. On this occasion, the Turks decided to attack Mdina first. As the Turks approached the city, many people from nearby farms and villages sought refuge behind the **city walls**. As the Turks approached, some civilians were worried that the city walls were not able to withstand an attack, and fled the city. Nearly all of them were captured and killed by the Turks. The city, however, did survive the attack, and possibly because of this when the Turks attacked again in 1565 they chose not to capture Mdina which was a disastrous decision for them. The attack on Mdina forms part of Dorothy Dunnett's novel, *The Disorderly Knights* (1966).

SLAVERY. During the rule of the Carthaginians and the Romans, there were many slaves on the island, and it seems likely that there were also many slaves during Arab rule. From the eleventh century, the Sicilian-Aragonese rulers also had many slaves, mainly captured Turks, and the Knights of St. John continued to have Muslim slaves. Dragut when he attacked Gozo in 1551 took away most of the population as slaves. And some of the knights including Jean de la Valette, had also spent some time as slaves of the Turks. In the seventeenth and eighteenth centuries, it has been estimated that slaves made up some 5% of the population. Of these, it has been calculated that some 40–45% were Moors with many others being Turks, Africans and Jews. When the French occupied Malta in 1798, they abolished slavery on the island.

References: Anthony Luttrell, 'Christian Slaves in Malta, 1271', *Melita Historica* vol 9, no 4 (1987), pp. 381–83; Anthony Luttrell, 'Slaves and captives on Malta: 1053/4 and 1091', *Hyphen* vol 7, no 2 (1992), pp. 97–104; Godfrey Wettinger, 'Coron captives in Malta: An episode in the history of slave-dealing', *Melita Historica* vol 2, no 4 (1959), pp. 216–23.

SPITERI, PAUL (1960–   ). Born in 1960 in Valletta, he was educated at Our Lady of Pillar School and Nazzar Secondary School, then at Upper Secondary School, Valletta. He studied management at the Maastricht School of Management and at Heriot-Watt University, working in a number of catering and tourism related businesses. The executive secretary of Mdina Local Council, he is married to Sabine (née Gehring), and they have a daughter, Tamira.

DE STANIGA, PIETRO. He was the **Capitano della Verga** of Mdina, 1521–22.

STIEFNU. By tradition, he was the bishop of Malta from 1154, and was said to have been the probable successor of Bishop **Rinaldus** as bishop and under his oversight it was claimed that much of the work on the Cathedral Church in Mdina was completed.

STRICKLAND, GERALD PAUL JOSEPH CAJETAN CARMEL ANTHONY MARTIN, BARON STRICKLAND (1861–1940). The prime minister of Malta from 1927 to 1932, he was the oldest son of Commander Walter Strickland (1824–1868), of the Royal Navy, and his wife, Donna Maria Aloysia Paula Bonici-Monpalao (1834–1907), daughter of Cavaliere Peter Paul Bonici of Malta, and niece and heir of Sir Nicholas Sceberras Bologna, fifth Count della Catena in Malta. Born on 24 May 1861 in Malta, he was educated at St. Mary's College, near Birmingham, England, and the Jesuit College of Mondragone, near Rome,

Italy, and then proceeded to Trinity College, Cambridge, and was called to the Bar by the Inner Temple. He returned to Malta and in 1886 was elected to the Maltese Council of Government. Helping draw up the country's constitution with Fortunato Mizzi, it resulted in the start of representative government in Malta and after some years there, Strickland was posted to the Leeward Islands and then to Australia (as Governor of Tasmania, 1904–08; Governor of Western Australia, 1909–13; and Governor of New South Wales, 1913–17), returning and running *The Times of Malta* as well as being elected a member of the British Parliament in 1924. His Anglo-Maltese Party merged with the Maltese Constitutional Party to form the Constitutional Party with Strickland becoming Prime Minister from 9 August 1927, a position he held until 21 June 1932. He had been preceded by Sir Ugo Pasquale Mifsud (1889–1942), who then went on to succeed him. Sir Gerald helped draw up plans to defend Malta in case of attach and died on 22 August 1940 at the Villa Bologna. He was buried on the following day at the **Cathedral** Church, Mdina.

Lord Strickland's daughter Mabel ran *The Times of Malta* for many years. Elected to the Maltese Parliament, and also a campaigner for many years, she was frequently battling with the Labour government of Dom Mintoff. When Mabel Strickland died on 29 November 1988, a Requiem Mass was held for her in Mdina Cathedral on 1 December. She was buried in the family vault at the Cathedral, and was commemorated on a postage stamp issued in Malta on 24 April 1996.

References: Joan Alexander, *Mabel Strickland*, Malta: Progress Press Co., 1996; Warren G. Berg, *Historical Dictionary of Malta*, Lanham, Md.: The Scarecrow Press, 1995, pp. 119–20; Joan Carnwath, 'Strickland, Gerald Paul Joseph Cajetan Carmel Antony Martin, Baron Strickland (1861–1940)', *Oxford Dictionary of National Biography*, Oxford University Press, 2004; Harrison Smith and Adrianus Koster, *Lord Strickland: servant of*

Mdina during World War II.

STROLOGO, ERIC REGINALD CHARLES ALEXANDER (c.1920–2008). A British officer in the Royal Artillery in World War II, he was posted to Malta and worked in Mdina. His father, Reginald Dello Strologo ran a tobacco plantation in Alexandria, Egypt. Eric was involved in an incident in Mdina on 31 July 1943 in which he found a young teenager loitering around his truck in the square outside the **Cathedral Church**. He then took the boy to Ta'Qali where he was locked in a cell. The parents alerted the police and Strologo was eventually charged and found guilty by three judges of kidnapping, and sentenced to 13 months with hard labour, the event was covered in *Time Magazine*. The matter was taken to the Privy Council in London, and after a few months he was released. Serving in the British Army of the Rhine, he later married Marianne Savica and they had a daughter Jacqueline, born on 26 August 1947 in Germany. He later worked for the Royal Automobile Club and died on 2 November 2008 at Riocaud, France.

References: Anne Agius Ferrante, *No Strangers in the Silent City*, Valletta: Andrew Rupert Publishing, 1992, pp. 108–12.

– T –

TELEPHONE SERVICES. Telephone services in Malta started in 1882 and these were initially run by the Malta Telephone Company, a private business. In 1933 it was taken over by the government. Much of the network was wrecked in the Axis bombing of Malta in **World War II** in which the telephone exchange was totally destroyed. However the service was rebuilt with an automated service from 1957. Mdina has always had good telephone connections with the rest of the island running from the **Rabat** telephone exchange, with Mdina **Cathedral Church** having the number Rabat 130. There was one public telephone box located in **Triq San Pawl** – this telephone was mentioned by Quentin Hughes in his 'Memories of Mdina' in *Mdina: Citadel of Memory*.

References: Richard England and Conrad Thake, *Mdina: Citadel of Memory*, Malta: Atlantis, 1995, p. 117.

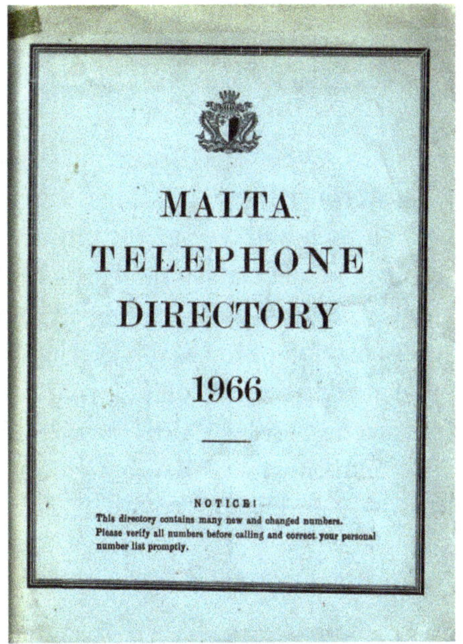

MALTA
TELEPHONE
DIRECTORY
1966

NOTICE!
This directory contains many new and changed numbers.
Please verify all numbers before calling and correct your personal number list promptly.

British-style telephone box in Mdina
Photograph © robert lerich / Fotolia.com

TELEVISION. The first television transmissions in Malta were in 1959 with Conte Consiglio d'Amato running the business which sold the first televisions in the country. There are now five countrywide free-to-view channels: TVM, One Television, NET Television, Smash Television, and Favourite Channel. There are also many other channels available by cable. Because of its geographical location, there has always been good reception for the free-to-view channels.

TEMPLE OF APOLLO. This famous **Roman** temple dedicated to the God Apollo, was located in what is now **Triq Villegaignon**. A Latin inscription was discovered in 1774 which referred to the temple which disappeared during the Arab period. It seems likely that the temple was raised on a podium and had a large gilded statue of Apollo. In early March 2002 during excavations to bury electricity cables, parts of the wall of the temple were uncovered. Professor Dennis de Lucca, Dean of the Faculty of Architecture at the University of Malta and the chairman of the **Mdina Rehabilitation Project**, said that this discovery was the most important finding made in three sites in Mdina.

References: Antonio Annetto Caruana, *Ancient Pagan tombs and Christian cemeteries in the Islands of Malta*, Malta: Government Printing Office, 1898; Antonio Annetto Caruana, *Ancient pottery from the ancient Pagan tombs and Christian cemeteries in the Islands of Malta*, Malta: Government Printing Office, 1899; Michael Testa, 'New find at Mdina most important so far in old capital', *The Times of Malta* 19 March 2002.

TENNIS. When the British maintained the Connaught Hospital (now the **Magisterial Palace**) in Mdina, they built a tennis court in the **Mdina Ditch** – in an area adjacent to the city walls. Initially it was only to be used by the doctors and staff at the hospital but gradually local school children were allowed to play there on Sunday mornings. When the hospital closed, the **Rabat** section of the Malta Playing Fields Association took over the running of what became the Malta Playing Fields Association Rabat Tennis Club. The first meeting of the Malta Lawn Tennis Association was held on 5 September 1966 and tennis was played there for many years until the site was closed in May 2012 amid many protests.

References: Stanley Vassallo, 'Battles at Mdina ditch', *The Times* (5 June 2012).

TERRAZZA, DIEGO. He was the **Capitano della Verga** of Mdina, 1414–15.

TERRAZZA, GIOVANNI LUPO. He was the **Capitano della Verga** of Mdina, 1415–17.

TERRIBILE, TONY (1945–). An author of many works on ecclesiastical history in Malta, Tony Terribile was born on 26 May 1945 in Sliema, and educated at Mount Carmel College, St. Venera. He was written 18 volumes in a series 'Treasures of Maltese Churches', a bilingual guide to the churches of Malta. He is also a member of staff of the **Cathedral Museum**, Mdina.

References: Michael J. Schiavone, *Dictionary of Maltese Biographies*, Malta: pubblikazzjonijiet Indipendenza, 2009, vol 2, pp. 1530–31.

TESTAFERRATA, FABRIZIO. The **Capitano della Verga** of Mdina, 1702–05, he was the son of Paolo Testaferrata and his wife Beatrice (née Cassia), inheriting the title of Baron of Castel Cicciano.

References: John Montalto, *The Nobles of Malta, 1530–1800*, Valletta: Midsea Books, 1979, p. 43.

TESTAFERRATA, D. MARIO. He was the **Capitano della Verga** of Mdina, 1689–92.

TESTAFERRATA, MARIO GALEA. He was the Mayor of Mdina from 2000, succeeding **George Attard**, and was in office until 2003 when he was succeeded by **Peter Dei Conti Sant-Manduca**.

TESTAFERRATA DE ROBERTIS, GIACOMO. The **Capitano della Verga** of Mdina, 1636–38, he was the son of Gian Tomaso Testaferrata. A noble of the Holy Roman Empire, he married Teodora Bonnici and they had four children: Mario, born in 1654; Camilla; Leonora; and Maria Rose.

References: John Montalto, *The Nobles of Malta, 1530–1800*, Valletta: Midsea Books, 1979, p. 102.

TESTAFERRATA-GHAXAQ, ALFIO (1911–1988). A nobleman and numismatist, he was born on 8 August 1911 the son of Senator Daniele Testaferrata-Bonici-Ghaxaq, 6th Baron of Qlejja, and 7th Marquis of San Vincenzo Ferri, and Marquis Testaferrata, and his wife the Noble Agnes Galea-Testaferrata del Baroni di San Marciano. He was educated in England at Stonyhurst College, and University College, Oxford. When his father died in 1945, he succeeded to his father's titles, and was recognised by the Committee of Privileges of the Maltese Nobility as the 8th Marquis of San Vincenzo Ferreri. He died on 8 January 1988.

References: Michael J. Schiavone, *Dictionary of Maltese Biographies*, Malta: pubblikazzjonijiet Indipendenza, 2009, vol 2, p. 1536.

TEUMA, BALDASSARE. The **Capitano della Verga** of Mdina, 1686–89, he was the son of Dr Pietro Paolo Teuma and Giustina (née Castelletti). In 1674, Baldassare Teuma married Anastasia d'Anastasio and they had five children.

THAKE VASSALLO, CLARE (1964–). A lecturer in semiotics, she was born on 19 July 1964 in Sliema, and was educated at St. Dorothy's Convent, Mdina, and then studied at the University of Malta, graduating BA (Hons) in English literature and philosophy. She then moved to Italy to take up a scholarship from the Istituto Italiano di Cultura, completing her doctorate in semiotics at the University of Bologna. Her tutor was the famous writer Umberto Eco. Clare Thake Cassallo was a member of the Board of Directors of the Public Broadcasting Services in 2000–03, and again from 2007, being promoted to chair of the board in June 2008.

References: Michael J. Schiavone, *Dictionary of Maltese Biographies*, Malta: pubblikazzjonijiet Indipendenza, 2009, vol 2, p. 1538–39; Carmel Vassallo and Clare Thake Vassallo (eds), *The Communist Manifesto: Karl Marx's Legacy to Humanity*, Msida: University of Malta Press: 2003.

L-R: General Sir (Henry Macleod) Leslie Rundle GCB, GCV, KCMG, DS; Capt Theuma Castelletti, Queen Mary, Lady Rundle, King George V, The Most Noble Mary Screrras d'Amico-Inguanez.

T(H)EUMA CASTELLETTI, Contino JOSEPH (1881–1942). The Aide de Camp to the Governor of Malta, he was born in Mdina, the second son of Count Peter Paul Theuma Casterlletti and Teresa de Marchesi Mallia Tabone. He served in the King's Own Malta Regiment of Militia rising to the rank of major by 1921 when he retired. He then became involved in running a ceramics and pipe manufacture business located at his palace which was close to the aerodrome – and was destroyed during Axis bombing in **World War II**. He died on 23 October 1942 at his home in **Rabat**'s Saqqajja Square. He was buried at St. Domenic's Church, Rabat. His first wife, whom he married in 1901, was Maria Rachele Azopardi dei Baroni du Buleben. After her death, in 1941 he married Mary Fenech Cabott.

References: Michael J. Schiavone, *Dictionary of Maltese Biographies*, Malta: pubblikazzjonijiet Indipendenza, 2009, vol 2, p. 1540.

TOWER OF THE STANDARD. This tower, known in Italian as Torre dello Stendardo, is sometimes called the Signal Tower of the Standard. Located to the left of the Main Gate, just inside the walls of Mdina, it replaced the original beacon tower, Torre Mastra. On the top of this tower, a fire was lit to warn the rest of the island at times of an invasion of Malta. The current tower dates from the early sixteenth century and was used during the **Great Siege** of Malta in 1565.

The tower was later remodelled and the arms of Grand Master António **Manoel de Vilhena** (r. 1722–36) were added. In recent years the tower has served as a **police** station on account of its location close to the **Main Gate**.

References: Can John Azzopardi, *Mdina, Rabat, Mosta*, Terni, Italy: Plurigraf, 1988, p. 12; Richard England and Conrad Thake, *Mdina: Citadel of Memory*, Malta: Atlantis, 1995, pp. 34–35; John Manduca, *Tourist Guide to City of Mdina*, Malta: Progress Press, 1975, p. 15; Edward Sammut, *The Monuments of Mdina*, Malta: Progress Press Co. Ltd, 1967, pp. 12–14.

de TRAFFORD, HUBERT EDMUND FRASER (1893–1974). Born on 27 November 1893, the son of Sir Humphrey de Trafford, 2nd Baronet, he was educated at Downside and served in World War I with the 1st Dragoons. He then moved to Malta where in 1927 he married Cecilia Strickland, daughter of 1st Baron Strickland of Sizergh Castle, Westmorland, and Villa Bologna, Malta. His daughter, Mary Roma de Trafford was married by Father Grahame Auchinleck to Philip James Gooding on 19 September 1964 at Mdina **Cathedral**. Hubert died in 1974 in Malta.

References: Marion Hill, *The Honeypot Killers*, Leighton Buzzard: Next Century Books, 2004, p. 231.

TRAJANU (TRAIANO). The bishop of Malta from 599 until around 603, he was at the old Christian Cathedral (on the site of the **Cathedral Church**) in Mdina and is the last known bishop before the Fatimid Arabs captured the island in 870. He was appointed by Pope Gregory I following his sacking of Lucillu. Because of the antagonims caused by the dismissal of his predecessor, Trajanu took with him, on the advice of the pope, four or five monks who helped him settle into the bishop's residence in Mdina.

References: Frederick Homes Dudden, *Gregory the Great: his place in history and thought,* London: Longmans, Green & Co., p. 386.

TRATTORIA AD 1530. *See* **Xara Palace**.

TURRENZI, ANTONIO. He was the **Capitano della Verga** of Mdina, 1629–33.

– U –

UNIVERSITÀ DEI GIURATI. This municipal body in Mdina consisted of the four men appointed as Giurati. They formed the Università which assisted the **Capitana Della Verga** in running the city, and also in administering the property of the **Cathedral Church**, the cumuli di carità (charity funds), and also the Hospital of Santo Spirito. It was formally recognised by the Parliament of Catania in Sicily in 1397. However with the arrival and installation of the Grand Masters, it was uncertain how this Università would operate. Grand Master **Juan de Homedes** decided to establish a new Università at Birgu which massively reduced the power of the body in Mdina.

References: John Montalto, *The Nobles of Malta, 1530–1800*, Valletta: Midsea Books, 1979, pp. 119–22.

UPTON, Sir THOMAS (d. 1551). An English knight who was elected to Turcopilier (cavalry commander) of the Knights of St. John on 5 November 1548, he was posted to Mdina during the Turkish attack on the city in 1551, and died in July 1551 fighting off the Turkish soldiers of Dragut. His use of horsemen was to lead to the cavalry being stationed at Mdina by the Knights of Malta during the **Great Siege** of 1565.

References: Denis de Lucca, *Mdina: A History of Its Urban Space and Architecture*, Valletta: Said International, 1995, p. 53; A. Mifsud, *Knights Hospitaller of the Ven. Tongue of England in Malta*, Malta: The Malta Herald, 1914, p. 149.

Mdina during World War II.

– V –

VASCO, VINCENZO. He was the **Capitano della Verga** of Mdina, 1545–48.

DE (LA) VALETTE, JEAN PARISOT (1495–1568). He was the Grand Master of the Knights Hospitaller (Knights of Malta) from 1557 until his death in 1568, and is one of the most famous Grand Masters. He came from a noble family from Quercy, in the south-west of France, his grandfather Bernard de Valette being a knight, and his father Guillot was a Chevalier de France, with some of the family having taken part in the Crusades.

Not much is known about the early life of de Valette but it is known that he fought in the siege of Rhodes in 1521. Seventeen years later there is a record of de Valette being sentenced to spend four months in a hole in the ground on Gozo after beating a layman and nearly killing him. He was then post to Tripoli where he spent two years and in 1541 he was captured by the Barbary pirates under Turgut Reis and made to toil as a galley slave for a year. In 1554 he was elected the Captain General of the galleys of the Hospitallers, and it was because of his skill and command of men during this time that he was elected in 1557 to succeed **Claude de la Sengle**.

Soon after taking over, Jean de Valette started work on strengthening the defences of Malta. This meant that he had to raise more funds and one of the methods he tried was to get the city of Mdina to contribute. Some of the local citizens protested and a petition was drawn and sent to King Phillip II of Spain. It was intercepted and a doctor called **Matthew Callus** and some others were arrested, with Callus found guilty of treason and executed.

De la Valette recognised that in any attack by the Turks, they were likely to land at Marsasirocco Bay and establish their camp there, then launch a landward attack on Fort St. Angelo, and Fort St. Elmo. To counter this, he bolstered the land defences of the forts, and expecting both places would have

Jean de Valette.
Drawing by Gordon Home

to withstand a siege, sent his cavalry to Mdina which would then serve as a base from which they could harry the Turkish supply lines, and possibly also the Turkish attackers. De Valette correctly anticipated the Turkish plans, and the forces at Mdina were crucial in a number of engagements. This led to him being able to withstand the Turkish siege gaining him, and his knights, much prestige around Europe.

A very strong military leader, de Valette's successful defence of Malta marked it out quite differently from many other sieges of the period. He allowed merchants in the city to stockpile and sell grain and other foods rather than seizing supplies at the start of the siege as usually happened. This and other moves by him ensured that he always had the support of the Maltese people. Another side to him was his ruthlessness when, on 24 June, after the all of Fort St. Elmo, he ordered that all the Turkish prisoners be executed and their heads fired from cannons at the lines of the attackers.

De Valette turned down the offer to be made a Cardinal in order to maintain the independence of the Hospitallers from the Papacy. In 1566 he started the construction of a new city, Valletta, laying the first stone himself. He died two years later and was buried in the Crypt of St. John's Co-Cathedral in Valletta. The inscription on his grave, written by his English secretary Sir Oliver Starkey, noted in Latin:

Here lies La Valette.
Worthy of eternal honour,
He who was once the scourge of Africa and Asia,
And the shield of Europe,
Whence he expelled the barbarians by his Holy Arms,
Is the first to be buried in this beloved city,
Whose founder he was

He was commemorated on two Maltese postage stamps issued on 1 September 1965, on the 300th anniversary of the siege of Malta, and on another issued on 28 March 1966. His armour was pictured on a Maltese postage stamp issued on 20 January 1977, and he was again commemorated on a Maltese postage stamp issued on 26 February 1999.

References: Warren G. Berg, *Historical Dictionary of Malta*, Lanham, Md.: The Scarecrow Press, 1995, pp. 133–34; Ernle Bradford, *The Great Siege*, London: Hodder & Stoughton, 1967; Maroma Camilleri, *Jean de la Valette 1495–1568: the man – a siege – a city*, Valletta: The National Library of Malta, 1995; Victor Mallia-Milanes & Louis J. Scerri, *An Uneasy Partnership: Malta 1530–1565*, Mdina: Midsea Books, 1985; Victor Mallia-Milanes, *Venice and Hospitaller Malta 1530–1798: aspects of a relationship*, Marsa: Publishers Enterprises Group, 1992; Bridget Cassar Borg Olivier, *The Shield of Europe: the life and times of La Valette*, Valletta: Progress Press, 1977; H.J.A. Sire, *The Knights of Malta*, New Haven: Yale University Press, 1994, pp. 68–73.

DE VASCONCELLOS, LUÍS MENDES (c1542–1623). The Grand Master of the Knights Hospitaller (Knights of Malta) from 1622 to 1623, he was born in about 1542 at Évora, Portugal, the son of Francisco Mendes de Vasconcelos, whose brother Luís da Costa worked for Henry of Portugal (King 1578–80). He was also the paternal grandson of Cristóvão Nunes da Costa, the illegitimate son of Luís Nunes da Costa and his wife Isabel Botelho. He had been the Portuguese governor of Angola from 1617 to 1621, and then moved to Malta, taking over from Grand Master Alof de Wignacourt. He was only Grand Master for six months, dying on 7 March 1623 in Malta, being succeeded by Antoine de Paule.

VASSALLO, FRANCIS J. (1948–). A banker, Francis Vassallo was born on 3 October 1948 in Mdina and studied at the Lyceum and then proceeded to the Royal University of Malta, graduating in 1970 with a BA (Hons) in economics. He initially worked for the Sciclunas Bank and then left Malta to work for the Chase Manhattan Bank in Milan, then moved to New York. In 1975 he was appointed the assistant general manager of the Chase Manhattan Bank in the Dominican Republic, and then was back in New York before being posted to London where he specialised in gold trading. He then moved to Spain and in 1991 was appointed the general manager of the Chase Manhattan Private Bank

in Switzerland, responsible for banking in southern Europe. In 1993 Francis Vassallo let the Chase Manhattan Bank to take up an appointment as governor of the Central Bank of Malta, a post he held until his retirement in 1997.

References: Michael J. Schiavone, *Dictionary of Maltese Biographies*, Malta: pubblikazzjonijiet Indipendenza, 2009, vol 2, p. 1566.

VASSALLO, LUIS ADRIAN (1933–1994). A professor of medicine, Luis Adrian Vassallo was born on 29 July 1933 in Mdina, and was educated at the Lyceum and the Royal University of Malta, gaining his BPharm in 1952, his BSc in the following year and his medical degree in 1955. Specialising in neurology, he worked as consultant physician at St. Luke's Hospital and also from 1965 he lectured at the Royal University of Malta, and was a member of the University Senate in the mid–1970s. However he left Malta after a trade union dispute in 1977 and worked at the Fahd Armed Forces Hospital in Saudi Arabia until 1994. He authored or co-authored a number of papers, and died on 28 June 1994.

References: Geoffrey Dean, *The Turnstone: a doctor's story*, Liverpool: Liverpool University Press, 2002, p. 183; Michael J. Schiavone, *Dictionary of Maltese Biographies*, Malta: pubblikazzjonijiet Indipendenza, 2009, vol 2, p. 1574; Luis Adrian Vassallo, 'An outbreak of lead poisoning of bread in Malta: interesting association with British Naval History', *Journal of the Royal Naval Medical Service* No 57 (1971), pp. 37–40; Luis Adrian Vassallo, 'Studies on Maltese Consanguinity', *Malta Medical Journal* vol 15, no 1 (May 2003), pp. 36–37.

VASSALLO, PETER (1941–). A professor of English and comparative literature at the University of Malta, he was born on 14 September 1941 at Mdina, and was educated at the Lyceum and proceeded to the University of Madrid. He then studied at the Royal University of Malta and at the University of Oxford, UK. He started teaching at the Junior College and was appointed head of the English department, becoming a lecturer at the University of Malta in 1974 and associate professor of English in 1988. In 1987 he was appointed the director of the Institute of Anglo-Italian Studies at the University of Malta, and has been visiting professor at a number of Italian universities and at Oxford. His main work is *Byron: the Italian literary influence* (London, 1984), and he has also edited *Byron and the Mediterranean* (1986).

References: Michael J. Schiavone, *Dictionary of Maltese Biographies*, Malta:

pubblikazzjonijiet Indipendenza, 2009, vol 2, p. 1580; Peter Vassallo (ed), *Byron and the Mediterranean*, Valletta: University of Malta Press, 1986.

de VAUBOIS, CLAUDE-HENRI BELGRAND (1748–1839). A French general, he was commissioned Lieutenant in the artillery in 1765. As a Captain Commander in 1789, he served under Napoleon Bonaparte in the Army of Italy. With the French landings in Malta in 11 June 1798, he took his soldiers straight to Mdina to capture the old capital of Malta. He then presided over the **French Occupation** which lasted over the whole island (including Mdina) for less than three months, and in Valletta until 1800. He was appointed a Senator in France during the siege, and after surrendering the city, he returned to France and was in charge of a division of the National Guard. In 1814 he was created a peer of France and decided not to support Napoleon in the 100 Days in 1815 culminating in the defeat of the French at Waterloo. He was commemorated on a Maltese postage stamp issued on 6 October 1999, on the 200th anniversary of the uprising against the French.

DE VERDALLE, HUGUES LOUBENX (1531–1585). He was the Grand Master of the Knights Hospitaller (Knights of Malta) from 1581 to 1595. Born on 13 April 1531 at the castle of Loubens in Gascony, he was from a prominent French noble family from Carcassonne. In 1547 he joined the Knights Hospitaller and five years later fought in the attack and capture of Zoara in North Africa. In 1565 de Verdalle was placed in command of the artillery and used it effectively against the Turks. He was then appointed as Grand Prior of Toulouse and then Grand Prior of the Langue de Provence. On 12 January 1572 he was elected Grand Master and on 18 December 1587 he was appointed a Cardinal by Pope Sixtus V. He did much to reform and modernise the Order and also commissioned Jacopo Bosio to write a history of the Order.

In 1587 Hugues de Verdalle started work on building a grand residence at the site which had been the location of a hunting lodge of Jean de la Valette. Located south of **Rabat**, it commands spectacular views of the southern walls of Mdina. Used as a military prison by Napoleon during the French Occupation, in 1858 it was converted to the official summer residence of the governors of Malta. Since 1987 it has been the summer residence of the Presidents of Malta. He died on 4 May 1585 in Rome and his body was brought back to Malta and buried in the crypt of St. John's Co-Cathedral. Hugues de Verdalle is the eponym of the Grand Verdala Hotel in Rabat.

References: Victor Mallia-Milanes, *Venice and Hospitaller Malta 1530–1798: aspects of a relationship*, Marsa: Publishers Enterprises Group, 1992; H.J.A. Sire, *The Knights of Malta*, New Haven: Yale University Press, 1994, pp. 66–73.

DE VILHENA, ANTÓNIO MANOEL (1663–1736). The Grand Master of the Knights Hospitaller (Knights of Malta) from 1722 to 1736, he was responsible for the regeneration of Mdina. From a Portuguese aristocratic family, his father was Sancho Manoel de Vilhena, the 1st Count de Vila Flor. He became actively involved in social projects in Malta and in 1731 helped built the Manoel Theatre in Valletta – it is now the oldest working theatre in the British Commonwealth, and the third oldest working theatre in Europe.

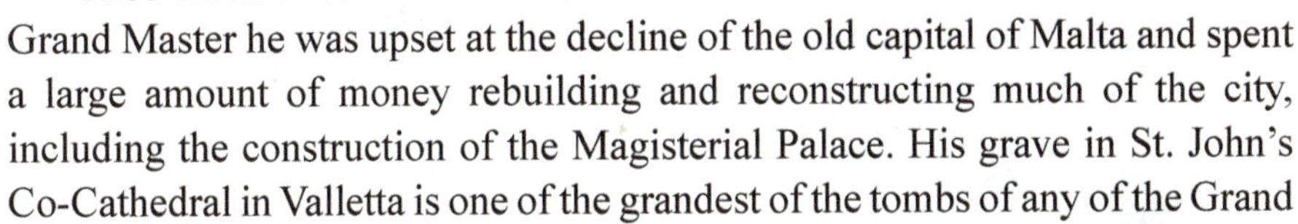

Also when António de Vilhena became Grand Master he was upset at the decline of the old capital of Malta and spent a large amount of money rebuilding and reconstructing much of the city, including the construction of the Magisterial Palace. His grave in St. John's Co-Cathedral in Valletta is one of the grandest of the tombs of any of the Grand Masters. There is also a statue of him at Floriana. It had been commissioned by the French knight Felician de Savasse in 1733 in recognition of Vilhena's accomplishments in Malta. His residence, the Palacio Vilhena, is now the Magisterial Palace. There was a prominent statue of him at Piazza Tesoreria in Valletta from 1858. Then in 1881 it was moved to the Maglio Gardens, and since 1989 it has been at Pope John

António Manoel de Vilhena
Photograph © McCarthys_PhotoWorks / Fotolia

XXIII Square, Floriana. The statue when it was in the Maglio Gardens appears on a postage stamp issued in the 1938–43 commemorative stamp series.

References: Dominic Cutajar, *Malta: A Presentation in Colour*, Valletta: MJ Publications, 1986, p. 27; Michael Galea, *Grandmaster Anton Manoel de Vilhena 1722–1735*, Malta: The Author, 1992; Victor Mallia-Milanes, *Venice and Hospitaller Malta 1530–1798: aspects of a relationship*, Marsa: Publishers Enterprises Group, 1992; 'Manoel de Vilhena memorial', *The Times* (26 June 2012).

VILHENA PALACE. *See* **Magisterial Palace**.

DE VILLEGAIGNON, NICOLAS DURAND (1510–1571). Born in 1510 in Villegaignon, in Seine et Marne, France, he was a nephew of **Philippe Villiers de L'Isle-Adam**, the Grand Master of the Order of Malta, with he himself being ordained as a Knight of the Order in 1521. He took part in the fighting against the Ottoman Turks, and in 1541 took part in the attack on Algiers. In the following year he fought in Hungary against the Turks at Budapest. In 1548 he was a commander of the French fleet which escorted the five-year-old Mary Queen of Scots from Scotland to France to allow her to marry Francis, Dauphin of France (later King Francis II). He returned to Scotland and took part in the capture of Feniehirst Castle and then went to Malta where in 1551 he was in charge of the garrison at Mdina from where the Knights managed to repel the Turkish attack.

In her novel, *The Disorderly Knights* (1966), Dorothy Dunnett has Villegaignon as one of the central figures with him, during his time in Scotland, recruiting the fictional Francis Crawford, a Scotsman, and the main character in the story. Villegaignon is with the Knights at their headquarters at Birgu when Dragut, the Corsair leading the Turks, attacks Mdina. After a messenger is sent from Mdina to plead for help, the Grand Master **Juan de Homedes** is eventually prevailed upon to send Villegaignon and six other knights to protect the city. His arrival results in a much-needed boost in morale, which, together with the Turks deciding to attack Gozo, saves the city.

Later the same year Villegaignon fought the Turks at Tripoli, and then took part in a plan by King Henry II of France to establish a French colony in South America. This saw him set up a base which was called Fort Coligny and was planned to be a settlement for French Huguenots and Swiss Calvinists, being named after the Huguenot leader who was to be murdered in the St. Bartholomew's Day Massacre in 1572. The Portuguese eventually took control of the fort in 1558 and it became the centre of Rio de Janeiro. Villegaignon tried to establish another colony in Florida and died on 9 January 1571. A street in Mdina is named after him to commemorate his role in the defence of the city in 1551.

References: Dorothy Dunnett, *The Lymond Chronicles 3: The Disorderly Knights,* London: Cassell & Company, 1966, reprinted London: Penguin Books, 1999; A. Heulhard, *Villegagnon, Roi d'Amérique: un Homme de Mer au XVIe Siècle*, Paris: E. Leroux, 1897; Lucian Provencal and Vasco Mariz, *Villegagnon: un chevalier de Malta au Brésil,* Paris: Editions Rive Droite, 2001.

VILLEGAIGNON, TRIQ (Villegaignon Street). This street was originally called Strada Reale (Royal Street) on account of the visit of King Alfonso V of Aragon in 1427, and remains the traditional route for processions through the city. It is now is named after **Nicolas Durand de Villegaignon** who led the defence of Mdina when the Turks attacked in 1551. At No 3 is the **Casa Inguanez**, with the **Caffè Medina** at No 19, and Maltese Falcon at No 27.

References: Can John Azzopardi, *Mdina, Rabat, Mosta*, Terni, Italy: Plurigraf, 1988, p. 30; Richard England and Conrad Thake, *Mdina: Citadel of Memory*, Malta: Atlantis, 1995, pp. 44–45, 68–69.

VILLEGAIGNON STREET. *See* **Villegaignon, Triq**.

VITALE, EMANUELE (1759–1802). One of the Maltese leaders during the insurrection against the French in 1798–1800, he was born on 30 April

1759, the son of Salvatore Vitale, a notary, and Rosa (née Caruana). In early 1785 he became a notary public in Mdina, and in March succeeded his father as the Chancellor of the Università of Mdina. He also had many commitments in **Rabat** and on 21 April 1794 he was appointed as the Rector of the Archconfraternity of St. Joseph.

The French appointed Vitale as a justice of the peace for Zurrieq. However he did not like the French and on 2 September 1798 resigned his position and together with 65 local farmers, led an attack on the French garrison in Mdina, chasing them from the city. Two days later he was chosen along with Count Salvatore Manduca, Marquis Vincenzo De Piro and Count Ferdinand Theuma Castelletti, to represent Mdina. He also represented Mdina, Rabat and Dingli to serve in the Maltese National Congress. When the French surrendered, Vitale became the Lieutenant of Senglea, and was later governor of Gozo, dying in Gozo on 8 October 1802. He was commemorated on a postage stamp issued in Malta on 18 October 2002, although there was some doubt cast over whether the stamp actually had an image of Vitale, or of somebody else.

References: Denis Damanin, 'Was the real Vitale depicted on stamp?' *The Sunday Times* (18 March 2012); Denis Damanin, 'Emmanuel Vitale on a stamp', *The Sunday Times* (1 July 2012); Michael J. Schiavone, *Dictionary of Maltese Biographies*, Malta: pubblikazzjonijiet Indipendenza, 2009, vol 2, p. 1629.

VUALGUERA, GIACOMO (d. 1501). He was the bishop of Malta being appointed on 30 March 1495 and ordained on 9 July, remaining in office until his death on 5 May 1501.

DE VULPONNO, ANTONIO. A Benedictine, he was the bishop of Malta from 15 October 1375 until his death in November 1392.

– W –

WARREN FAMILY. Prominent British residents in Mdina, the Warren family descend from Rev. Robert Warren, the fifth son of Sir Robert Warren, 1st Baronet. The Rev. Robert Warren's son, also Rev Robert Warren, his second son was Major General Richard Warren, whose second son Herbert Lauder Warren was a staff paymaster in the Royal Navy. Herbert Warren was born on 1 April 1855, he married Ella Christian Hoyer, and they had two daughters: Ella Christian Louise Lauder, born on 11 January 1891; and Kathleen 'Kay' Pelham Lauder, born on 30 August 1892. Herbert Warren died on 9 January 1897 at Portsea, Hampshire, England.

His widow and the two daughters then moved to Malta, initially settling at 44 Strada Mezzoli, Valletta, and then moved to Mdina. Anne Ferrante wrote, 'she was thin and tall and walked round Mdina as if she owned it, wearing a long high collared dress, a hat and carrying a parasol.' Ella, the mother, died on 12 March 1945, and was buried at Ta'Braxia Cemetery. The two daughters continued living at 2 St. Paul Street (**Triq San Pawl**), Mdina, their telephone number was 'Rabat 107'. Ella was awarded the MBE for her service to the British war effort in World War I. She was the Hon. Secretary of the Malta Amateur Dramatic Club from 1927, and in World War II, she worked as a cipher officer for the British, becoming Secretary of the British Council in Malta, 1945–53. Ella later lost her sight, but Kay continued to wander around Mdina driving a battered 1946 Ford Prefect. When Maggie Smith visited Malta, they met up and showed the visiting actress around the Manoel Theatre in Valletta. Kay, also awarded an MBE, returned to England and lived at Heath Mount (now Heathmount), a care centre in Rake, Liss, Hampshire, and died on 14 November 1984, aged 92.

References: Burke's *Peerage and Baronetage*, p. 2516; Debrett's *Illustrated Baronetage 1976*, p. 2110; Anne Agius Ferrante, *No Strangers in the Silent City*, Valletta: Andrew Rupert Publishing, 1992, pp. 19–22; *Malta Telephone Directory 1960*, p. 388; *Malta's Who's Who 1964*, p. 195; *Malta's Who's Who 1965*, p. 252; *Malta's Who's Who 1968*, p. 373; *Malta's Who's Who 1969/70*, p, 387.

DE WIGNACOURT, ALOPH (1547–1622). He was the Grand Master of the Knights Hospitaller (Knights of Malta) from 1601 until his death in 1622. From France, he succeeded **Martin Garzes** as Grand Master and continued the work of his predecessor in improving the defences of Malta and Gozo

with the construction of the Wignacourt Towers at St. Paul's Bay. These were completed in 1610. He befriended the painter **Caravaggio** who had fled to Malta in 1606 after having killed a man in Rome. In Malta he painted Aloph de Wignacourt and also the famous *The Beheading of John the Baptist* which is on display at St. John's Co-Cathedral in Valletta. The Wignacourt Aqueduct was completed on 21 April 1615. He died on 14 September 1622 and was succeeded by Luís Mendes de Vasconcellos. A full-length portrait of him by Lionello Spada (1576–1622) survives. His armour was pictured on a Maltese postage stamp issued on 20 January 1977.

Malta in 1602.

References: Michael Galea, *Grand Master Aloph de Wignacourt 1601–1622: a monograph*, San Gwann: Publishers Enterprises Group, 2002; Nicholas de Piro, *The International Dictionary of Artists who Painted Malta*, Valletta: Audio Visual Centre Limited, 2003, p. 438–39; Victor Mallia-Milanes, *Venice and Hospitaller Malta 1530–1798: aspects of a relationship*, Marsa: Publishers Enterprises Group, 1992; H.J.A. Sire, *The Knights of Malta*, New Haven: Yale University Press, 1994, pp. 76–77.

WILKINSON, Mrs NORAH GRACE (d. 1966). From England, she ran the English Guest House in Holy Cross Street, Mdina, serving, according to **Anne Agius Ferrante**, 'excellent teas with strawberries and cream, muffins and sandwiches, but we never tasted them till the war when they were less good due to the food shortage'. She also apparently advertised in *The Times of Malta*, 'English Guest House – Tea Rooms Open on Good Friday' in the hope of annoying the religious Maltese. And Ferrante also noted that even though it was advertised as a 'guest house', it served teas but did not have guests to stay overnight. Norah Wilkinson died on 13 February 1966, aged 84, and was buried at Ta'Braxia Cemetery.

References: Anne Agius Ferrante, *No Strangers in the Silent City*, Valletta: Andrew Rupert Publishing, 1992, p. 22; *Malta Telephone Directory 1960*, p. 389; *Malta Telephone Directory 1966*, p. 251.

WORLD WAR I. With the outbreak of World War I, Malta as a British colony entered the war and served as an important naval base for the British. With large numbers of British, Australian, New Zealand and other allied soldiers and sailors passing through Malta, large numbers had some spare time on the island and many visited Mdina with many surviving photograph and postcard collections of service personnel having images of the old city. And there were also people from Mdina who served in the war including Guido de Piro d'Amico (1879–1921) who fought on the Western Front.

WORLD WAR II. With the outbreak of World War II, the British reinforced Malta which became even more important when Italy entered the conflict on 10 June 1940. The British had evacuated all civilians from Gibraltar but it was impossible to do this with Malta. Although some Maltese civilians did leave voluntarily, many others remained on the island which was attacked by Italian aircraft for the first time on 11 June 1940. Gradually the raids intensified with 262 in January 1942. During March and April 1942 twice the tonnage of

bombs was dropped on Malta than had been dropped on London during the Blitz. There were food shortages, and a typhoid epidemic in Malta. The British sent a number of naval convoys bringing supplies which alleviated some of the suffering. Many British planes were based at Ta'Qali, close to Mdina, and as a result, some Royal Air Force pilots were billeted in Mdina in some of the large empty houses. In spite of its location close to the airfield, the old city of Mdina largely escaped unscathed from the Axis aerial attacks.

From 30 January – 3 February 1945, the Malta Conference took place between the British Prime Minister Winston Churchill and US President Franklin Delano Roosevelt (who arrived on 2 February). On the afternoon of his arrival, Roosevelt went by car to tour Malta and this included Mdina.

References: Warren G. Berg, *Historical Dictionary of Malta*, Lanham, Md.: The Scarecrow Press, 1995, pp. 61–62; Ernle Bradford, *Siege: Malta 1940–1943*, London: Hamish Hamilton, 1985; Joseph Galea, 'Malta and the Second World War: A bibliography', *Melita Historica* vol 1, no 1 (1952), pp. 33–51; John Alfred Agius, 'Malta and the second world war. Some additions to Dr. Galea's bibliography', *Melita Historica* vol 2, no 1 (1956), pp. 14–18; J. Hogan, *Malta: The Triumphant Years 1940–1943*, London: Robert Hale Ltd, 1978; Stewart Perowne, *The siege within the walls: Malta 1940–1943*, London: Hodder & Stoughton, 1970.

– X –

DE LA XABICA, GIORGIO. The **Capitano della Verga** of Mdina, 1470–71, 1475–76, and again from 1480–81, he was the son of **Giovanni De La Xabica** and his wife Leanora de Caro. In 1448 he married Margherita d'Alagona, and they had a son Manfred, and two daughters Zuna and Caterina.

DE LA XABICA, GIOVANNI. The **Capitano della Verga** of Mdina, 1457–58, he was the son of Giacomo Fabica who was a Spanish soldier who moved to Malta. His son **Giorgio De La Xabica** was later the **Capitano della Verga**.

References: John Montalto, *The Nobles of Malta, 1530–1800*, Valletta: Midsea Books, 1979, p. 170.

XARA, ANTONIO. He was the **Capitano della Verga** of Mdina, 1658–59, 1664–68, and 1678–80.

XARA, PIETRO. A scholar, he joined the Dominican Order, probably when studying in Sicily, having graduated with a degree in theology. In 1508 he was sent to Malta and settled in **Rabat**, working with the Dominicans in Mdina. In 1511 he asked King Ferdinand II of Aragon to help the order in Malta, with Xara being prior of the Dominicans in 1513–14 and 1518.

References: Michael J. Schiavone, *Dictionary of Maltese Biographies*, Malta: pubblikazzjonijiet Indipendenza, 2009, vol 2, p. 1639.

XARA, STANISLAO. The **Capitano della Verga** of Mdina, 1671–73, he was the son of Paolo Xara and Maruzzia Bonnici who were married in 1633. Stanislao Xara himself married Domenico Xara Cassia; they had no children. He was the deputy to the Inquisitor Ranuccio Pallavicino from 1676 and was recognised as the Baron of Gariexem and Tabia on 21 August 1689 by Grand Master Gregorio Carafa.

References: John Montalto, *The Nobles of Malta, 1530–1800*, Valletta: Midsea Books, 1979, p. 35, 37, 117, 194.

XARA PALACE. This palace is located at the end of **Triq San Pawl**. Constructed in the seventeenth century, it was the residence of the Moscati Parisio family and was then owned by the **Stricklands**. During **World War**

The Xara Palace.

The Xara Palace.

For XMAS and NEW YEAR
Book at the
XARA PALACE HOTEL, MDINA
Terms and Brochures from Manageress
Cables: Xarapal, Malta.

II it was a mess for the Royal Air Force officers at nearby Ta'Qali. It was converted into a hotel in 1949, and has operated continuously since 1964 (see advertisement from 1974 above). Recently restored, in 1999 the palace was reopened as a boutique hotel with 17 luxury suites and an atrium bar, with the Trattoria AD 1530, a stylish restaurant, next door.

References: *1000x European Hotels*, Berlin: Braun, 2008, p. 972; Carolyn Bain, *Malta & Gozo*, Footscray, Vic, Australia: Lonely Planet, 2004, pp. 121–22; Roland Flamini, 'The Xara Palace: Once home to Maltese nobility, a Baroque dwelling is reborn behind Mdina's ancient walls', *Architectural Digest* vol. 62, no. 4 (April 2005), pp. 192–99; Laddie Lucas, *Malta: The Thorn in Rommel's Side – Six Months that Turned the War*, London: Stanley Paul, 1992; 'Wake up a princess in one of the world's most beautiful palaces', *Hello! Daily News* (8 August 2013), http://www.hellomagazine.com/travel/2013080813926/palace-hotels-where-you-can-stay/ (accessed August 2013); Xara Palace, www.xarapalace.com.mt.

XERRI (or **SCERRI**), **GREGORIO (d. 1623)**. The **Capitano della Verga** of Mdina, 1584–87, 1592–95, 1599–1601, 1605–09, 1611–13, and 1615–23, he was the Baron of Castel Cicciano. The third child and oldest son of Gio Francesco Scerri (Xerri) and his wife Imperia Surdo, he married Imperia Cassia in 1579 and they had three children: Gio Francisco, Catarina, Margarita. He also had two illegitimate sons Giovanni and Gio Maria, and an illegitimate daughter, Maddelena.

XERRI, GIOVANNI DOMENICO. He was the **Capitano della Verga** of Mdina, 1603–05.

XIMENES, GIOVANNI. A Franciscan, he was the bishop of Malta from 16 March 1418 until his death, being succeeded on 21 August 1420 by **Mauro de Albraynio**.

– Z –

The organ in Mdina Cathedral
Photograph willmac / Big Stock Photo

ZAHRA, MIKIL (1574–1646). The organist at the **Cathedral Church** in Mdina, he was ordained priest in 1598 and after working at the Cathedral Church, he went to study **music** at Palermo. The Cathedral authorities paid for him to go to Sicily providing he returned to Mdina afterwards. He was then appointed the organist in Mdina until his death. He left his music books to the Cathedral.

References: Michael J. Schiavone, *Dictionary of Maltese Biographies*, Malta: pubblikazzjonijiet Indipendenza, 2009, vol 2, pp. 1662–63.

ZAMMIT CIANTAR, JOE (1942–). A lawyer, historian and poet, he was born on 8 May 1942 at Ta' Sannat, Gozo, and was educated at Victoria, becoming a teacher in a number of schools in Malta ending up as Head of the Department of Education. He graduated from the University of Malta in 1973, and completed his doctorate in Maltese in 2005. The author of a number of books on Malta, he edited *A Benedictine's notes on seventeenth-century Malta*, and has composed much thoughtful poetry on the city of Mdina.

References: Michael J. Schiavone, *Dictionary of Maltese Biographies*, Malta:

pubblikazzjonijiet Indipendenza, 2009, vol 2, pp. 1689–90.

ZAMMIT MONTEBELLO, ALFRED (1933–2001). A psychologist, he was born on 1 September 1933 in Mdina, and studied at the Lyceum and then at St. Michael's Training College. After proceeding to the University of Liverpool in England, he then went to Queen's University and the University of Toronto in Canada, specialising in applied psychology. Back in Malta Alfred Zammit Montebello worked as a teacher in the department of education, and then focused on special education. Returning to St. Michael's Training College to lecture, he also worked at the Royal University of Malta. In 1971 he became the first educational psychologist to be appointed by the government, and 17 years later became director of welfare. He has also worked with the International Labour Organization in the Cayman Islands, China, Jordan, Lesotho, and in Jerusalem. He retired in 1994 and died on 10 December 2001.

References: Michael J. Schiavone, *Dictionary of Maltese Biographies*, Malta: pubblikazzjonijiet Indipendenza, 2009, vol 2, pp. 1698–99.

ZUKI, PIETRO (d. 1503). The founder of the Dominican Order in Malta, he was born in Mdina and studied in Sicily where he joined the Dominicans, returning to Malta in about 1450 to establish the Order in his homeland. He was granted some land by the church and just outside Mdina he built a church and convent in a grotto after there were sightings of the Virgin Mary there. He died in 1503 and the church was finished two years later.

References: S. L. Forte, 'Prior of Valletta and Vicar of Malta – a chapter in the history of the Maltese Dominicans', *Archivum Frater Praedicatorum* vol. 34 (1964); Michael J. Schiavone, *Dictionary of Maltese Biographies*, Malta: pubblikazzjonijiet Indipendenza, 2009, vol 2, p. 1712.

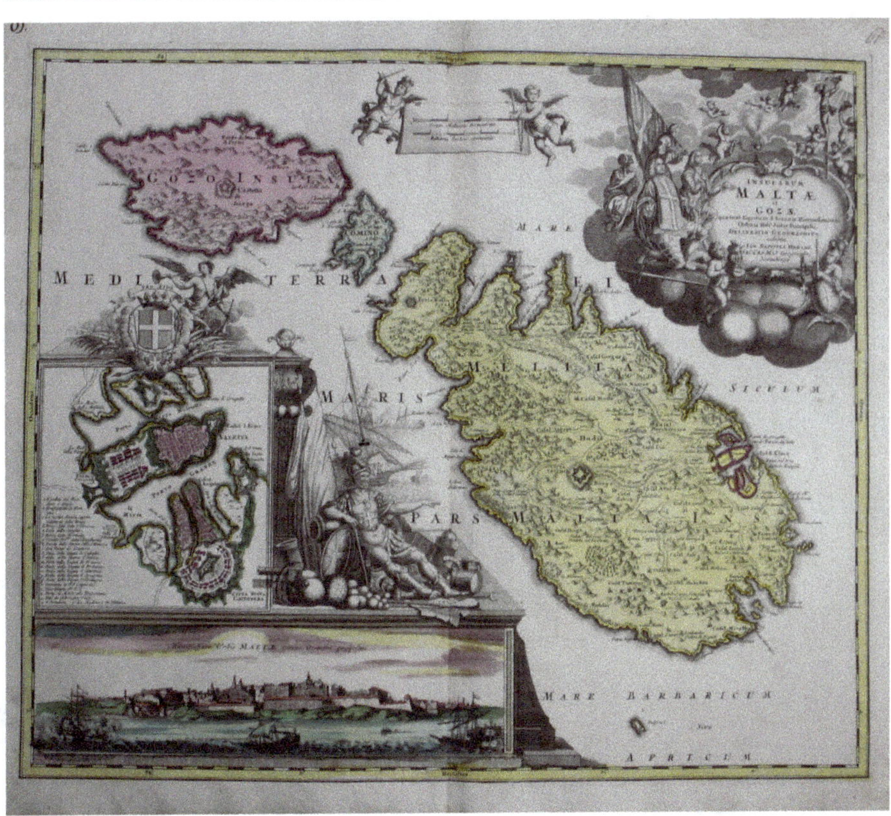

Malta in 1720.

APPENDIX I

Heads of State and Heads of Government of Malta

Abbasid Caliphs

870 – 15 Oct. 892	Al-Mu'tamid
892 – 5 April 902	Al-Mu'tadid
902 – 13 Aug. 908	Al-Muktafi
908 – 909*	Al-Muqtadir

Fatimid Caliphs

909 – 934	Abdullah al-Mahdi Billah
934 – 17 May 946	Muhammad al-Qa'im Bi-Amrillah
946 – 953	Ismail al-Mansur
953 – 975	Al-Mu'izz li-Din Allah
975 – 996	Abu Mansur Nizar al-Aziz Billah
14 Oct. 996 – 13 Feb. 1021	Al-Hakim bi-Amr Allah
1021 – 1036	Ali az-Zahir
1036 – 1091*	Ma'ad al-Mustansir Billah

Counts of Sicily

1091 – 22 June 1101	Count Roger I (Count since 1071)
22 June 1101 – 28 Sept. 1105	Count Simon
1105 – 27 Sept. 1130	Count Roger II

* denotes the date of the person holding that position in Malta. In some cases they remained in control for longer outside Malta.

Kings of Sicily

27 Sept. 1130 – 26 Feb. 1154	King Roger II
26 Feb. 1154 – 7 May 1166	King William I
7 May 1186 – 11 Nov. 1189	King William II
Nov. 1189 – 20 Feb. 1194	King Tancred
1193 – 24 Dec. 1193	King Roger III
Dec. 1193 – Oct. 1194	King William III
1194 – 27 Nov. 1198	Queen Constance
25 Dec. 1194 – 28 Sept. 1197	King Henry I
1198 – 13 Dec. 1250	King Fredrick I
Feb. 1212 – 1217	King Henry II
13 Dec. 1250 – 21 May 1254	King Conrad I
21 May 1254 – 1258 (*de jure* until 29 Oct. 1268)	King Conrad II
1258 – 26 Feb. 1266	King Manfred
1266 – 1282	King Charles I
4 Sept. 1282 – 2 Nov. 1285	King Peter I
2 Nov. 1285 – 20 June 1295	King James I
11 Dec. 1296 – 25 June 1337	King Fredrick II
1337 – 15 Aug. 1342	King Peter II
15 Aug. 1342 – 16 Oct. 1355	King Louis
16 Oct. 1355 – 27 Jan. 1377	King Fredrick III
27 July 1377 – 25 May 1401	Queen Maria
1392 – 25 July 1409	King Martin I
25 July 1409 – 20 Jan. 1410	King Martin II
1412 – 2 April 1416	King Ferdinand I
2 April 1416 – 27 June 1458	King Alfonso
27 June 1458 – 20 Jan. 1479	King John
20 Jan. 1479 – 23 Jan. 1516	King Ferdinard II
23 Jan. 1516 – 26 Oct. 1530	Queen Joanna (until 12 April 1555 as Queen of Sicily)
23 Jan. 1516 – 26 Oct. 1530	King Charles II (until 27 Aug. 1558 as King of Sicily)

Grand Masters of the Knights Hospitaller

26 Oct. 1530 – 21 Aug. 1534	Philippe Villiers de L'Isle-Adam (Grand Master since 1521).
26 Aug. 1534 – 17 Nov. 1535	Piero de Ponte
22 Nov. 1535 – 26 Sept. 1536	Didier de Saint-Jaille
20 Oct. 1536 – 6 Sept. 1553	Juan de Homedes y Coscon
11 Sept. 1553 – 18 Aug. 1557	Claude de la Sengle
21 Aug. 1557 – 21 Aug. 1568	Jean Parisot de la Valette
23 Aug. 1568 – 26 Jan. 1572	Pietro del Mante
30 Jan. 1572 – 1581	Jean de la Cassière
1581 – 4 Nov. 1581	Mathurin Romegas (de facto Grand Master)
4 Nov. 1581 – 21 Dec. 1581	Jean de la Cassière (restored)
12 Jan. 1582 – 4 May 1595	Hugues Loubenx de Verdalle
8 May 1595 – 7 Feb. 1601	Martin Garzez
10 Feb. 1601 – 14 Sept. 1622	Alof de Wignacourt
17 Sept. 1622 – 7 March 1623	Luís Mendes de Vasconcellos
10 March 1623 – 9 June 1636	Antoine de Paule
16 June 1636 – 14 Aug. 1657	Giovanni Paolo Lascaris
17 Aug. 1657 – 6 Feb. 1660	Martin de Redin
9 Feb. 1660 – 2 June 1660	Annet de Clermont-Gessant
5 June 1660 – 20 Oct. 1663	Raphael Cotoner
23 Oct. 1663 – 29 April 1680	Nicolas Cotoner
2 May 1680 – 21 July 1690	Gregorio Carafa
24 July 1690 – 4 Feb. 1697	Adrienne de Wignacourt
7 Feb. 1697 – 10 Jan. 1720	Ramon Perellos
13 Jan. 1720 – 16 June 1722	Marc'Antonio Zondadari
19 June 1722 – 10 Dec. 1736	Manoel de Vilhena
16 Dec. 1736 – 15 Jan. 1741	Ramon Despuig
18 Jan. 1741 – 23 Jan. 1773	Manuel Pinto da Fonseca
28 Jan. 1773 – 9 Nov. 1775	Francisco Ximenes de Texada
12 Nov. 1775 – 14 July 1797	Emmanuel de Rohan-Polduc
17 July 1797 – 11 June 1798	Ferdinand von Hompesch zu Bolheim (in Malta as Grand Master until 6 July 1799).

French Commandant

12 June 1798 – 5 Sept. 1800	Claude Henri Belgrand de Vaubois

French Commissioners

June 1798 – 9 Nov. 1799	Regnaud de Saint Jean d'Angely
Nov. 1799 – Sept. 1800	Pierre Jean Louis Ovide Doublet

Presidents of the Provisional Government (during the Malta Rebellion)

1798 – Feb. 1799	Emanuele Vitale & Francesco Saverio Caruana
Feb. 1799 – Sept. 1800	Alexander John Ball

British Monarchs

4 Sept. 1800 – 29 Jan. 1820	King George III (since 25 October 1760 in the United Kingdom)
29 Jan. 1820 – 26 June 1830	King George IV
26 June 1830 – 20 June 1837	King William IV
20 June 1837 – 22 Jan. 1901	Queen Victoria
22 Jan. 1901 – 6 May 1910	King Edward VII
6 May 1910 – 20 Jan. 1936	King George V
20 Jan. 1936 – 11 Dec. 1936	King Edward VIII
11 Dec. 1936 – 6 Feb. 1952	King George VI
6 Feb. 1952 – 21 Sept. 1964	Queen Elizabeth II

Queen of Malta

21 Sept. 1964 – 13 Dec. 1974	Queen Elizabeth II

British Representatives

8 Sept. 1800 – 19 Feb. 1801	Alexander John Ball
19 Feb. 1801 – July 1801	Henry Pigot

Civil Commissioners

July 1801 – 5 June 1802	Charles Cameron

5 June 1802 – 20 Oct. 1809	Sir Alexander John Ball
20 Oct. 1809 – 5 Oct. 1813	Sir Hildebrand Oakes

Governors

5 Oct. 1813 – 17 Jan. 1824	Sir Thomas Maitland
7 June 1824 – 1826	Francis Rawdon-Hastings, Marquess of Hastings
2 Dec. 1827 – May 1835	Sir Frederic Cavendish Ponsonby
1 Oct. 1836 – 1843	Sir Henry Frederic Bouverie
13 July 1843 – Oct. 1847	Sir Patrick Stuart
18 Dec. 1847 – 1851	Richard More O'Ferrall
27 Oct. 1851 – 1858	Sir William Reid
30 Apr. 1858 – 1864	Sir John Gaspard Le Marchant
15 Nov. 1864 – 1867	Sir Henry Knight Storks
15 May 1867 – 1872	Sir Patrick Grant
3 June 1872 – 1878	Sir Charles Thomas Van Straubenzee
13 May 1878 – Apr. 1884	Sir Arthur Borton
13 June 1884 – 28 Sept. 1888	Sir John Lintorn Arabin Simmons
28 Sept. 1888 – Nov. 1889	Sir Henry D'Oyley Torrens
11 Jan. 1890 – 1893	Sir Henry Augustus Smyth
9 Dec. 1893 – 6 Jan. 1899	Sir Arthur James Lyon Fremantle
6 Jan. 1899 – 1903	Sir Francis Wallace Grenfell (from 18 July 1902, Francis Wallace Grenfell, Baron Grenfell)
2 Mar. 1903 – 1907	Sir Charles Mansfield Clarke
9 Aug. 1907 – 1909	Sir Henry Eugene Walter Grant
3 Aug. 1909 – 1915	Sir (Henry Macleod) Leslie Rundle
27 Jan. 1915 – May 1919	Paul Sanford, Baron Methuen of Corsham
10 June 1919 – 1924	Herbert Charles Onslow Plumer, Baron Plumer
29 June 1924 – 28 Feb. 1927	Sir Walter Norris Congreve
1927 – 1931	Sir John Philip du Cane
June 1931 – 1936	Sir David Graham Muschet Campbell
1936 – 1940	Sir Charles Bonham-Carter
Apr 1940 – 1942	Sir William Dobbie

1942 – 26 Sept. 1944	John Standish Surtees Prendergast Vereker, Viscount Gort
26 Sept. 1944 – 10 July 1946	Sir Edmond Charles Acton Schreiber
10 July 1946 – 16 Sept. 1949	Francis Campbell Ross Douglas (from 1947, Sir Francis Campbell Ross Douglas)
16 Sept. 1949 – 3 Aug. 1954	Sir Gerald Hallen Creasy
3 Aug. 1954 – 13 Feb. 1959	Sir Robert Edward Laycock
13 Feb. 1959 – 2 July 1962	Sir Guy Grantham
2 July 1962 – 21 Sept. 1964	Sir Maurice Henry Dorman

Governors-General (who represent the British monarch as Head of State)

21 Sept. 1964 – 4 July 1971	Sir Maurice Henry Dorman
4 July 1971 – 13 Dec. 1974	Sir Anthony Joseph Mamo

Presidents

13 Dec. 1974 – 27 Dec. 1976	Sir Anthony Joseph Mamo
27 Dec. 1976 – 27 Dec. 1981	Anton Buttigieg
27 Dec. 1981 – 15 Feb. 1982	Albert V. Hyzler (acting)
15 Feb. 1982 – 15 Feb. 1987	Agatha Barbara
15 Feb. 1987 – 4 Apr. 1989	Paul Xuereb (acting)
4 Apr. 1989 – 4 Apr. 1994	Censu Tabone
4 Apr. 1994 – 4 Apr. 1999	Ugo Mifsud Bonnici
4 Apr. 1999 – 4 Apr. 2004	Guido de Marco
4 Apr. 2004 – 4 Apr. 2009	Eddie Fenech Adami
4 Apr. 2009 – 4 Apr. 2014	George Abela
4 Apr. 2014 –	Marie Louise Coleiro Preca

Prime Ministers

26 Oct. 1921 – 13 Oct. 1923	Joseph Howard
13 Oct. 1923 – 22 Sept. 1924	Francesco Buhagiar
Sept. 1924 – Aug. 1927	Ugo Pasquale Mifsud (1)

Aug. 1927 – 21 June 1932	Gerald Strickland, Count Della Catena, (from 1928 Baron Strickland)
21 June 1932 – 2 Nov. 1933	Sir Ugo Pasquale Mifsud (2)
4 Nov. 1947 – 26 Sept. 1950	Paul Boffa
26 Sept. 1950 – 20 Dec. 1950	Enrico Mizzi
20 Dec. 1950 – 11 Mar. 1955	George Borg Olivier (1)
11 Mar. 1955 – 26 Apr. 1958	Dom Mintoff (1)
5 Mar. 1962 – 21 June 1971	George Borg Olivier (2)
21 June 1971 – 22 Dec. 1984	Dom Mintoff (2)
22 Dec. 1984 – 12 May 1987	Carmelo Mifsud Bonnici
12 May 1987 – 28 Oct. 1996	Eddie Fenech Adami (1)
28 Oct. 1996 – 6 Sept. 1998	Alfred Sant
6 Sept. 1998 – 23 Mar. 2004	Eddie Fenech Adami (2)
23 Mar. 2004 – 11 Mar. 2013	Lawrence Gonzi
11 Mar. 2013 –	Joseph Muscat.

Photograph © JackF / Fotolia.com

Photograph © Lotharingia / Fotolia.com

APPENDIX II

Administrators of Mdina

Capitani della Verga of Mdina

1365–	Giacomo di Pellegrino
1371–72	Giovanni d'Aragona
1372–	Guglilmo Murina
1399–	Giulio Riccari
1403–06	Francesco Gatto
1406–08	Francesco di Santa Colomba
1413–14	Diego de Portocarrero
1414–15	Diego Terrazza
1415–17	Giovanni Lupo Terrazza
1418–21	Ruggiero de Serrano
1428–29	Paolo de Pellegrino
1429–	Antonio d'Esguanez
1431–33	Francesco Gatto
1433–38	Antonio d'Esguanez
1438–39	Francesco Platamonte
1439–40	Antonio d'Esguanez
1440–42	Gerardo d'Esguanez
1442–54	Antonio d'Esguanez
1454–55	Carlo di Paterno'
1455–56	Leonardo di Bordino
1456–57	Stafano Pierrera
1457–58	Giovanni de la Xabica
1458–60	Pietro Giovanni di Mazara

1460–61	Pietro de Baldes
1461–62	Batolommeo de Clementis
1462–66	Paolo de Nasis
1466–67	Raimondo de Parisio
1467–68	Giovanni di Mazara
1468–	Trissano de Guevara
1470–71	Giorgio de la Xabica
1471–73	Giovanni di Mazara
1473–74	Simone di Mazara
1474–75	Giovanni di Mazara
1475–76	Giorgio de la Xabica
1476–77	Giovanni di Mazara
1477–	Simone di Mazara
1479–80	Giovanni de Guevara
1480–81	Giorgio de la Xabica
1481–82	Torres de Guevara
1482–84	Pietro de Ribera
1484–86	Pietro de Baldes
1486–87	Simone di Mazara
1487–93	Carlo de Guevara
1493–99	Antonio Gatto d'Esguanez
1500–06	Giovanni de Guevara
1513–14	Giacome Falzone
1514–15	Manfredo Caxaro
1516–17	Matteo de Guevara
1517–18	Giovanni di Mazara
1518–19	Ambrogio Falzone
1519–20	Inguaterra de Nava
1520–21	Giovanni di Mazara
1521–22	Pietro de Staniga
1522–23	Leonardo di Bordino
1523–24	Ambrogio Falzone
1524–25	Giovanni di Mazara

1525–26	Michele Falzone
1526–27	Pietro Falzone
1527–28	Giovanni de Nava
1528–30	Antonio d'Esguanez
1530–31	Leonardo Calava'
1531–32	Paolo de Nasis
1532–33	Antonio Falzone
1533–34	Antonio Manduca
1534–36	Matteo Falzone
1536–38	Antonio Manduca
1538–40	Antonio Goffredo Inguanez
1540–42	Matteo Falzone
1542–45	Antonio Manduca
1545–48	Vincenzo Vasco
1548–50	Antonio Inguanez
1550–57	D. Girolamo d'Alagona
1557–63	Matteo Falzone
1563–65	D. Antonio de Guevara
1565–68	Matteo Falzone
1568–70	Antonio de Guevara
1570–71	Alfonso de Nava
1571–73	Francesco d'Alagona
1573–74	Giuseppe de Nava
1574–78	D. Ferdinando de Guevara
1578–79	Francesco d'Alagona
1579–80	Ferrante de Guevara
1580–81	Salvatore Montagnes
1581–82	Francesco d'Alagona
1582–84	Alonso de Nava
1584–87	Gregorio Xerri
1587–90	Ugolino Navarra
1590–92	Giovanni Maria Cassia
1592–95	Gregorio Xerri

1595–97	D. Pietro de Guevara
1597–98	Ambrogio Falzone
1598–99	Antonio Inguanez
1599–1601	Gregorio Xerri
1601–03	Pietro de Guevara
1603–05	Giovanni Domenico Xerri
1605–09	Gregorio Xerri
1609–11	Michele Cassar
1611–13	Gregorio Xerri
1613–15	Giovanni Maria Cassia
1615–23	Gregorio Xerri
1623–24	Antonio Cumbo
1624–25	Giovanni Domenico Felici
1625–27	Giovanni Vincenzo Castelletti
1627–29	Francesco Mamo
1629–33	Antonio Turrenzi
1633–35	Francesco Perticomati
1635–36	Diego Ferriolo
1636–38	Giacomo Testaferrata de Robertis
1638–40	Diego Ferriolo
1640–42	Ignazio Bonnici
1642–44	Lorenzo Cassar
1644–52	Silvestro Fiteni
1652–53	Pietro Cassar
1653–54	Gio' Batta Micallef
1654–56	Gregorio Bonnici
1656–58	Gio' Batta Micallef
1658–59	Antonio Xara
1659–60	Pietro Cassia
1660–62	Gio' Domenico Muscat
1662–64	Gio' Maria Cardona
1664–68	Antonio Xara
1668–69	Giacinto Macedonia

1669–71	Gio' Domenico Muscat
1671–73	Stanislao Xara
1673–75	Pietro Mompalao
1675–77	Giacinto Macedonia
1677–78	Alessandro Mompalao
1678–80	Antonio Xara
1680–82	Domenico Bonnici
1682–84	Pietro Mompalao
1684–86	Gio' Batta Bonnici
1686–89	Baldassare Teuma
1689–92	D. Mario Testaferrata
1692–98	Giovanni Gourgion
1698–1700	Antonio Perticomati Bologna
1700–02	Calcerano Mompalao
1702–05	Fabrizio Testaerrata
1705–09	Marcantonio Inguanez
1709–10	Cosmano Cassar
1710–13	Antonio Bonnici
1713–15	Marcantonio Inguanez
1715–17	Antonio Muscat
1717–21	Pietro Mompalao
1721`–30	Marcantonio Inguanez
1730–33	Pietro Paolo Galea
1733–40	Ferdinando Castelletti
1740–61	Marcantonio Inguanez
1761–64	Salvatore Manduca
1764–75	Gio' Francesco D'Amico Inguanez
1775–97	D. Pasquale Sciberras Testaerrata
1797–99	Gregorio Bonici
1799–1801	Francesco Gauci
1801–14	Giovanni Francesco Sant
1814–15	Giuseppe Bonnici
1815–18	Giuseppe Muscat

Mayors of Mdina

1994–2000	George Attard
2000–2003	Mario Galea Testaferrata
2003–	Peter dei Conti Sant-Manduca

APPENDIX III

Bishops and Archbishops of Malta

Bishops of Malta

60–67	St. Publius
451	Acacius
501	Kostantinu
533/553	Julianus (Giuliano)
592–599	Lucillu (Lucillo)
599	Trajanu (Traiano)
1091	Gualtieri
1095	Brialdo
1113	Gwanni
1122	Rinaldus
1154	Stiefnu
1167–1169	Johannes I (Giovanni I)
1211–24	Johannes II (Giovanni II)
1251	Ruggerius (Ruggerio) of Cefalù
1253-	Domenico
1259	Jacobus
1267	Marinus (Marino di Sorrento)
1268	John (Johannes) Normandus
c1270	Andrea Bancherini
1274–97	Jacobus of Malta
1304–22	Nicolaus (Niccolò)
1332–33	Alduinus (Alduino)
1334–41	Henericus of Cefalù

1342–43	Nicolaus Boneti
1343–46	Ogerius
1346–56	Jocobus
1356-	Mario Corrado
1370-	Antonio
1371-	Corrado
1375–92	Antonio de Vulponno
1393–1408	Mauro Cali
1408–09	Andrea de Pace
1409-	Antonio
1414-	Andrea
1418-	Giovanni Ximenes
1420-	Mauro de Albraynio
1432-	Senatore di Noto
1445-	Jaime
1447-	Antonio de Alagona
1479–89	Giovanni Paternò
1489–90	Pierre (Pietro) di Foix (*Apostolic Administrator*)
1491–95	Paolo Della Cavalleria
1495–1501	Giacomo Vualguera
1501–03	Antonio Corseto
1506	Juan de Castro (*Apostolic Administrator*)
1506–09	Bandinello Sauli
1506–12	Bernardino da Bologna
1512	Juan Pujades
1514–16	Juan de Sepúlveda
1516	Bernardino Cateniano
1516–20	Raffaele Sansoni Riario della Rovere (*Apostolic Administrator*)
1520-	Bonifacio Cateniano (*Bishop elect*)
1523–38	Girolamo Ghinucci (*Apostolic Administrator*)
1538–39	Tommaso Bosio
1540–66	Domingo Cubels
1572–77	Martín Rojas de Portalrubio

1578–1614	Tomás Gargal
1615–33	Baldassarre Caglieres
1635–63	Miguel Juan Balaguer Camarasa
1666–68	Lucas Buenos
1670–77	Lorenzo Astiria
1678–82	Miguel Jerónimo de Molina y Aragonés
1684–1711	Davide Cocco Palmeri
1713–21	Joaquín Cánaves
1722–27	Gaspare Gori-Mancini
1728–57	(Paul) Alpheran de Bussan
1757–69	Bartolomeo Rull
1770–80	Giovanni Carmelo Pellerani
1780–1807	Vincenzo Labini of Bitonto
1807–29	Ferdinand Mattei
1831–47	Francesco Saverio Caruana
1847–57	Publio Maria dei Conti Sant
1848–66	Annetto Casolani (Auxiliary Bishop of Malta)
1857–74	Gaetano Pace dei Baroni Forno
1875–88	Carmelo Scicluna
1889–1914	Pietro Pace
1914–43	Maurus Caruana
1943–44	Michael Gonzi

Archbishops of Malta

1944–76	Michael Gonzi
1976–2006	Joseph Mercieca
2006–2014	Paul Cremona.
2015–	Charles J. Scicluna

Administrator-Bishop of Malta

1884–88	Antonio Maria Buhagiar.

Auxiliary Bishops of Malta

1899–1906	Salvarore (Saviour) Gaffiero
1914–27	Angelo Portelli
1942–74	Emmanuel Galea
1974–76	Joseph Mercieca
1998–2011	Annetto Despasquale
2012–15	Charles J. Scicluna

Coadjutor Archbishop of Malta

1967–73	Emmanuel Gerada

APPENDIX IV

Telephone Subscribers in 1960

Extracted from *Malta Telephone Directory 1960*

Agius Ferrante, Dr T J	3 St Peter Square	157
Anthony. Lt Cdr C K, RN	Palazzo Santa Sofia	224
Apap Bologna, The Noble A	11 Holy Cross St	161
Apap Bologna, Navarra Cassia	1 Greek Gate Sq	343
Archbishop of Malta	- – -	80
Attard Montalto, The Noble G	Beaulieu	36
Bonnici, The Most Rev Mgr C	14 Villegaignon St	74
Bugeja, The Rev Canon S	23 Mesquita St	137
Busuttil, M A	15 St Nicholas St	174
Buttigieg, The Very Rev Mgr Paul	1 Bastion Square	284
Camilleri, Joseph	8 Mesquita St	362
Carmelite Priory	- – -	24
Cassar, Dr M	3 Mesquita St	305
Catholic Church	- – -	136
Christin's Store	9 Villegaignon St	52
Cox, D H	4 St Saviour's St	189
De Piro Cowley, Major W	20 Magazines St	115
De Piro Gourgion, Mrs G P	2 St Paul's Square	190
Farrugia, Mrs Benedetta	30 Villegaignon St	355
Farrugia, C / Christin's Store	9 Villegaignon St	52
Farrugia, C	3 Aragon Lane	52
Farrugia, The Very Rev Canon Treas S	5 St Paul's Square	101
Farrugia, Mrs P	5 St Paul's Square	101

Formosa Gauci, Mrs A	12 Villegaignon St	365
Galea, Joseph, BA FSA (Scot)	5 Villegaignon St	71
Galea Testaferrata, The Noble Mrs B	Mangion Palace	41
Green Hand Leathercraft / John Attard	2 Magazine St	268
Guest House (Mrs Wilkinson)	7 Holy Cross St	169
Hamilton-Rose, Cdr J A, RNR (Retd)	Beaulieu, 21 Villegaignon St	322
Leopardi, E R	1 Archbishop's Square	72
Lloyd, Dr D B	3 St Nicholas St	324
Mallia, Michael	6 St Peter's St	286
Millar, Capt W H	10 Holy Cross St	279
Moore, Mrs Wilfred	Casa Isabella, King Ferdinand's Lane	259
Pullucino, The Hon Sir Philip Kt LLD, BLitt	8 The Bastions	11
St Dorothy's Convent	5 St Roque St	143
St Dorothy's Convent	3 Bastion St	143
Sant Manduca, The Noble J A	5 St Saviour's St	2
Sant Manduca, The Noble J A	6 St Saviour's St	299
Stagno Navarra, Major A, ED KOMR	3 St Agatha's Esplanade	59
Teuma Castelletti, The Noble Nina	15 Villegaignon St	77
Van Someren, Lt Cdr E, RN	3 Carmel St	206
Vella, Nicola	The Old Stores, 3 Magazine St	76
Warren, The Misses E & K Lauder	2 St Paul's St	107
Wilkinson, Mrs N G	The Guest House	169
Xara Palace Hotel	St Paul's Square	300

Sorted by address:

- - -	Archbishop of Malta	80
- - -	Carmelite Priory	24
- - -	Catholic Church	136
1 Archbishop's Square	Leopardi, E R	72
3 Aragon Lane	Farrugia, C	52
1 Bastion Square	Buttigieg, The Very Rev Mgr Paul	284
3 Bastion St	St Dorothy's Convent	143
8 The Bastions	Pullucino, The Hon Sir Philip Kt LLD, BLitt	11
3 Carmel St	Van Someren, Lt Cdr E, RN	206
1 Greek Gate Sq	Apap Bologna, Navarra Cassia	343
7 Holy Cross St	Guest House (Mrs Wilkinson)	169
10 Holy Cross St	Millar, Capt W H	279
11 Holy Cross St	Apap Bologna, The Noble A	161
[Holy Cross St]	Wilkinson, Mrs N G	169
King Ferdinand's Lane	Moore, Mrs Wilfred	259
2 Magazine St	Green Hand Leathercraft / John Attard	268
3 Magazine St	Vella, Nicola	76
20 Magazines St	De Piro Cowley, Major W	115
3 Mesquita St	Cassar, Dr M	305
8 Mesquita St	Camilleri, Joseph	362
23 Mesquita St	Bugeja, The Rev Canon S	137
3 St Agatha's Esplanade	Stagno Navarra, Major A, ED KOMR	59
3 St Nicholas St	Lloyd, Dr D B	324
15 St Nicholas St	Busuttil, M A	174
2 St Paul's Square	De Piro Gourgion, Mrs G P	190
5 St Paul's Square	Farrugia, The Very Rev Canon Treas S	101
5 St Paul's Square	Farrugia, Mrs P	101
St Paul's Square	Xara Palace Hotel	300
2 St Paul's St	Warren, The Misses E & K Lauder	107
3 St Peter Square	Agius Ferrante, Dr T J	157
6 St Peter's St	Mallia, Michael	286

5 St Roque St	St Dorothy's Convent	143
4 St Saviour's St	Cox, D H	189
5 St Saviour's St	Sant Manduca, The Noble J A	2
6 St Saviour's St	Sant Manduca, The Noble J A	299
5 Villegaignon St	Galea, Joseph, BA FSA (Scot)	71
9 Villegaignon St	Christin's Store	52
9 Villegaignon St	Farrugia, C / Christin's Store	52
12 Villegaignon St	Formosa Gauci, Mrs A	365
14 Villegaignon St	Bonnici, The Most Rev Mgr C	74
15 Villegaignon St	Teuma Castelletti, The Noble Nina	77
[21 Villegaignon St]	Attard Montalto, The Noble G	36
21 Villegaignon St	Hamilton-Rose, Cdr J A, RNR (Retd)	322
30 Villegaignon St	Farrugia, Mrs Benedetta	355
[Villegaignon St]	Galea Testaferrata, The Noble Mrs B	41
Palazzo Santa Sofia	Anthony. Lt Cdr C K, RN	224

Addresses in squared brackets from other sources.

www.ingramcontent.com/pod-product-compliance
Lightning Source LLC
Chambersburg PA
CBHW070345100426
42812CB00005B/1437
* 9 7 8 1 8 7 6 5 8 6 3 6 2 *